PUTTING FAMILIES FIRST

MODERN APPLICATIONS OF SOCIAL WORK

An Aldine de Gruyter Series of Texts and Monographs

SERIES EDITOR

James K. Whittaker

Ralph E. Anderson and Irl Carter, **Human Behavior in the Social Environment: A Social Systems Approach** (fourth edition)

Richard P. Barth and Marianne Berry, **Adoption and Disruption: Rates, Risks, and Responses**

Richard P. Barth, Mark Courtney, Jill Duerr Berrick, and Vicky Albert, **From Child Abuse to Permanency Planning: Child Welfare Services Pathways and Placements**

Kathleen Ell and Helen Northen, **Families and Health Care: Psychosocial Practice**

Marian Fatout, **Models for Change in Social Group Work**

Mark W. Fraser, Peter J. Pecora, and David A. Haapala, **Families in Crisis: The Impact of Intensive Family Preservation Services**

James Garbarino, **Children and Families in the Social Environment** (second edition)

James Garbarino, Patrick E. Brookhouser, Karen J. Authier, and Associates, **Special Children—Special Risks: The Maltreatment of Children with Disabilities**

James Garbarino, Cynthia J. Schellenbach, Janet Sebes, and Associates, **Troubled Youth, Troubled Families: Understanding Families At-Risk for Adolescent Maltreatment**

Roberta R. Greene, **Social Work with the Aged and Their Families**

Roberta R. Greene, **Human Behavior Theory: A Diversity Framework**

Roberta R. Greene and Paul H. Ephross, **Human Behavior Theory and Social Work Practice**

André Ivanoff, Betty J. Blythe, and Tony Tripodi, **Involuntary Clients in Social Work Practice: A Research-Based Approach**

Paul K. H. Kim (ed.), **Serving the Elderly: Skills for Practice**

Jill Kinney, David A. Haapala, and Charlotte Booth, **Keeping Families Together: The Homebuilders Model**

Robert M. Moroney, **Shared Responsibility: Families and Social Policy**

Robert M. Moroney, **Social Policy and Social Work: Critical Essays on the Welfare State**

Peter J. Pecora, Mark W. Fraser, Kristine Nelson, Jacqueline McCroskey, and William Meezan, **Evaluating Family-Based Services**

Peter J. Pecora, James K. Whittaker, Anthony N. Maluccio, Richard P. Barth, and Robert D. Plotnick, **The Child Welfare Challenge: Policy, Practice, and Research**

Norman A. Polansky, **Integrated Ego Psychology** (second edition)

John R. Schuerman, Tina L. Rzepnicki, and Julia H. Littell, **Putting Families First: An Experiment in Family Preservation**

Betsy S. Vourlekis and Roberta R. Greene (eds). **Social Work Case Management**

Heather B. Weiss and Francine H. Jacobs (eds.), **Evaluating Family Programs**

James K. Whittaker, Jill Kinney, Elizabeth M. Tracy, and Charlotte Booth (eds.), **Reaching High-Risk Families: Intensive Family Preservation in Human Services**

James K. Whittaker and Elizabeth M. Tracy, **Social Treatment, 2nd Edition: An Introduction to Interpersonal Helping in Social Work Practice**

PUTTING FAMILIES FIRST

An Experiment in Family Preservation

John R. Schuerman, Tina L. Rzepnicki, and
Julia H. Littell

ALDINE DE GRUYTER
New York

About the Authors

John R. Schuerman is Professor, School of Social Service Administration, and a Faculty Associate at the Chapin Hall Center for Children, University of Chicago. He was also co-principal investigator of evaluations of the placement prevention and family reunification programs of the State of Illinois. Dr. Schuerman is the editor of *Social Service Review* and the author of *Research and Evaluation in the Human Services,* and *Multivariate Analysis in the Human Services.*

Tina L. Rzepnicki is Associate Professor and Associate Dean in the School of Social Service Administration and a Faculty Associate at the Chapin Hall Center for Children, University of Chicago. She served as co-principal investigator of evaluations of the placement prevention and family reunification programs of the State of Illinois.

Julia H. Littell is Assistant Professor, Graduate School of Social Work and Social Research, Bryn Mawr College. As a research fellow at the Chapin Hall Center for Children, University of Chicago, she was project director for the evaluation of the Illinois Placement Prevention program.

ALDINE DE GRUYTER
A division of Walter de Gruyter, Inc.
200 Saw Mill River Road
Hawthorne, New York 10532

This publication is printed on acid-free paper ∞

Library of Congress Cataloging-in-Publication Data

Schuerman, John R.
    Putting families first : an experiment in family preservation /
John R. Schuerman, Tina L. Rzepnicki, and Julia H. Littell.
      p.   cm. — (Modern applications of social work)
    Includes bibliographical references and index.
    ISBN 0-202-36091-1. — ISBN 0-202-36092-X (pbk.)
    1. Family services—United States. 2. Family social work—United
States. 3. Child welfare—United States. I. Rzepnicki, Tina L.
II. Littell, Julia H. III. Title. IV. Series.
HV699.S38 1994
362.82′8′0973—dc20   94-30535
                                             CIP

Manufactured in the United States of America

10 9 8 7 6 5 4 3 2 1

Contents

Acknowledgments   *ix*

Foreword by James K. Whittaker   *xi*

PART I

1   The Safety of Children and the Preservation
         of Families   3

                 The Explosion of Foster Care   9
                 Family Preservation   18
                 Notes   29

2   Previous Research on Family Preservation   33

                 Placement Prevention   33
                 Prevention of Subsequent Child
                         Maltreatment   43
                 Impact on Child and Family
                         Functioning   43
                 Cost Effectiveness of Family
                         Preservation Services   44
                 Prevention of Child Abuse and Neglect   45
                 Summary and Conclusions   47
                 Notes   48

3   The Evaluation of Family First   53

     Tier 1: Understanding the Family First
          Program   55
     Tier 2: Assessing the Effects of the
          Program   65
     Tier 3: Interviews with Parents   73
     Limitations of the Study   79
     Notes   79

PART II

4   The Families   85

     Demographic and Household
          Characteristics   86
     Reports of Abuse and Neglect   90
     Family Problems as Viewed by the
          Family First Caseworkers   92
     Client Views   96
     Summary   103
     Notes   104

5   Services Provided and Issues in Implementation   107

     Model of Service   107
     Services Received by Family First and
          Regular Service Families   109
     Family First Workers and Their Work
          Environment   124
     Issues in Program Implementation   132
     Summary and Conclusion   138
     Notes   140

6   The Outcomes of Family First   143

     Tier 1: All Family First Cases   143
     Tier 2: The Experiment   148
     Tier 3: Interviews with Parents   170

Summary and Conclusions   187
Notes   191

PART III

7   Issues in the Evaluation of Family Preservation
     Programs   199

     Outcomes   200
     The Black Box and the Million Models   205
     The Design of Studies   206
     Problems of Data Quality   211
     What Do We Need to Learn?   213
     Notes   215

8   The Recent Evolution of the Family First Program   217

     July 1990 to June 1991   217
     July 1991 to June 1992   221
     July 1992 to the Present   224

9   What We Have Learned—Directions for Reform
     in Child Welfare   229

     The Outcomes of Family First   229
     The Present and Future of Child
        Welfare   240
     The Basis of a New Vision   244
     Conclusion   248
     Notes   249

Appendix A
Summary of Controlled Studies of
Family Preservation Programs   251

Appendix B
Selection of Proportional Hazard Models   267

Appendix C
Examination of Simultaneous Equations Using
Two-Stage Least Squares   271

Appendix D
Variables in the Hazard and Two-Stage
Least Squares Analysis   277

Appendix E
Additional Tables   281

References   285

Bibliography of Reports on the Evaluation of the
Illinois Family First Placement Prevention Program   299

Index   305

Acknowledgments

A study such as that reported in this book requires the involvement of a large number of people, in this case, hundreds of people. We begin by thanking our staff, listed on the following page. They have been an extraordinary group of colleagues, often laboring far beyond the call of duty. The ideas in this book have been largely shaped in vigorous discussions among us.

The Chapin Hall Center for Children at the University of Chicago has been the home of this project. Chapin Hall is an exceptional organization, having a staff that is simultaneously wonderfully supportive and eager to dispute. We are particularly appreciative of the support and tolerance of its director, Harold Richman.

This research was conducted under contracts with the Illinois Department of Children and Family Services (DCFS) and grants from the United States Children's Bureau of the Administration on Children and Families. The assistance of DCFS went far beyond financing—dozens of its staff have helped in many ways. Various administrators in the department have provided us with support and valuable criticism at many points in the course of our work. Staff at all levels of the department, from high-level administrators to caseworkers, have spent many hours talking with us about their work. We cannot list here all of the DCFS staff who were helpful to us, but three people must be mentioned: our two contract monitors, Barry Colvin and Craig Bailey, and the first coordinator of the Family First program in Illinois, Diane Yost. At the Children's Bureau, we were fortunate to have the wise counsel of Cecelia Sudia and Penny Maza.

The program we investigated was carried out by over sixty private child welfare agencies. We put many demands on the staff of these agencies: We asked them to fill out many forms and to spend many hours talking with us about their work. Our research is largely about their efforts, and we owe them a great debt. The research is also about the efforts of parents to overcome great social and personal problems. We talked with a number of parents in our work, and we are indebted to them for their patience in answering our questions and for the insights they gave us into their lives.

A draft manuscript for this book was reviewed by Craig Bailey, Susan Campbell, William Reid, Harold Richman, Peter Rossi, Jim Gleeson, Kathleen Wells, Jim Whittaker, Richard Barth, and Duncan Lindsay. Cecelia Sudia reviewed portions of the work. We greatly appreciate their insistence that we be clearer and that we avoid a number of obfuscations and contradictions. However, we did not take all of their suggestions, so they cannot share in the blame for problems that remain.

Finally, we are appreciative of, and for, our families. They took the brunt of our preoccupations during the four years of this project and during the writing of this book. We dedicate the book to them, and to families everywhere.

Staff of the
Evaluation of Illinois Family First
Placement Prevention Program

Lead Interviewer-Liaisons
Stephen Budde, Jeanne Howard, and Penny Johnson

Interviewer-Liaisons
Cynthia Chrisman, Brenda Eckhardt, Mark Hugel, Diane Pellowe,
Phyllis Richards, Sandra Rick, and Kathleen B. Smith

Control Group Interviewers
Javondlynn Dunagan, Linda Gorham, Marisa Mitchell,
Jean O'Mahoney, Jennifer Norton, and Susan Smith

Parent Survey Coordinator
Marva Lopez

Data Management Supervisors
Lucinda Fox, Christian Gustafson, and John Juergenson

Coders
Stephen Baker, Thomas Lawless, LaRasz Moody, and David Rodnitsky

Data Management Staff
Rodd Campbell, Albert Chang, Lauren Heberle,
Gayle Johnson, Debra Menas, Carolyn Shannon,
Linda Simon, and Ginger Wegner

Data Analysts
Amy Chak, Eric Fong, Tammy Dee Jones,
Hye Lan Kim, and Karen Rolf

Administrative Assistants
Synita Booker-Capler, Deborah Pieczynski

Foreword

As a permanent home for the early years of dependent children, the orphan asylum should go out of business.

R. R. Reeder, "Our Orphaned Asylum" (1925)

The foster home is not a panacea for social ills and should not be advertised as the "Soothing Syrup" of social work.

Samuel Langer, "Reply" (Ibid)

Fashions change. Thus, while ironic, it should not surprise that:

1. Nearing the midpoint of the last decade of the twentieth century, we should observe serious public policy discussion directed toward resurrection of that Dickensian sounding social invention so roundly condemned in the century's first decade: the "orphan asylum."
2. That a significant stimulus to this discussion should be the growing disquiet over the apparent shortcomings of the latest child welfare remedy, "family preservation," only recently offered up as a policy response designed to correct serious faults ("premature and unnecessary placement" and "drift") apparent in an earlier response, "family foster care," itself offered as a preferred alternative to asylums.
3. That a central stage for this spirited debate should be Chicago.

Where else but in that urban crucible of social service ferment that earlier produced the likes of Jane Addams and Hull House, Healy and Bronner, and the juvenile court, and more recently has given birth to such innovations as "wrap-around service" (Project Kaleidoscope) and the "Ounce of Prevention" project? Indeed, one should have predicted that some of the clearest voices among the leading contributors to the current conversation would share common affiliation with that long respected center of reasoned discourse on the great child welfare issues, the School of Social Service Administration at the University of Chicago.

Professors John Schuerman and Tina Rzepnicki and their colleague Julia Littell at the Chapin Hall Center for Children at the University of Chicago follow in the footsteps of such luminous predecessors as Grace Abbott, whose classic, *The Child and the State*, set out one of the key propositions in the present discourse: "The progress of a state may be measured by the extent to which it safeguards the rights of its children" (v. 1: vii).

And one would add today, "family," for the story these authors tell is at its core about preserving that delicate balance between two of society's most basic and fundamental obligations: protecting its young and assuring the dignity, support, and autonomy of its fundamental social unit: the family. Minimally, one would hope that society's rules and laws in carrying out these obligations would not be in conflict, ideally they would be complementary. That is, the great power of the state would recognize that the safest haven for children, the optimum institution for their care and nurture, is the family and would thus direct its policies toward strengthening the family unit, offering help, support, and encouragement when needed and staying out of the way when not.

This book and the ambitious service experiment it describes are about what happens when things go awry. When the specter of extreme physical or sexual abuse or neglect intrudes on what Lasch calls the "safe haven" of the family and turns it into a living hell for children. Its lessons are many for those who would create, implement, or evaluate services for families and children. Recent news accounts from Chicago of egregious harms to children perpetrated by some parents and caretakers give urgency to the multiple lessons contained in this volume.

At one level this is a book about evaluation research and the thoughtful attempts of a premier research team to match their methodology to a bold statewide initiative in family preservation designed to prevent unnecessary out-of-home placement by offering alternative, intensive, in-home service to those families deemed at "imminent risk" of placement. This major study has already sparked a lively debate in the child welfare research community about the adequacy and appropriateness of the design, the significance of the primary criterion variable (placement prevention), the quality of the interventions offered, and the meaning of the findings. Notable was the relatively low level of predictive validity of the primary intake criterion: "imminent risk of placement." Simply put, many children deemed as such never entered care. The authors anticipate and deal with many of these methodological questions in their presentation and in a particularly rich discussion section in the book's latter half. Like the earlier and much discussed efforts of Lloyd Ohlin and his colleagues in Massachusetts to evaluate the "Massachusetts experiment" in closing delinquency institutions in the early 1970s, this volume will be the focal point for much fruitful debate and discussion in the research community for years to come: What is an appropriate research design for immature and nascent family intervention programs and what implications may be drawn from this study for the design of future research?

At quite another level, this is a fascinating case history of program development and policy implementation. Might an initiative with more modest objectives (pilot developmental sites?) or a more defined and prescriptive service protocol have yielded different results? The authors offer much data and commentary to temper the enthusiasm surrounding much current program implementation. It is an exceedingly complex task. Schuerman, Rzepnicki, and Littell challenge us to think of placement critically and to avoid the mistaken concreteness that sees it as either a uniform or uniformly negative event. They offer some sensible advice to those who, like themselves, still value the contribution of high-quality, time-limited family preservation services and suggest a proper place for such services in an overall continuum of care and treatment.

At its most basic level, this is a book about values toward families and children and the lengths to which a state can or should go to ensure the health and safety of its citizens. The authors enumerate the multiple handicapping conditions besetting the families they studied—poverty, racism, inadequate housing, drug abuse, poor education, and community violence—and rightly take issue with the mistaken presumption that *any* short- or long-term service strategy can adequately address these pervasive concerns. In the authors' words: "Family preservation is often expected to solve major social problems one case at a time." Students of social policy and child welfare reform will find much of benefit here in an analysis with implications far beyond the particular intervention studied.

In the final analysis the authors leave us with hope, or, in their words: "The message . . . is one of caution but not despair." This densely packed and thoughtful volume offers much to those who would reform, study, or deliver services in the present system of child and family services. Schuerman, Rzepnicki, and Littell provide careful analysis and thoughtful comment. Their message will and should provoke much healthy debate. We are in their debt.

James K. Whittaker

PART I

Chapter 1

The Safety of Children and the Preservation of Families[1]

This book is about the response of our society to the abuse and neglect of children. There are two main elements in that response: the provision of services to prevent further maltreatment and allow families to stay together; and substitute care for children when the risks of further harm are too great. We focus on services designed to prevent the removal of abused and neglected children from their families, programs that are called *family preservation services.* We report on a large-scale evaluation of family preservation services in one state, Illinois. From that study we attempt to draw lessons for family preservation efforts generally and for the reform of child welfare services.

Until the middle of this century, child welfare was concerned with the care of children who were orphaned, abandoned, or otherwise dependent, including those who had suffered severe abuse or neglect. During the 1960s our society began to take on expanded responsibilities for the protection of children from abuse and neglect (Antler 1978, 1981; Nelson 1984; Costin 1992; Anderson 1989). In the last thirty years we have seen increasing efforts to identify children who have been harmed or who are at risk of harm and to provide them protection. Hence, the child welfare system has become focused more and more on the problem of abuse and neglect.

The increased concern about the plight of children who are abused or neglected has resulted in a system in which persons who suspect that children are being harmed or even at risk of harm are encouraged to report their suspicions to state authorities. Some individuals, by virtue of their professional standing, are required to report their suspicions and everyone is encouraged to do so.[2] These reports are screened and those which are deemed to be significant are investigated.

A substantial proportion of the reports that are investigated are "unfounded." Nationwide, the percentage is about 60%, in Illinois the proportion is about two-thirds. But in those cases in which abuse or neglect is determined to have occurred, state or local child welfare staff must decide what to do about it. A number of cases are simply closed, because the situation is not considered serious enough to require action and the child is thought to be unlikely to incur further serious harm in the foreseeable future. In a relatively small proportion of cases, the child is deemed to be at such risk of further harm that he or she is removed from the home and placed in foster care or other substitute care (in Illinois the percentage is about 17% of founded cases). Court orders are required to maintain the placement of a child in substitute care. The cases in between, that is, those which are neither closed nor placed, are opened in the child welfare system and are provided a variety of in-home services. Some are simply monitored, that is, watched to see if further harm occurs; others are provided services meant to reduce the risk of further harm. In these nonplacement cases, the courts may or may not be involved.

In recent years there has been an increase in the number of children in foster homes or institutions. That increase is considered to be the major problem facing the field since it has caused great strains in child welfare systems and has led to a considerable increase in the costs of child welfare services. Efforts to contain the increase have centered on the development of family preservation programs.

Central to the choice between substitute care and in-home services is the tension between two values, the value of ensuring the safety of children from harm and the value of respecting the integrity of the family. In the "integrity of the family" we include respect for individual preferences in manner of child rearing and a sense that family life ought to be private. Hence, families ought to be able to regulate the extent to which their ways of relating are known to others, as long as those ways of relating do not cause harm to their members. Perhaps most important, maintaining the family is thought to be in the best interests of the child in most, though not all cases.

The investigator of abuse and neglect must balance these two values or, more properly, must determine which holds precedence in an individual case. The society and its child welfare system influence that decision through custom, law, regulations, and available responses (such as services). The default position is to respect the integrity of the family, that is, nonintervention. This default is overturned only if the child has been harmed significantly or is at risk of significant harm. We cannot prevent all harms to children. The problem here is that harm and particularly risk of harm lie on a continuum. No child survives without some harm and all children live with some risk. The alternative of taking all children from their families at birth to put them in safer circumstances is neither desirable nor feasible. So we have a threshold problem: Where do we draw the line between state intervention and nonintervention? And where do we draw the multiple lines between various interventions?

In the past fifteen years three principles have dominated the search for the lines in individual cases. These principles—permanency planning, reasonable efforts, and least restrictive alternative—have dominated the development of child welfare systems.[3]

The Parent-Child Bond

Two of these principles, reasonable efforts and permanency, grew out of a belief that, in the absence of serious contraindications, children are better off in their homes of origin than anyplace else and a belief that children are harmed by foster placement. The belief that children belong in their own homes comes out of child development research and is based at least in part on evidence of a special bond between children and mothers. It is claimed that the interaction that comes from biological relatedness and perhaps from the closeness involved in bearing and being borne (and born) cannot be duplicated in other relationships (Bowlby 1952, 1969–1973, 1988).[4] This biologically based altruism ought not be disrupted and barriers to its expression ought to be removed when possible.

The notion of a special bond is supplemented by an almost religious belief on the part of some advocates in child welfare that "all families want to do right for their kids." While there is considerable evidence that a special bond exists between most parents and their children, experience suggests that it may not be quite universal. Some parents do reject their children or fail to display the most elemental of caring or nurturing behaviors. This phenomenon is sometimes attributed to lack of knowledge, lack of resources, the temporary influence of drugs, emotional or psychological problems, or other barriers to performance. In any event, the desire to do right for one's children appears to be submerged in some parents.

The idea that foster care is detrimental to children is even more problematic, both theoretically and empirically. We encounter here a conflict of time horizons, between concerns for the immediate safety of children and their long-term development. While some children are abused or neglected in foster care, the rate of abuse and neglect in foster care is less than in families in which harm has previously occurred. So, statistically at least, children who are placed are safer than if they had been left in their own homes. But it is claimed that foster care is detrimental to the long-term emotional, cognitive, and social development of children.

This is because a foster home is not the child's real home and "natural" bonds are missing.

In assessing such claims, one must make distinctions among ideal foster care, bad foster care, and average expectable foster care. Children are often exposed to multiple placements and these frequent moves are clearly devastating to their growth. Foster homes are sometimes approved after inadequate investigation or are inadequately supervised, with the result that children experience neglect and abuse in them. But there is little evidence that children in stable, adequate foster homes fare significantly worse than similar children left in their own homes (Wald, Carlsmith, and Leiderman 1985; Fanshel and Shinn 1978; Kadushin 1978; Institute for Research on Poverty 1992).

Reasonable Efforts

As codified in the Adoption Assistance and Child Welfare Act of 1980 (PL 96-272), states are required to show, in each case in which a child is placed in substitute care, that alternatives to placement have been tried or at least considered. Judicial certification of these "reasonable efforts" must accompany court orders for substitute care. Further, states are required to make reasonable efforts to reunify with their families children who are placed in substitute care.

How has the reasonable-efforts principle worked in practice? We may have here the problem of whether the glass is half full or half empty. On the one hand, nearly every state now has some version of a family preservation program intended to prevent the placement of children. But it has taken a long time for these programs to develop and they vary in their coverage and their effectiveness. There is also some evidence that many workers with responsibility for decisions about placement (notably investigators of abuse and neglect allegations) have largely adopted the reasonable-efforts principle in that they place children only when it is truly the last resort (for an extensive review of the reasonable-efforts principle, see Shotton 1989–1990).

On the other hand, there continue to be substantial barriers to full implementation of the reasonable-efforts principle. First is the problem of interpretation. *Reasonable* is quite ambiguous and given to multiple interpretations. It has not been adequately defined by the federal government. In many locations, adherence to the reasonable-efforts requirement is purely formal and perfunctory. Judges have a standard form they sign to certify compliance, perhaps adding a phrase or two in a bow to individualization. Instead of recognizing that reasonable efforts is a requirement in each case, compliance is sometimes claimed simply on the basis of the existence of a family preservation program that might or might not be available for a particular case.

Implementation has also been hampered by lack of resources. The federal government has not provided adequate funds to the states to meet the mandate. One response to the reasonable-efforts requirement is the establishment of family preservation programs, but most states have failed to implement these programs on a wide scale or with adequate resources. Furthermore, most of the emphasis has been on placement prevention, while reunification efforts have gotten short shrift.

Permanency

The permanency principle requires that efforts be made to provide the child with a permanent home.[5] It is well established that children need a "psychological parent," a nurturing relationship that is stable over the long term (Goldstein, Freud, and Solnit 1973, 1979). The permanency principle is often linked with the idea of least restrictive alternative to produce the notion that children should be in a permanent situation that is as "homelike" as possible. Curiously, the permanency principle is expressed as a requirement for *permanency planning,* thereby seeming to put the emphasis on planning rather than doing. Thus, the stage is set for formal rather than substantive compliance since the criterion for compliance is the existence of paperwork rather than some outcome for children.

In its narrowest form, the permanency principle might be thought of as combating the "bounce" phenomenon, the fact that many children in foster care experience multiple placements. But as used in practice, the emphasis is on keeping children in or returning them to their own homes, rather than finding the best long-term living situation (Fein and Maluccio 1992; Maluccio, Warsh, and Pine 1993). When children are placed, the permanency plan (or "permanency goal") is almost always "return home." Our observations in Illinois indicate that this goal is rarely changed, no matter how unlikely its achievement. The reluctance to give up on returning children home no doubt arises in part from the belief that all parents want to do right for their children and that family ties should be broken only as a last resort, but it is also related to the reluctance of the state to commit the resources required for long-term placement. This reluctance is at times not beneficial for children and in fact is a violation of the permanency principle.

Least Restrictive Alternative

The least-restrictive-alternative principle is grounded in the basic idea in our society that freedom should be maximized. The notion of least restrictive alternative found its first expression in the context of responses to psychiatric disorder: Persons with mental illnesses were to be restrained only as far as necessary to ensure their own and others' safety (*Lake v. Cameron* 1966).[6] They should be provided a setting for their care that is as unrestrictive as possible. Beyond the apparently inherent American suspicion of state authority, the least-restrictive-alternative principle is based on the idea that people develop best when they are given maximum freedom.

The combination of permanency planning and least restrictive alternative in child welfare has resulted in a hierarchy of alternatives for children.[7] Most desirable is living in the home of origin, followed by adoption, foster care in the home of a relative, long-term foster care in the home of a stranger, and finally care in an institution. When the child is old enough, independent living is added to the hierarchy. There are subalternatives, like group homes and guardianship, which must be fit into the hierarchy, and there is sometimes argument about the precise location in the hierarchy of certain alternatives, like kinship care, but the idea of a hierarchy is well established in the minds of child welfare practitioners and provides guidance for their decisions.

The Principles Considered Together

As noted above, these principles are vague and therefore do not provide clear guidance for action. The fact that they are both vague and codified in law gives rise to no end of bureaucratic and legal maneuvering to stretch interpretations of the law and produce questionable evidence of compliance. Compliance may become largely formal and nonsubstantive. These conditions, present in nearly every state, provide openings for class action lawsuits alleging noncompliance and demanding reform. In fact, they make litigation nearly inevitable.

Another problem with the principles is that they are potentially in conflict, at least in some cases. In dealing with a very troubled child, the principles of reasonable efforts and least restrictive alternative often lead workers to begin with the least restrictive placement, perhaps foster care (with relatives or others) and resort to other alternatives only when that alternative does not work out. The child may then be subjected to a series of successively more restrictive placements (sometimes because it is claimed that the child needs more intensive treatment). Thus the principle of permanency is violated in the bouncing of the child from one placement to another. Because his or her needs have not been met, the child is likely to be worse off because of the bouncing around than if he or she were placed in a more restrictive environment in the first place (Testa 1982).

The principle of reasonable efforts exists to combat a supposed tendency to place children when that is not necessary and to prod authorities to try to return children home when they are in placement. But it is particularly ambiguous. Besides the difficulty in determining what is reasonable, there are at least two shadings of meaning, depending on whether one puts the emphasis on *reasonable* or on *efforts*. One might interpret the phrase to mean that *efforts* should be taken but that they should not be unreasonable. Hence, twenty-four-hour-a-day surveillance might be interpreted as unreasonable, while daily visits might be reasonable. A service that is not available might also be considered unreasonable (it is unreasonable to be required to provide a nonexistent service). Alternatively, emphasis on *reasonable* focuses attention on the family and its circumstances, so that if it is unreasonable to expect that the child can be adequately protected with services short of placement, efforts to prevent placement need not be taken. The distinction between these two meanings might also be put in the form of a question: Must reasonable efforts be made or only considered? It is likely that child welfare practice uses a combination of these meanings but we believe that the emphasis is on the first, that is, efforts should be made unless there are very compelling contraindications.

But sometimes efforts to avoid placement or to return children home are not appropriate. Some situations require placement and some children require restrictive environments, and those children should not have to suffer attempts to keep them at home or in environments that they cannot handle. Countering that observation is the suggestion that in many cases we do not know what is best for the child, that we are often not in a position to assess the risk to the child, or that we cannot assess the likely response of a family to services. The principle of reasonable efforts provides a guideline for action in situations of uncertainty. The point raises an important problem: the limitation in assessment technology. The reasonable-efforts principle may be justified if we do not have adequate technology for determining the most appropriate action at the outset, leaving us to engage in a process of trial and error. When that is the case, it seems appropriate to begin by trying to keep the child at home. However, while there are considerable limitations in assessment technology, there are cases in which it is not reasonable to leave children at home and then there is no point in invoking the principle.

THE EXPLOSION OF FOSTER CARE

While children are placed in substitute care in only a small proportion of cases in which harm has occurred, in recent years there has been a substantial increase in the numbers of children in substitute care. Unfortunately, national data on substitute care are incomplete and quite problematic, making it difficult to develop a full understanding of the reasons for changes in caseload. Data currently available depend on the voluntary provision of data by states and states sometimes fail to submit information or to submit complete information. Usually the data are in aggregate form; rarely are case-level data available for analysis. States vary considerably in definitions of important terms. For example, what is included as a *placement* differs considerably. States treat placements with relatives in various ways (see below). They also treat short-term and shelter placements differently. Furthermore, definitions and practices have changed over time, making interpretation of changes problematic. Some states, including Illinois, do have relatively sophisticated data systems that allow for greater confidence in interpretation. We present here some national data and data from Illinois.

The Voluntary Cooperative Information System (VCIS) of the American Public Welfare Association has collected data from the states on substitute care since 1982. Data for fiscal years 1986 to 1992 are shown in Table 1.1. These data must be taken as estimates because of problems such as those suggested above. The data suggest an increase of 60% (from 273,000 to 442,000) in the substitute care population of the United States from 1985 to 1992. The most substantial increases occurred in 1988 and 1989, with a reduction in the rate of increase since.

The number of children in foster care at any one time is a function of the numbers of children entering care and the numbers leaving care. The number leaving care is influenced by the length of time they spend in care. Foster care caseloads may increase either because there are more children entering care or because children are spending more time in care (that is, fewer children are leaving care). Both entries and exits

Table 1.1:   Estimates of Numbers of Children in Substitute Care in the United States (in Thousands)

Fiscal year	First day[b]	Entered care	Left care	Last day	% Change
1986	273	183	176	280	
1987	280	222	202	300	7.1
1988	312	199	171	340	13.3
1989	340	222	182	380	11.8
1990	379	238	210	406	6.8
1991	412	224	207	429	5.7
1992[a]	421	238	217	442	3.0

Source: VCIS Research Notes, No. 2-9, January 1990–August 1993.

[a] Data for FY 1992 are preliminary estimates.

[b] Discrepancies between last day and first day figures are due to problems in the data as discussed in the text.

Table 1.2: Foster Care Entries and Exits, Illinois

Calendar year	Entries	Exits	Total end of year	% Change	First admissions	% First admissions
1981	7,429	7,212	14,390		5,742	77.3
1982	7,320	7,141	14,569	1.2	5,787	79.1
1983	6,856	6,953	14,472	−0.7	5,393	78.7
1984	7,299	7,101	14,670	1.4	5,718	78.3
1985	7,239	7,281	14,628	−0.3	5,541	76.5
1986	7,188	6,974	14,842	1.5	5,562	77.4
1987	8,562	6,431	16,973	14.4	6,720	78.5
1988	8,578	6,658	18,893	11.3	6,884	80.3
1989	9,093	6,798	21,188	12.1	7,384	81.2
1990	9,315	6,647	23,856	12.6	7,451	80.0
1991	11,430	6,666	28,620	20.0	9,359	81.9
1992	11,960	6,803	33,777	18.0	9,873	82.6

Source: Chapin Hall Multistate Data Archive and Illinois Department of Children and Family Services (1993). Placements of three days or less are excluded.

increased sharply in 1987, dropped in 1988, and have been generally increasing since, with a dip in entries in 1991.

Table 1.2 presents similar data for Illinois. As can be seen, foster care admissions and discharges remained stable and about equal through 1986, so the caseload was also stable. Beginning in 1987, entrants rose to a new level while exits remained at previous levels, so that the caseload steadily rose. Children entering care may be further divided between those entering care for the first time and "recidivists." Over the period from 1981 to 1992, the number of first entrants rose much more (71.9%) than reentrants (23.7%). Infants and African-Americans increased as percentages of first entrants. The percentage of first entrants who were children under 1 year of age rose from 15% in 1981 to 21.4% in 1992; the percentage of African-Americans rose from 39.9 to 68.6% in the same period.

The fact that more children were entering than leaving care indicates that they were spending more time in care. From 1981 to 1985 lengths of time in care dropped (larger percentages were leaving care earlier). In 1985, length of time in care began to increase. Of children placed in 1985, 55% left care within one year, 75% within three years. For children entering care in 1990, the figures were 35 and 50%[8] (see also Tatara 1993).

Kinship Care

The expansion of kinship foster care has been a major component of the explosion in foster care. In Illinois, placements in homes of relatives account for nearly all of the recent increase in numbers of children entering care. Between 1981 and 1992, the proportion of children in relative care increased from 24 to 53% of all children in foster care.[9]

Relatives have been caring for children since the beginning of time. Previously, such arrangements did not involve the state but now the state actively supports them by paying relatives for care, often at the same rate as other foster homes (Department of Health and Human Services 1992a).[10] When placement is deemed necessary, many jurisdictions now require consideration of placement with a relative and relatives are often asked if they are willing to take a child. The burgeoning of kinship care has raised many issues, some of which we note here.

Kinship care often embodies conflicts between the principles enunciated earlier and the need of the state to restrain the costs of foster care. Workers think of kinship care as upholding the principles of least restrictive alternative and permanency. It is thought that homes of relatives are usually similar to the natural home of the child and thus serve the principle of least restrictive alternative. In fact, workers think of homes of relatives as being almost the same as the natural home (or better because the risk of harm is less) so they are legitimate permanency plans. Kinship care may also be thought of as meeting the requirements of reasonable efforts. Thinking of such arrangements as potentially permanent, with ongoing state support, obviously conflicts with policymakers' desires to reduce placement in order to reduce the costs of foster care. As would be expected, given the attitudes of workers, lengths of time in relative foster care are, on average, longer than in other forms of care.[11]

It has been observed by many that the availability of state support for kinship care arrangements has created perverse financial incentives (Testa 1993). Relatives who care for children may realize that they can be paid for this care if they report the child's parent for neglect. Furthermore, in most jurisdictions foster care payments substantially exceed public assistance payments (Testa 1993; Link 1990; Department of Health and Human Services 1992b).[12] Hence, a family unit consisting of a mother, children, and grandmother that receives public assistance for the children would receive more money if the grandmother were to become the children's foster parent. Although these incentives for kinship foster care exist, the extent to which they have resulted in more placements is not clear (for a suggestion that this may not be a major issue see Department of Health and Human Services 1992b).[13]

Kinship care arrangements also raise issues for the maintenance of foster care standards and the assurance of children's safety. In many jurisdictions, the investigation of a kinship foster home is considerably less detailed than that for other foster homes and standards for acceptance are much less stringent. Furthermore, workers have expressed concern about the safety of children placed with a grandparent who also may have been an abuser. Kinship care may result in inadequate protection of children because of unrestricted and unsupervised contact with parents. Conversely, kinship care may result in the parent being denied access to a child because of conflict between the parent and the caretaker.

Finally, kinship foster homes often receive inferior services from child welfare agencies compared to nonkin homes (Testa 1993; Link 1990). In the face of high caseloads, workers sometimes ignore kinship placements and kin may be less likely to demand services. In some jurisdictions (e.g., Mississippi) relative foster parents are not required to be licensed, and those who are not licensed are excluded from services provided to licensed foster parents (Department of Health and Human Services 1992a).

Clearly, much more needs to be understood about kinship foster care. Research is needed on the motivations of kin for taking on the care of children, on the extent to which kinship care is being used for income maintenance, on the extent to which it is viewed as and becomes a permanent plan, on the adequacy of care in kinship homes, and on the dynamics of reunification in kinship care.

Foster Care Bounce

One of the most problematic aspects of foster care for many children is the instability of placement, the fact that many children experience multiple placements during their time in the care of the state. Multiple placements may occur for many reasons, including changes in circumstances in foster homes and problems foster parents have in caring for sometimes difficult children. Goerge (1993) tracked a sample of 851 children placed in Illinois in 1988. Through June 30, 1992, 26% of these children experienced five or more placements and slightly more than half (51%) had three or more. Only 24% had one placement. Children who were not reunified during the observation period were much more likely to experience multiple placements (93% of those not reunified had more than one placement compared to 59% of those who were reunified). Reduction of the bouncing of children among foster care placements is clearly a major challenge to the field of child welfare (see also Tatara 1993).

Reentry

While most children who are placed in foster care are reunified with their parents, some later return to foster care. Goerge and Wulczyn

(1990) followed children placed in fiscal 1986 in two states, New York and Illinois. Children in Illinois were followed until June 30, 1988, while those in New York were followed until March 31, 1989. Of those who left foster care, about a quarter returned to care during this period (26% in Illinois and 27% in New York). Of course, this is an underestimate of the proportion returning to care, since these children were followed for relatively short periods of time. Other estimates suggest that about one-third of children returned home will again experience a foster care placement.

From Report to Placement

Our concern in this book is with child abuse and neglect, but although maltreatment is the reason for a substantial proportion of placements, the above numbers include placements for other reasons, most notably for dependency and child behavior problems. In some states the data include placements for delinquency. Unfortunately, it does not appear to be easy to separate out those cases in which placement occurred because of abuse or neglect. Furthermore, much of this book is concerned with placement prevention programs. These programs usually target services on cases in which there has been a recent allegation of abuse or neglect. However, placements also occur in cases that enter the substitute care system through other routes. For example, in the course of work with a family in which abuse or neglect had previously occurred it may be determined that placement is in the best interests of a child even though there has not been a recent incident of harm.

The number of children who enter foster care during an investigation of abuse or neglect may be thought of as a function of the number of reports, the proportion of those reports that are founded, and the proportion of the founded reports that result in the placement of a child. National longitudinal data of this kind do not appear to be available. Estimates of the number of children reported are available and are shown in Table 1.3. This table indicates that the number of reports has risen by 133%, from 1,154,000 to 2,695,000 in the period 1981 to 1991. In 1990 the National Center on Child Abuse and Neglect began collecting data on number of reports, number of cases founded, and number of children taken into custody (National Center on Child Abuse and Neglect 1993). Data from 40 states for 1991 indicate that 39.3% of reported children were substantiated victims (see also Daro and McCurdy 1991).[14] In that year, 33 states reported that about 79,000 children were removed from their homes, about 4,000 more than in 1990.[15]

Data on reports and what happened to them for Illinois are shown in Table 1.4.[16] The number of reports of abuse and neglect has increased each year, with a huge increase in 1987, a large increase in 1989, and

Table 1.3: National Estimates of Numbers of Children Reported for Abuse or Neglect (in Thousands)

Year	Number	% Increase
1980	1,154	
1981	1,225	6.2
1982	1,262	3.0
1983	1,477	17.0
1984	1,727	16.9
1985	1,928	11.6
1986	2,086	8.2
1987	2,178	4.4
1988	2,243	3.0
1989	2,411	7.5
1990	2,568	6.5
1991	2,695	4.9

Source: National Center on Child Abuse and Neglect (1993).

another very large increase in 1992. The proportion of reports that are indicated has steadily dropped, to about one-third in 1992, somewhat less than the national figure. The drop in proportion of cases indicated may be due to an increased number of reports of situations that are "truly" not abuse or neglect or it may be due to changes in the threshold of what is considered abuse or neglect in the child welfare system. It is possible that one way the system adjusts to pressures of more reports is to restrict the meaning of abuse and neglect. The percentage of indicated reports resulting in protective custody of one or more children has stayed in a fairly narrow range from 17.2 to 19.8% except for 1985, when it was 20.8%. In 1992, this increased to 19.7% from levels below 18% in the previous years. The number of children taken into protective custody has varied, sometimes increasing and sometimes decreasing, with a vary large increase in 1992. However, the data on number of protective custodies in years before 1992 are questionable, as indicated in the note to Table 1.4.[17] The number of protective custodies is not an indication of the number of children entering foster care following an investigation of abuse or neglect. The taking of protective custody by an investigator must be followed within 48 hours by a court hearing at which time the child is placed in "temporary custody" or released to his or her care-taker. In some cases the protective custody is terminated before the court hearing while in others the court vacates custody. We know of no very good data on the numbers of cases in which protective custody is terminated without temporary custody.

We believe that the increase in the number of reports is due to a

Table 1.4: Illinois Reporting Statistics

Fiscal year	Children reported		Family reports		Indicated investigations		Protective custody reports		Children taken into protective custody	
	Number	Increase (%)	Number	Increase (%)	Number	Family reports (%)	Number	Indicated reports (%)	Number	Increase (%)
1980	37,476	51.1								
1981	51,548	37.5								
1982	59,194	14.8								
1983	63,432	7.2	36,018		15,848	44.0	2,725	17.2	4,382	
1984	67,058	5.7	39,232	8.9	17,858	45.5	3,539	19.8	5,473	24.9
1985	69,627	3.8	41,463	5.7	19,537	47.1	4,057	20.8	6,452	17.9
1986	70,422	1.1	41,498	0.1	20,143	48.5	3,770	18.7	5,956	−7.7
1987	91,723	30.2	53,229	28.3	22,707	42.6	4,083	18.0	6,480	8.8
1988	94,098	2.6	55,070	3.5	23,877	43.4	4,342	18.2	6,729	3.8
1989	102,267	8.7	60,093	9.1	23,604	39.3	4,078	17.3	6,524	−3.1
1990	103,485	1.2	60,730	1.1	22,068	36.3	3,929	17.8	6,152	−5.7
1991	107,310	3.7	62,481	2.9	21,609	34.6	3,667	17.0	5,954	−3.2
1992	130,585	21.7	73,962	18.4	24,532	33.2	4,845	19.7	7,878	32.3

Source: Illinois Department of Children and Family Services, Annual Reports, Child Abuse and Neglect Statistics.

Note: The 1992 report says, "Although it appears that the number of children taken into temporary protective custody during fiscal 1992 represents a 32 percent increase over the number of children taken into temporary custody in fiscal year 1991, this is a statistical anomaly. In January 1991 (mid fiscal year 1991), the Department's computerized child abuse and neglect tracking system was enhanced for the more accurate tracking of data. Before this date, some information, including protective custody data, was not consistently recorded among the various regions in the state; and it is likely that the number of protective custodies was underreported."

number of factors: changes in what is considered to be abuse and neglect, changes in reporting practices by those who are in a position to
report abuse and neglect, changes in the conditions in families, and
changes in broader social conditions that may affect the conditions in
families. We discuss each of these factors below.

There has been a steady enlarging of the definition of abuse and
neglect in the past thirty years. It has expanded beyond actual physical
harm to children to risk of physical harm, to emotional harm, and, in
some jurisdictions, even to "educational neglect" (many cases of educational neglect were formerly considered the child's problem and labeled
"truancy"). But there have been more subtle changes as well. In the past,
grandparents have often provided care for grandchildren when parental
duties were shirked; now the state may become involved in these arrangements (an Illinois appeals court has found presumptive reason to
conclude that neglect has occurred in a case in which a mother left her
children with their grandmother without making arrangements with the
grandmother for their care; see *In re B.T.* 1990). The ability to detect
abuse and neglect has also improved, resulting in further widening of
the net, beginning with advances in radiology that led to the labeling of
the "battered-child syndrome" (Kempe et al. 1963).[18] There is increasing
concern for "failure-to-thrive" infants, and physicians are exploring
cases of "sudden infant death syndrome" to detect situations in which
the child was suffocated.[19] Physicians are also detecting more cases in
which violent shaking has resulted in injury or death.

Those who are in a position to report abuse and neglect appear to be
increasingly doing so. Public education efforts and the ready availability
of hotlines have contributed to this trend, as has publicity about the
prevalence of harms to children. Public sensitivity has been raised, and
people appear to be more likely to entertain suspicions about their
neighbors and relatives, and to report those suspicions. Laws man-
dating reports of suspected abuse and neglect by professionals have
increased professional responsibility for reporting (Antler 1981; Meriwether 1986; Myers 1986; Hutchinson 1993). And grandparents who are
saddled with the care of grandchildren are more likely to report their
children for neglect.

Conditions in families and in society that lead to increases in the
numbers of reports of abuse and neglect are intertwined. Among these
are well-documented increases in the numbers of children in families in
poverty, the increase in violence, particularly in the inner city, the increase in the use of drugs, and increases in the numbers of children
being raised in one-parent families (often headed by teenaged mothers).
In fact, the child welfare system is now largely concerned with mother-
child families.

While all of these factors have contributed, the effects of drugs are perhaps most salient for workers who investigate allegations of abuse and neglect. A substantial proportion of their cases involve abuse of drugs or alcohol. An important subgroup that has grown dramatically in the last few years is that of "cocaine babies," infants who are found to have cocaine in their bodies at birth. In Illinois, the number of reports involving "substance-affected infants" (primarily cocaine) jumped from 181 in 1985 to an estimated 2,770 in 1991 (Illinois Department of Children and Family Services 1991). There is considerable confusion in the child welfare system as to what to do about cocaine babies. In many jurisdictions, medical personnel are required to report such cases to state abuse and neglect hotlines and in some jurisdictions (e.g., Illinois) the diagnosis of cocaine baby results in an automatic finding of child abuse by the mother. But should such children be considered to be ipso facto at risk and placed in substitute care? There appears to be much variation in the answers to this question (Larson 1991; Madden 1993). In some areas, placement of cocaine babies occurs frequently, while in others, placement occurs only if a previous child was a cocaine baby or if there is evidence of serious abuse or neglect. The confusion is fed by lack of understanding about the long-term effects of *in utero* exposure to cocaine and evidence that there is a great range of responses of young children to such exposure, with some children unaffected while others may be seriously damaged (Zuckerman 1991; Kronstadt 1991).

It should also be noted that this is another area in which advances in technology have had substantial influence. The ingestion of intoxicating, addictive, and harmful substances appears to have begun before recorded history (*Encyclopedia Britannica* 1990; Barber 1967; Roueche 1960).[20] Use of these substances by pregnant women is probably just as ancient in origin. But it is only recently that we have become aware of the possible effects of such use and been able to detect it. These observations also raise the question as to how far the state should go in attempting to govern the behavior of pregnant women. For example, it is known that smoking may be detrimental to fetal growth, so should a woman who smokes during pregnancy be convicted of abuse of her child?

FAMILY PRESERVATION

The family preservation movement in child welfare developed as a way to implement the ideals outlined above while addressing the foster care explosion. By maintaining the nuclear family we uphold the principles of least restrictive alternative and reasonable efforts and we hope that the family will stay together, thus serving the goal of permanency. We also avoid the heavy cost of foster care.

Family preservation programs have now been implemented in nearly every state, at least on a trial basis. The programs vary considerably in conception and in the activities they undertake. Typically, the programs are intended to be delivered to families in which there is a risk of placement of a child and families are referred to them during investigations of allegations of abuse or neglect. Versions of these services are also used to facilitate the reunification of families in which a child has been placed and, in Illinois at least, a version has been implemented to intervene in cases in which adoptions might be disrupted.

Various advocates for family preservation services have suggested lists of the hallmarks of such services. These lists often include such things as the following:

1. Services should be *family centered* rather than child centered, that is, services should be directed at enhancing family functioning as a whole so that the child can remain in the family.
2. Services should be *home based,* that is, insofar as possible they should be delivered in the home, not in an agency office.
3. Services should be *crisis oriented,* taking advantage of the dynamics of crisis to bring about change. As such, services should begin immediately upon identification of the crisis, should be intensive in nature, and should be time limited. Services should be available twenty-four hours a day, seven days a week. An implication of this principle is that caseloads should be small.
4. Services should *empower* families, which we take to mean developing in families the ability to solve their own problems. This involves the belief that families have strengths that can be developed in the service of problem-solving.
5. Services should be *community oriented.* Families should be "connected" with extended family and community resources, both formal and informal.
6. *Case management* approaches should be used to obtain, coordinate, and monitor resources for the family.

The idea of family preservation is often traced to the first White House Conference on Children in 1909, although there are probably earlier sources. In response to the extensive use of foster care and institutions in the latter half of the nineteenth and early part of the twentieth centuries, the conference declared that "home life is the highest and finest product of civilization." The conference went on to suggest that children should not be deprived of home life "except for urgent and compelling reasons" (*Proceedings of the Conference on the Care of Dependent Children* 1909; see also Bremner 1971; McGowan 1990; Jones 1989; Mayer, Richman, and Balcerzak 1977; Pecora 1991). However, the pronouncements of the conference did not result in concrete steps to reduce the numbers of children in care. McGowan observes that the Aid to Dependent Children provisions of the Social Security Act of 1935 and its successor program, Aid to Families with Dependent Children, "undoubtedly contributed more than any other social program to the goal of enabling children at risk of placement to remain in their own homes" (McGowan 1983:69).

The roots of many of the approaches of current family preservation programs may be found in the early history of social work. Home visiting was a central feature of social work with families in the early years of this century. Social work was heavily involved in the development of short term crisis intervention work in the years after the Second World War. In the 1950s the St. Paul Family Centered Project, focusing on "multiproblem" families, had many of the characteristics of current family preservation work, including home visiting, a focus on the provision of concrete services, and a crisis orientation (Birt 1956; Frankel 1988; Horejsi 1981; Wood and Geismar 1989). However, an approach developed by two psychologists in Washington state has come to dominate much of the discussion about ways to approach family preservation. This approach, called *Homebuilders*, was originally developed for work with families of adolescents who had become involved with the juvenile justice or mental health systems. Homebuilders pushes the short-term and intensive features of the work almost to the limit. Families are to be seen for four to six weeks and caseloads are to be kept to not more than two families so that workers can spend many hours a week with families. Workers are to be available to clients twenty-four hours a day, seven days a week. Cases are served by a single therapist (with backup), a feature that contrasts with other approaches using teams of workers. The approach has a strong "cognitive-behavioral" component. Clear, specific, and concrete goals are set for family members and use is made of the armamentarium of tracking devices popularized by behavioral psychology and behavioral social work, devices such as behavioral checklists. Also prominent in the Homebuilders model is the provision of concrete services (Kinney, Haapala, and Booth 1991; Whittaker, Kenny, Tracy, and Booth 1990).

Homebuilders has been widely (though not universally) adopted. It has a great deal of appeal largely because it is a well-developed, systematic approach, focused on the practical needs of families and on their dysfunctional relationships. Its systematic character may make it less subject than other approaches to "model drift." But other approaches to family preservation are in use, most notably, the *family systems* approach, which uses ideas from *structural family therapy* developed by Salvador Minuchin and his colleagues in Philadelphia (Minuchin 1974; Minuchin and Fishman 1981). As the name implies, the family systems approach focuses on the family as a social system and on subsystems within the family (Nelson and Landsman 1992). Relationships with larger systems are also important, with attention given to improving connections with the community. Among the notions employed is that dysfunctional patterns of relationships develop over multiple generations. Some programs have used approaches found in the standard family therapy literature, usually centering around interviews with the entire family. Families tend to be seen for longer periods of time than in the Homebuilders approach (3 to 12 months).

Other models have sometimes been employed in family preservation programs, usually involving longer periods of contact with families. These include models based on psychodynamic theories and behavioral approaches.[21]

Differences in the prescriptions of various models for the activities of workers presumably arise out of differences in views as to the causes of human problems and in how they should be addressed. The models differ in the extent to which they provide explicit theories of human problems and problem resolution.

A great deal of emphasis has been put on the matter of "models" in family preservation. In particular, researchers have been urged to determine which of the several models are most effective. However, it is possible that the most important elements in a family preservation program (those things that "explain the most variance" in outcomes) are not the activities that distinguish models of practice. Instead, characteristics of practice that are peripheral to model formulations or that all models attempt to incorporate may be most important. We are thinking here about such things as the imagination and zeal of the worker. Of course, in the end, the question of whether models matter is empirical.

Are Short-Term Models Effective?

Since the beginning of the family preservation movement, the idea that services should be short term has been perhaps its most controversial element. Time-limited services have long been advocated for their ability to "concentrate the mind" (Reid and Epstein 1972; Reid 1978, 1992; Epstein 1988, 1992). Time limits put the onus on both the worker and the client to get things done. It is thought that client motivation and concentration can be better maintained if there is a clear time limit at the outset. In contrast, the greater leisureliness of services without time limits may dissipate energy and lead to a bogging down of the process. Furthermore, most episodes of casework treatment are fairly short anyway, because of "unplanned terminations" precipitated by the client. Finally, there is cost. The cost of short-term service is both limited and predictable.

The idea of short-term service is often connected to the notion of crisis intervention, another central tenet of many family preservation approaches. Crisis intervention attempts to marshal energy around the resolution of the crisis in ways that will result in a higher level of functioning than the family previously displayed. The state of crisis is thought to provide opportunities for growth that may not otherwise occur. But crisis intervention was originally developed as a way to respond to disasters, and social crises may have quite different characteristics.

It is thought that families referred to family preservation programs are in a state of crisis. This proposition is based on the assumption that the incident of abuse or neglect and the events leading up to that incident must have constituted a crisis for the family. The investigation and the threat of losing the children intensify the crisis. Finally, there is the coerced involvement in services, which may deepen the sense of crisis further.

However, crisis may not always accompany an investigation of abuse or neglect. In many families, abuse or neglect has been occurring for some time before the state becomes aware of it. The conditions leading to the report are often long-standing. Many of these families have had a number of contacts with state agencies, including the child welfare agency, so that state involvement, while no doubt usually unwanted, is familiar. They are aware that the state more often threatens action than takes action, so they may quite reasonably perceive threats as empty.[22] Besides, some families would be quite relieved to be rid of their children.

The Problem of Targeting

As we will see below, a significant problem in the implementation of family preservation has been that of targeting. The intended target group for family preservation programs is families in which there is an "imminent risk of placement." It is not entirely clear what is meant by that phrase, but it is evident in a number of studies, including ours, that relatively few of the families served would have had a child placed in substitute care in the absence of services [for discussions of efforts to define imminent risk, see Berry (1991) and Tracy (1991)]. To the extent that this is true, family preservation programs cannot be expected to reduce the rate of placement and, in fact, the term *family preservation* becomes something of a misnomer.

Problems in the targeting of social programs are not new. Observers have pointed out that many programs appear to "cream," that is, favor the acceptance of "better" or "easier" cases, cases that are relatively less needy. A prominent example is community mental health centers, many of which were originally set up to serve chronically mentally ill patients being discharged from large state psychiatric hospitals and now devote most of their resources to treatment of less severely ill patients. Other examples of creaming are family support centers, job training programs, and many Head Start centers.

A related problem in social programs is that of "net-widening." Net-widening occurs when more families become involved in the public system than would have without the program. As we shall see, there is evidence of some net-widening in our evaluation of the Illinois family preservation program. The net-widening effect has also been observed in some other social programs, most notably programs to deflect juveniles from involvement in the juvenile corrections system (Ezell 1989; Binder and Geis 1984; Blomberg 1977, 1983; Polk 1984). Net-widening is a particularly disturbing phenomenon, since it means that the program has caused more families to become involved in a system that by its nature contains coercive elements. Thus, at least in part, programs having the intent of diverting families from the public child welfare system may have had the opposite effect.

The Risks in Family Preservation

On those occasions that family preservation services are targeted on cases in which placement of a child is imminent, it must be recognized that there are risks, to the child and to the system. No program is perfect and mistakes will be made. Hence, it is practically inevitable that the incidence of serious harm to children, including child deaths, will be higher in a program in which children at risk are left at home rather than taken into foster care. Although some children are harmed in foster care, the incidence of harm in foster care is considerably lower than in families in which there has been a founded incident of abuse or neglect.[23] In family preservation programs attempts are made to minimize risks to children through frequent monitoring and surveillance but these efforts are unlikely to be successful in all cases. Hence, family preservation programs may result in more harm and deaths of children. Traded off against this higher (one hopes, only slightly higher) mortality is that many more children will presumably benefit from growing up in their own families. Of course, trade-offs involving higher mortality are common in the making of public policy. Speed limits are raised, we decide not to provide adequate funding for immunizations of children, and we decide not to prohibit the production and sale of handguns, all actions that result in increased deaths. The fact that such trade-offs are made is usually ignored by policymakers.

The Beginnings of the Illinois Family First Program

The Illinois Family First initiative was authorized by the Illinois Family Preservation Act (Ill. Rev. Stat., 23, Sect. 2057.4) adopted in 1987. To a large extent the private sector took the lead in advocating the passage of the act. This leadership came from provider groups (e.g., the Child Welfare Advisory Council, composed of private-sector providers of services under contract with the Department of Children and Family Services) and advocacy groups (e.g., the Chicago Legal Assistance Foundation and Voices for Illinois Children). The Family Preservation Act was initially drafted by the Legal Assistance Foundation. Although the act was effective January 1, 1988, it was not funded until the 1988 legislative session, at which time an appropriation of approximately three million dollars was provided. The act provided for services "to prevent the placement of children in substitute care, to reunite them with their families if so placed and if reunification is an appropriate goal, or to maintain an adoptive placement." The act required that these services be "uniformly available throughout the State" by January 1, 1993, a deadline that was later extended to July 1995. The definition of those eligible for services was quite broad:

> The child and his [sic] family shall be eligible for services as soon as the report is determined to be "indicated." The Department may offer services to any child or family with respect to whom a report of suspected child abuse or neglect has been filed, prior to concluding its investigation. . . . The Department may also provide services to any child or family who is the subject of any report of suspected child abuse or neglect or may refer such child or family to services available from other agencies in the community, even if the report is determined to be unfounded, if the conditions in the child's or family's home are reasonably likely to subject the child or family to future reports of suspected child abuse or neglect. Acceptance of such services shall be voluntary.

The Illinois Plan

As described above, a number of models for family preservation services existed at the time Illinois began its program. The approach adopted by the state was close to the Maryland model, a three-month intervention involving teams of workers that included paraprofessionals. A pilot homebuilders program in Chicago, together with some other family preservation efforts in the state, also provided guidance for the development of the plan. After the inception of the program, DCFS encouraged the use of the *multisystems approach* (Cimmarusti 1992) and training was provided in that model. The multisystems approach is similar to the family systems model described above. It places emphasis on four systems levels: the family, the extended family, the community, and the family preservation group. Also emphasized is "empowerment" of the family and a focus on family strengths. Families are thought to be abusive or neglectful "because they are constrained from being otherwise" (p. 246).

The Illinois program was conducted through contracts with private agencies. These agencies had a great deal of latitude in constructing their programs. The initial request for proposals for the program specified that a family would be eligible for the program if it was the subject of an abuse or neglect report or investigation, there was a child 6 or under (later changed to 12 or under) in the home who was in imminent danger of out-of-home placement, the child's safety was not immediately jeopardized by remaining at home if family preservation services were provided, and the family had been the subject of three or fewer previous investigations in which harm to a child had been confirmed.

According to the initial request for proposals (RFP):

The services sought through the Families First Initiative are intended to:
1. Increase the accessibility of services for abusing or neglectful families.
2. Establish a comprehensive range of services that assess the risk of harm to children while responding to the immediate and long term needs of referred families.
3. Increase the family's level of functioning to prevent the reoccurrence of abuse or neglect.
4. Increase the use of community based services to support families and prevent the placement of children.

The RFP further specified that the

program model . . . encompasses the following criteria:
    An approach to services that enables a family to recognize and build upon their own strengths, to increase the quality of interaction between family members and to become self-sufficient in its community;
    The capacity to provide services as intensely as needed in order to stabilize the family as quickly as possible and to reduce the risk of harm to the child(ren);
    A mix of services that includes, but is not limited to, the following:

emergency caretakers, homemakers, housing assistance, individual and family counseling, parenting and child development education, respite care, child care, transportation, job finding, emergency food assistance, emergency cash assistance and household management education;

Comprehensive case management responsibility that includes: needs assessment, service planning, case coordination, service brokerage linkages with community resources, monitoring the family's utilization of provided services, monitoring the family's progress toward meeting case goals and objectives, and the development of recommendations for ongoing services, when necessary;

The capacity to begin services (face-to-face contact) within twenty-four hours of the agency's receipt of a telephone or written referral. In exceptional situations a shorter response time may be negotiated by the department with the agency;

The availability of staff seven days per week, twenty-four hours a day;

The provision of services in the family's home or a setting convenient to the family;

The availability of staff to appear/testify at Juvenile Court on behalf of a referred family as requested by the Department;

The arrangement or provision of an aftercare plan or follow-up services for referred families in consultation with department staff;

The capacity to assist in the development and collection of client tracking data, to document the delivery of services and to cooperate with the evaluation of the Families First Initiative.

The goals of the program, as specified in the RFP, were that 85% of families would remain intact during the service period and for a period of six months following the termination of services and that 80% of families would not be the subjects of indicated reports during that time. Other goals were process measures: 90% of families would receive at least one service through a community provider and 100% would have face-to-face contact with the agency within twenty-four hours of referral. The goals were refined in the course of the program, but not materially changed.

Initial Implementation

DCFS is a large bureaucracy with over three thousand employees and an annual budget in fiscal year 1994 of about 900 million dollars. The department provides many of its services under contract with private agencies. At the time the Family First initiative was begun, the administration of DCFS was largely decentralized in eight regional offices. The regions had a great deal of autonomy so there was some variation in the interpretation of goals of the program and in approaches to achievement of those goals. A statewide coordinator was responsible for facilitating the implementation of the program but this was a staff rather than a line position and therefore did not have authority over program implementation in the regions. In each of the regions a Family First coordinator was appointed. Coordinators wore various other hats; for example, they might be assistant regional administrators, managers of the local offices for investigation of abuse and neglect, or grants and contracts administrators.

The initial RFP to provide family preservation services was issued by DCFS in August 1988. The department received seventy-one proposals, which were reviewed by panels composed of regional and central office staff. Each review panel operated quite independently. Twenty-five contracts involving services at thirty-one sites were awarded. Thirteen of the contracts were awarded in Cook County and twelve downstate. In October 1988, the department issued an RFP for evaluation of family preservation services. Approximately ten proposals were submitted and these were reviewed by a panel composed of departmental and private agency personnel. The evaluation contract was awarded to the Chapin Hall Center for Children at the University of Chicago.

The first agency to begin operations received its initial referral in December 1988. Press conferences were held in each region to kick off the Family First initiative, beginning with one in Chicago on January 9, 1989, attended by Governor James Thompson and DCFS director Gordon Johnson. As referrals to the Family First programs began, the department held several types of orientation sessions for DCFS and private agency staff. These meetings focused on problems in substitute care and the historical and philosophical underpinnings of family preservation services. The early training sessions were devoted to convincing DCFS investigative staff and private agency personnel at various levels that this new way of working with protective service cases—involving intensive, in-home intervention with families to prevent substitute care placement—had promise as a response to serious social problems. In addition, there was a great deal of emphasis in these sessions on procedural issues, eligibility requirements, and the coordination of referrals from DCFS to the private agencies. Considerable attention was also given to the development of "disaster protocols," plans to deal with tragic circumstances, particularly those with public relations implications, such as the death of a child in the program.

The Family First initiative was fully launched by DCFS at a two-day meeting in Chicago in January 1989 for private agency executives, program directors, and DCFS regional and central office staff. Eighty-two people attended this meeting. The keynote address was given by Jane Knitzer from the Bank Street College of Education in New York. Other speakers included DCFS Director Gordon Johnson and Jerome Stermer

(president of the advocacy organization Voices for Illinois Children).
DCFS central office staff described the department's long range plans for
Family First, approaches to family assessment, and plans for training,
evaluation, and community education.

Following this opening meeting, 20 two-day training sessions were
held for line staff in both the public and private agencies. These were
attended by a total of 653 DCFS child protective services staff and private
agency workers. Sponsored by DCFS, these meetings focused on historical and philosophical perspectives on family preservation services, enabling legislation and reasonable efforts, risk assessment, eligibility
requirements, engaging families, planning services, and referral processes. This was the beginning of a fairly extensive investment in training throughout the period of the initiative.

The Growth of Family First

By June 30, 1989, the program involved about 30 agencies in selected
areas of the state and had served approximately 450 cases. During fiscal
year 1990 (July 1, 1989, to June 30, 1990), the Family First program grew
markedly. The appropriation for fiscal year 1990 was $12.3 million, but
since most of that was to be spent in the last half of the year, this
amounted to an annualized allocation of $20.6 million (compared to an
appropriation of about $3 million in the first year, an annualized amount
of about $6.3 million). By June 30, 1990, 60 agencies throughout the state
were involved and had served over 2,000 families. The referral criteria
for the program were broadened from families with children under 6 to
include families with at least one child age 12 or under at risk of placement. In addition, a reunification program was begun with 13 private
agency programs and 5 internal DCFS programs. This program was
designed to facilitate the return home of children in placement (Chapin
Hall was also responsible for the evaluation of that program). The year
also saw the beginning (in April 1990) of an experiment in which cases in
selected regions were randomly assigned to the Family First program or
to the regular services of the department, an experiment designed to
provide definitive information on the effects of the program. The experiment continued until April 1992.

The rapid expansion of the Family First program in fiscal 1990 resulted
in a number of strains in the program. Some agencies new to the program had difficulties in starting their programs, primarily because of
problems in recruiting staff. Staff turnover in this very demanding program became an issue in some agencies. DCFS staff experienced difficulty in properly monitoring the new agencies. Concern was expressed
about the ability of the private sector to respond to the demands of the

new program; it was thought that the private sector might have reached a saturation point with the expansion of the placement prevention program and the initiation of the reunification program. At the same time, it became evident that in some locations the supply of slots in the program exceeded the demand for services and the criteria for referral were relaxed in some instances.

In the following chapters we consider Illinois's implementation of family preservation services. To a substantial extent, the Illinois program did not live up to its billing. The shortcomings of this program were largely due to the fact that most of the children in the families served by the program would not have been placed in substitute care in the absence of the program. That is, the intended target group was not served. Despite these problems, the program did provide many needed services to many families, services that would not have been available otherwise. As we seek to further reform the child welfare system, it is important that we learn the lessons of this and other experiments.

NOTES

1. Substantial assistance in the preparation of this chapter was provided by Tom Lawless.
2. In some states, all residents are theoretically under the obligation to report (see Hutchinson 1993).
3. The principles were codified in the federal Adoption Assistance and Child Welfare Act of 1980 (PL 96-272), which conditioned federal financial participation in states' costs of foster care on the provision of services based on these principles.
4. This view is at variance with that of Goldstein et al. (1973): "Normally, the physical facts of having begotten a child or having given birth to it have far-reaching meaning for the parents as confirmation of their respective sexual identities, their potency and intactness. . . . By contrast, for the child, the physical realities of his conception are not the direct cause of his emotional attachments" (pp. 16–17).
5. See the discussion below of the origins of this principle in the first White House Conference on Children in 1909.
6. An early case requiring the states to pursue their purposes with minimal restrictions on individual liberties is *Shelton v. Tucker* 1960. An Illinois case is the *Chicago Board of Education v. Terrile* 1977, concerning the state's handling of habitual truants, a case that helped close the Chicago truancy schools.
7. The 1909 White House Conference on Children developed a very similar hierarchy (*Proceedings of the Conference on the Care of Dependent Children* 1909).
8. Data are from the Chapin Hall Multistate Data Archive. Children in care for three days or less are excluded.
9. Other states are also experiencing this trend (see Wulczyn and Goerge 1992).

10. States vary in their eligibility requirements for relative foster care payments and in their levels of payment. Most require that relative homes be licensed or otherwise certified. Nine states also require that children be eligible for Title IV-E foster care funds, a requirement that has been affirmed by the Ninth Federal Circuit in an Oregon case (*Lipscomb v. Simmons* 1992).

11. Testa (1993) estimates that for Illinois children entering care in 1987–1988, reunification rates for children who were ever placed in home of relative care are 50–60% lower than for those never placed with relatives.

12. A federal Supreme Court decision requires that payment for licensed kinship care be made at the same rate as for nonkin care (*Miller v. Youakim* 1979). However, the Illinois Department of Children and Family Services pays the nonkin rate for all kinship care. An Illinois appellate court decision in 1990 (*In re B.T.*) increased the likelihood that DCFS would take custody of children in cases in which parents leave children with relatives. Countering this tendency, the law was changed in 1993 to remove from the definition of neglect situations in which parents place their children with relatives by plan.

Testa (1993) notes that in Illinois, rates for foster care (whether with kin or nonkin) increase linearly with increasing numbers of siblings, while AFDC rates level off. Thus, with larger sibling groups the disparity between AFDC and foster care payments is greater. This is likely the case in other states as well.

13. Recent analyses of data on the movement of Chicago children at the time of initial placement indicates that the "percent of children placed with relatives that did not move rose steadily from 1987 (11.3%) to 1990 (20.3%) and then decreased slightly in 1991 (17.7%)" (Goerge, Harden, and Lee 1993:3). The percentages are highest for African-American children (see also Testa 1993).

14. Some states use two different categories: (1) substantiated or founded and (2) indicated or reason to suspect.

15. These data are for calendar years. California and New York are not included among the 33 states so it is difficult to interpret this number. The number reported for Illinois is 7,320, which compares to the Illinois DCFS annual report figure of 7,878 for fiscal 1992. Note also that "children removed from their homes" includes children in care for brief periods, perhaps in shelters, and those in care awaiting a court hearing.

16. Actually, these data do not reflect reports per se. Rather, the numbers of reports shown here are numbers of reports *investigated*. Workers at the Illinois child abuse and neglect hotline screen reports to determine whether they should be investigated and a substantial number of reports are not investigated. DCFS reports the total number of calls to the hotline but this does not indicate the number of reports since it includes callbacks when the caller was unable to get through the first time or was told to call back later, multiple calls on the same incident from different reporters, and simply requests for information. As a result, accurate data on the number of incidents reported do not exist.

17. These problems with the data make it impossible to use them to determine the effects of the DCFS placement prevention program (which has operated from 1989 to the present) on total numbers of placements in the state.

It is of interest to compare the numbers of children taken into protective custody in fiscal 1992 (7,878) with the number of children entering foster care in calendar 1992 (from Table 1.2, 13,925). The number entering foster care is much higher than the number taken into protective custody. For reasons stated earlier, the data on placements and the data on protective custodies are not strictly comparable (besides the fact that one is a fiscal year and the other a calendar year number). Some children taken into protective custody are almost immediately returned home from shelters and may not show up in the foster care numbers. On the other hand, as explained above, there are a number of foster care entries that do not come through the abuse and neglect reporting system, a fact that is evident in the comparison of these figures.

18.   Kempe et al.'s (1963) famous article galvanized the concern of medical and social service professionals for the "battered child." However, it is of interest that the radiological advances occurred much earlier, along with the recognition that intentional mistreatment might be the cause of mysterious fractures in the long bones of children (see Caffey 1957; Antler 1981).

19.   The identification of the failure-to-thrive syndrome dates back at least to Chapin's observations of institutionalized children in 1915. After the phenomenon disappeared from the literature for a while, Spitz (1945) refocused attention on it (see Oates 1986). For discussions of SIDS, see Christoffel (1992), Berger (1979), and Lundstrom and Sharpe (1991).

20.   According to the *Encyclopedia Britannica* (1994) "The origin of alcoholic beverages is lost in the mists of prehistory" (p. 199). Roueche (1960) writes, "That epochal hour [when people first encountered alcohol], like so many beginnings, is lost in the ambiguous deeps of time" (pp. 3–4). And Barber (1967) says "Opium in some form has been used in many different parts of the world, and apparently for as far back as we can read history" (p. 3).

21.   For more extensive descriptions of models of family preservation practice, see Nelson et al. (1990), Nelson and Landsman (1992), and Barth (1990).

22.   For a further discussion of limitations in use of crisis theory see Barth (1990).

23.   Barthel (1992) quotes National Center on Child Abuse and Neglect statistics indicating that 30 out of 1,000 children in foster care are abused. Recidivism rates for families with founded reports are at least ten times higher.

Chapter 2

Previous Research on Family Preservation

What is known about the effects of family preservation programs? In this chapter we review previous research on programs designed to prevent out-of-home placement of children. We also review what is known about the effects of social interventions aimed at preventing child abuse or neglect. We find little evidence that family preservation programs result in substantial reductions in the placement of children. Claims to the contrary have been based largely on nonexperimental studies that do not provide solid evidence of program effects. The results of controlled studies suggest that difficulties in targeting services to families at risk of placement contribute to the lack of program effects on placement. Prevention of child maltreatment has also been an elusive objective in family preservation and family support programs.

PLACEMENT PREVENTION

Since the central concern of family preservation programs has been the prevention of placement, this has been a major, sometimes singular focus of evaluations. Most evaluations of programs designed to prevent placement have used nonexperimental designs.[1] The results of these studies suggest that most families remain intact during and shortly after family preservation services. One of the earliest studies of the Homebuilders' model (Kinney, Madsen, Fleming, and Haapala (1977) found that 97% of 80 families remained intact three months after the intervention had ended. Since then, evaluations of the Homebuilders program have found that 73 to 91% of families were intact at 12 months after referral for service (Kinney et al. 1991). Studies of other programs have found that at least two-thirds of families remain together within a year after the end of services. For example, 66% of 747 families who received family preservation services in Iowa remained intact one year after termination (Thieman, Fuqua, and Linnan 1990). A study of family preservation services in Connecticut found that 69% of 591 families remained intact one year after services and 82% of the 1,588 children in these families were not placed during this period (Wheeler, Reuter, Struckman-Johnson, and Yuan 1993). Eighty-eight percent of 367 families in the In-home Family Care Program in northern California were intact one year after services ended (Berry 1992).

The Families First program in Michigan has received a great deal of attention because of its claimed success in preventing placement. An evaluation of the program compared 225 children who were thought to be at "imminent risk of placement" at the time their families were referred to the program with a matched comparison group of 225 children who had recently exited foster care.[2] It is not clear to us how this group can be considered to be an adequate comparison group. Children at risk of placement and those recently discharged from care are likely to differ in many respects, including their likelihood of experiencing future placement. An adequate comparison group should be composed of children who are in similar circumstances and who have similar probabilities of placement at various points in time. It is not at all clear that the comparison group here meets these requirements. With that caveat in mind, 76% of the children in the Families First group remained in their homes for 12 months after the intervention, while 65% of children in the comparison group remained in their homes for 12 months after they had returned from foster care (Bergquist, Szwejda, and Pope 1993). Additional claims for the effectiveness of the program, made by the State of Michigan, have been based on a decrease in the number of children placed in foster care in 1992, four years after the initiation of the Families First program.[3] However, Schwartz and his colleagues (forthcoming) examined the Michigan data in terms of rates of foster placement per thousand children; their results are inconclusive.[4] In any event, changes in foster care rates over a few years do not provide evidence of the effects of family preservation programs because such rates are affected by many other factors. In many jurisdictions, foster care caseloads are increasing despite the presence of family preservation services; it is possible that these increases would be greater in the absence of family preservation efforts or, as we shall suggest in Chapter 6, intensive in-home services may actually contribute to the rise in foster care rates.

These findings have been used to suggest that family preservation programs reduce the need for out-of-home placement of children.[5] However, nonexperimental studies such as these do not provide convincing evidence of program effects, since it is not clear whether families would have experienced placement of children in the absence of these services.

Claims that children were at imminent risk of placement at the time of referral have not been supported by evidence. Although referring workers are often uncertain about whether and when placement may (and should) occur, they may assert that placement is imminent in order to obtain intensive services for families.[6] Randomized experiments provide the only means to determine what would have happened in the absence of family preservation services and, thus, experiments provide the best estimates of the effects of these programs. Below we review the results of controlled studies of family preservation programs; these studies are described in greater detail in Appendix A.[7] Early studies (those conducted in the late 1970s and early 1980s) involved smaller groups of clients than more recent evaluations. We pay particular attention to the methods and findings of larger and more recent studies.

Early Studies

The New York State Preventive Services Demonstration Project, conducted in the mid-1970s, provided intensive services to families over approximately 14 months (Jones, Neuman, and Shyne 1976). The project may be considered a precursor to current family preservation programs. During the spring and summer of 1974, the project served cases in which placement was thought to be imminent, families with children in placement, and those in which children had recently been returned home. The goals of the project were to prevent placement, reunify families, and prevent reentry into foster care. Here we focus on the subgroup of families in which children were living at home at the time of referral. Families of 525 children were randomly assigned to the program or a control group. At the end of treatment, placement rates were significantly lower in the experimental group than in the control group (7 versus 18%). Six months after the termination of services, 8% of children in the program group and 23% of those in the control group had been placed (Jones et al. 1976). A follow-up study of a subsample of 243 children in the experiment was conducted five years after the project ended. At that time, 34% of the children in the experimental group and 46% of those in the control group had been placed in foster care, a statistically significant difference (Jones 1985). Thus, the program appears to have had beneficial effects on placement, although the differences between the experimental and control groups were not large, and sample loss at the time of the five-year follow-up (less than 50% were followed) limits the usefulness of the data.

Special Services for Children, a public agency in New York City, provided intensive services to families with children "at risk of placement." Halper and Jones (1981, reviewed in Stein 1985) reported the results of a randomized experiment involving 120 families with 282 children. During the project, 4% (6) of the 156 children in the experimental group and 17% (22) of 126 in the control group were placed in substitute care (a statistically significant difference).

The Hudson County Special Service Project was conducted in New Jersey in the late 1970s. The program served families whose children were thought to be at "risk of placement within the next two years" (Magura 1981, Stein 1985). Ninety families were randomly assigned to program and control groups. At the end of the three-year demonstration project, 24% (11) of families in the program and 18% (8) of those in the control group experienced placement (a nonsignificant difference). Children in the control group were more likely to be placed in restrictive settings (such as residential treatment) and less likely to be placed with relatives than those who received more intensive services (Willems and DeRubeis 1981).

Nebraska Intensive Services to Families at Risk served families at risk of placement because of actual or suspected child maltreatment (Leeds 1984, reviewed in Stein 1985). One hundred and fifty-three families were randomly assigned to experimental or control groups. Control cases required more public foster care, compared with experimental cases, which were more likely to be placed with relatives and friends. Although the exact number of children placed is not known,[8] available data show that 4% (3) of 80 families in the experimental group and 11% (8) of 73 families in the control group had one or more children placed in out-of-home care (Stein 1985), a nonsignificant difference.

The *Home Based Services Demonstration Project* of the Ramsey County (St. Paul), Minnesota, child protective services department (Lyle and Nelson 1983) involved random assignment of 74 families to one of three traditional child protection units or an experimental, family-centered, home-based unit (Frankel 1988). Three months after services ended, 33% of families in the experimental group had experienced placement of one or more children, compared with 55% of families in the control group. Of the children who were placed, those in the experimental group spent significantly less time in substitute care (Frankel 1988).

The *Family Study Project in Hennepin County*, Minneapolis, involved random assignment of 138 cases to experimental and control units of the county agency (Hennepin County Community Services Department 1980, reviewed in Stein 1985). The families served had children under age 15 who "were at risk of placement, but who were judged by intake workers not to be at imminent risk of abuse or neglect" (Stein 1985:116). The experimental group had a higher number of children placed in foster care (123 versus 84 children in the control group); however, the total number of children in each group was not reported (Stein 1985). Of those placed, children in the experimental group spent slightly fewer days in placement (mean of 199 days) than those in the control group (mean of 208 days).

A Social Learning Treatment Program in Oregon, reported by Szykula and Fleischman (1985), involved a randomized experiment with families of 48 children to test the effects of a social learning treatment program compared with regular child protective services.[9] Clients were parents with children between the ages of 3 and 12 who were considered at risk of placement because of child abuse and neglect. Cases were identified as more or less difficult by workers, based on numbers of prior abuse reports and types of family problems.[10] Cases within each difficulty group were randomly assigned to program or control services. The experimental program appeared to reduce the risk of placement among less difficult cases: 8% (1 of 13) of the children in the less difficult experimental group and 38% (5 of 13) of those in the comparable control group were placed. However, there was no significant difference between program and control groups in placement rates for more difficult cases: 64% (7 of 11) of children in the more difficult experiment group versus 45% (5 of 11) in the control group. The overall effect of the program (for both groups) was not significant.

FamiliesFirst in Davis, California, an intensive, in-home service program was based on the Homebuilders model (Wood, Barton, and Schroeder 1988). An overflow comparison study was conducted in conjunction with researchers at the University of California at Davis. Families were referred to the project by child protective services staff. Eligible families had children who had been abused or neglected and were thought to be at risk of having at least one child placed out of the home. One year after intake, 25% (15) of the 59 children in the in-home services group were placed compared with 53% (26) of 49 children in the comparison group (a statistically significant difference). Children who were the focus of intervention were placed more often than their siblings.

Thus, the results of early experimental studies of family preservation programs were mixed: Some found little or no effects on placement, while others found that the programs achieved slight reductions in placement. However, in all studies, relatively few control group families experienced placement. This means that services were generally not delivered to the target group of families at risk of placement.

More Recent Studies[11]

Family Preservation Services in Hennepin County, the second study conducted in Hennepin County, was an evaluation of a program conducted by the county Child Welfare Division (Schwartz and AuClaire 1989; Schwartz, AuClaire, and Harris 1991). The program consisted of intensive home-based services delivered by eight "specially trained social workers." The service was intended to last for four weeks. The evaluation of this program involved a nonrandom comparison group. There were 58 cases in each group, selected during the period August through December 1985. Three of the experimental group cases were in placement during the entire follow-up period and were excluded from outcome analyses. Follow-up extended until December 31, 1986. The authors believed that since the comparison group was almost certain to have a placement at the beginning of the study period (actually, 5 were never placed during the study period), it would be appropriate to compare their placement experience after that placement with that of the home-based service group. These "adjusted" comparisons are reported here. There were 76 placement episodes involving 31 (56%) of the 55 experimental cases and 81 (adjusted) placements involving 34 (59%) of the 58 comparison cases.

The Bronx Homebuilders Program, modeled after Homebuilders, began accepting clients in May 1987 (Mitchell, Tovar, and Knitzer 1989). A preliminary evaluation involving 45 families referred in the first year is available. Cases were referred from two sources: the city Child Welfare Administration (CWA) and the Pius XII Court Designated Assessment Service (Pius). The average length of service was 35 days. A one-year follow-up was conducted. An overflow comparison group of 12 families was available for the Pius group (1 of these 12 families was lost to follow-up). Families in the overflow group had relatively fewer placements than those in the service group. At 3 months, 19% (4 of 21) CWA, 23% (5 of 22) Pius treatment, and 9% (1 of 11) Pius comparison families had experienced a placement. At 12 months, 24% (5) of the CWA, 27% (6) of the Pius treatment, and 18% (2) of the Pius comparison families had experienced placement. Apparently, all children who were placed were still in placement at the end of the follow-up period.

The Family-Based Intensive Treatment (FIT) Study (Pecora, Fraser, and Haapala 1992) involved 453 Utah and Washington families in intensive home-based services based on the Homebuilders model and 26 families in an overflow comparison group in Utah.[12] A 12-month follow-up was conducted with 263 families. In Utah a 60-day service model was provided in two sites by the state child welfare department, while in Washington a 30-day service was provided in four sites by Homebuilders (under contract with the state agency). The criteria for referral were risk of imminent placement, safety of the child with service, and willingness of at least one parent to cooperate with service. At termination, 9% of the 172 Utah children and 6% of the 409 Washington children in the treatment groups had been placed. At the 12-month follow-up, 41% of 97 Utah children and 30% of 245 Washington children had been placed. In the Utah comparison group of 27 children, 85% were placed during the 12-month follow-up period.

Unfortunately, 54% of the cases served in the Washington project during the study period did not participate in the study.[13] In addition, 32% of the cases in the overflow comparison group were not tracked. The biasing effects of these losses are not known. The researchers note that the overflow comparison group was quite small and that they relied on interviews with referring workers for information on outcomes for this group (in contrast, placement data were obtained from both clients and workers in the Homebuilders programs). Missing data for the overflow comparison group seriously compromise the interpretation of differences. In addition, referring workers can often manipulate an overflow design in order to ensure that cases that really "need" intensive services receive them. For example, some cases may be referred repeatedly until there is an opening for services.

California's AB 1562 In-home Care Demonstration Projects, evaluated by Walter R. McDonald and Associates (1990), was an intensive, in-home services program conducted in eight counties. The program operated from 1986 to 1989. Cases thought to involve "imminent risk of placement" due to abuse or neglect were referred by county child protective services offices.[14] Families were served for an average of 7 weeks in programs conducted in eight sites by seven private agencies and one public mental health agency. Data were collected on 709 (96%) of the 741 families served by these programs over a 3-year period.

A substudy involving the random assignment of cases to the new services and to regular services of the county child welfare agencies was conducted with 152 families in each group. Five of the eight in-home service programs participated in this substudy. Families in the control group received "traditional services" provided by the local child protective services office, either directly or through referrals to other community resources. Detailed data on the types and amounts of services provided to cases in the control group are not available.

Cases were followed for 8 months after random assignment. Outcome data were available for 293 (96%) of the cases in the randomized experiment. It was found that in 20% of the control group families and 25% of the experimental group families a placement occurred between two and 8 months after referral—a difference that is not statistically significant.[15] (A similar proportion of the entire group of 709 families experienced placement in the study period.) There were no substantial differences in lengths of time in placement and costs of placement.[16] Of the children placed, those in the control group were more likely to be placed with relatives.

The *New Jersey Family Preservation Services* (FPS) program was modeled after Homebuilders. Services were provided by private agencies in five counties for a median of 6 weeks. Referrals came from local child welfare offices, county family court or crisis intervention units, and regional community mental health centers. The FPS programs served "several waves" of families before a randomized experiment was instituted by the state. Data are available on 117 experimental and 97 control cases that were randomly assigned in four of New Jersey's 21 counties (Feldman 1991). Another 33 families were "turned back" after random assignment to the experimental services (because they did not meet selection criteria, the caretaker refused to participate in the program, or the children were deemed at imminent risk of harm and were removed from the home); these cases were not included in the analysis. The exclusion of 22% of the cases assigned to the experimental group casts doubt on the initial comparability of the experimental and control groups.

During the intervention period (approximately 6 weeks) 17% of the families in the control group experienced placement of at least one target child, compared to 6% of families in the experimental group. At 6 months posttermination, 50% of control group families and 27% of families in the experimental group had experienced at least one placement.[17] At one year posttermination, 57% of families in the control group and 43% of those in the experimental group had experienced placement. (Differences between groups were statistically significant at each point in time.)[18] There is some evidence that the program delayed placement, but the magnitude of this effect dissipated over time. For the first target child to enter placement in each family, there were no significant differences between the experimental and control groups in types of placements,[19] numbers of placements, or duration of time in placement.

Other outcomes that were examined included changes in measures of family functioning, perceived social support, goal attainment, and client satisfaction. There were some differences between experimental and control groups in the amount of change in these measures (favoring the experimental group) but they were quite limited (Feldman 1990, 1991).

The Family Support Project in Los Angeles provided in-home family support services to families referred by the Los Angeles County Department of Children's Services to two private child welfare agencies. Referrals were based on "caseworker judgment about need for the services" and were not limited to cases in which children were thought to be at imminent risk of placement (Meezan and McCroskey 1993).[20] Families referred to the project ($N = 240$) were randomly assigned to in-home services or regular child protective services. Data on placements were available for 231 families. At the beginning of the project 37 (34%) of the 108 families in the program group and 30 (24%) of 123 families in the control group had one or more children in placement. During the project, 19 (6%) of the 335 children in the experimental group were placed, compared with 34 (8%) of 424 children in the comparison group. At the end of the project (12 months after services ended), families in the experimental group had more children in out-of-home placements than those in the comparison group (38 versus 24%) (McCroskey and Meezan 1993). Below we report the study's findings regarding program effects on family functioning.

Studies Currently Under Way. Several other studies are now under way. Most notably, Betty Blythe and her colleagues are conducting a randomized experiment in Detroit. This study is designed to address the targeting problems evident in previous evaluations. Random assignment to family preservation or control groups will occur after placement has been authorized by the Wayne County Juvenile Court. The Detroit study is being conducted from January 1993 through September 1995. Evaluations of family preservation programs are also underway in Arkansas, California, Hawaii, New York, North Carolina, and Texas.

Relationships between Case Characteristics and Placement Rates. Several studies have reported results of analyses of the characteristics of families that are likely to experience placement during or soon after family preservation services.[21] These findings have sometimes been used to describe the kinds of cases in which family preservation services are more or less likely to be "successful." However, analysis of relationships between case characteristics and outcomes within groups receiving intensive services does not provide information about the relative effects of services for various subgroups. This is because the "base rates" of outcomes, in the absence of these services, vary across subgroups. To identify subgroups that benefit most, it is necessary to look within subgroups, comparing cases that received family preservation services with those that did not. Two studies have conducted this type of analysis, although findings in both are based on very small numbers of cases. Feldman (1991) found that family preservation services appeared to result in reduced risk of placement for single-parent families. Overall, single-parent families were more likely to experience placement within one year after program termination. Approximately two-thirds (68%) of the single-parent families in the control group experienced placement, compared with 49% of the single-parent families who received family preservation services. The study by Szykula and Fleischman (1985) described above suggested that efforts to prevent placement may be more successful for families in which child abuse and neglect are not chronic and other family problems are relatively less severe.

Relationships between Service Characteristics and Placement. Several studies have examined correlations between service characteristics and placement outcomes.[22] However, since these studies did not randomly assign clients to different types of treatment these findings are difficult to interpret. It is not clear how case characteristics were related to differences in the provision of services.

Summary. Although many nonexperimental studies have suggested that high percentages of families remain intact after intensive family preservation services, the results of randomized experiments provide more convincing tests of the extent to which "placement prevention rates" can be attributed to the effects of these programs. The findings of the controlled studies we reviewed are decidedly mixed: Six of the 10 randomized experiments (Willems and DeRubeis 1981; Leeds 1984; Hennepin County Community Services Department 1980; Szykula and Fleischman 1985; McDonald and Associates 1990; Meezan and McCroskey 1993) and two comparison group studies (Mitchell et al. 1989; Schwartz et al. 1991) found that the programs did not produce significant overall reductions in placement. Four randomized experiments (Jones et al. 1976; Halper and Jones 1981; Lyle and Nelson 1983; Feldman 1991) and two overflow comparison studies (Wood et al. 1988; Pecora et al. 1992) found significant reductions in placement in favor of the experimental groups.

In studies that found significant reductions in placement, differences between groups were relatively small. For example, in New Jersey, the difference between groups in the proportion of cases in placement at one year after treatment ended was 14% (Feldman 1991). Although larger differences were found in the overflow studies, serious questions about the comparability of groups in these studies remain. Small sample sizes are also a concern, particularly in the earlier projects.

The fact that placement occurred within a short period of time after group assignment in less than half of the control or comparison cases in most studies suggests that these programs were generally not delivered to families with children at risk of placement. (The placement rate in a control group is an estimate of the risk of placement for both groups in the absence of experimental services.) When the risk of placement among family preservation clients is low, it is unlikely that a program will demonstrate significant reductions in placement. It is not meaningful to talk about preventing an event if the event would not have happened anyway.

Finally, available evidence sheds little light on whether family preservation programs have differential effects on placement for different kinds of families or on the relative effectiveness of different approaches to placement prevention.

PREVENTION OF SUBSEQUENT CHILD MALTREATMENT

The hope in family preservation programs is to prevent the placement of children without further harm to them. Few studies have examined the effects of family preservation programs on the recurrence of child maltreatment. In her 5-year follow-up study, Jones (1985) found that 21% of 98 families in the experimental group had experienced one or more indicated reports of child maltreatment, compared with 25% of 44 control group families. The difference between groups was not statistically significant. Similarly, McDonald and Associates (1990) reported that approximately one-quarter of families in both the program and control groups experienced an investigation of child abuse or neglect within 8 months after referral. As with placement, the rates of maltreatment in both the experimental and control groups in these studies were fairly low. Had placement been prevented, the results could be taken as indicating that this benefit was attained without increased harm to most children. However, most children in both groups remained in their homes, and the results indicate that the experimental services did not reduce an already low rate of subsequent harm.

IMPACT ON CHILD AND FAMILY FUNCTIONING

Several studies have compared measures of family functioning obtained before and after family preservation services, but few controlled studies have examined program effects on child and family functioning.[23]

In the New Jersey study, both the treatment and control groups made gains on the Family Environment Scale, Interpersonal Support Evaluation List, and Child Well-Being Scales, but there were few statistically significant differences between groups in the amount of change (Feldman 1991). In Meezan and McCroskey's (1993) study, family functioning was measured on six scales: parent-child interactions, living conditions of the family, interactions between caregivers, supports available to parents, financial conditions of the family, and developmental stimulation of children. Families who received in-home services and those in the regular services comparison group generally reported that they did not have significant problems in family functioning at case opening and did not see significant change in these areas at case closing. However, families in the in-home services group reported more improvements in living conditions and financial conditions at one year after termination, compared to families who received regular child protective services. Parents in the program group also reported more improvements in their children's behavior between referral and case closing, although there were no differences between groups one year after services had ended. In contrast to parents' views of family functioning, workers who provided home-based services reported that the families had significant problems in all areas of family functioning at case opening and made significant improvements in four of six domains at case closing.[24] (The four areas in which improvements were noted were parent-child interactions, living conditions, supports available to families, and developmental stimulation given to children.) The validity of workers' ratings of change in cases in which they are invested is open to question. Further, since caseworkers' reports were not available for the control group, we cannot be sure that changes reported by workers were due to the services provided.

COST EFFECTIVENESS OF FAMILY PRESERVATION SERVICES

Family preservation programs have been promoted as a cost-effective alternative to foster care. However, claims of cost savings are based largely on nonexperimental studies that assume that some or all of the families who receive intensive, home-based services would have required placement in the absence of these services. The costs of intensive services are then compared with estimated costs of placements.[25] As we have shown, the assumption that placement would have occurred in the absence of services is highly problematic.

Few controlled studies have examined costs in treatment and control groups. In an overflow comparison group study, Wood et al. (1988) reported that the cost of 4 to 6 weeks of in-home services for 26 FamiliesFirst cases plus the cost of placements that occurred in these cases over a one-year period totaled $124,783, compared with $176,015 in placement costs alone for 24 cases in the comparison group. Information on the costs of other services provided to program and comparison cases was not available.

Only one randomized experiment has examined costs in both treatment and control groups. McDonald and Associates (1990) found that the placement costs for in-home services and control cases were comparable ($141,375 versus $145,388) for the 152 families in each group. In addition, the average cost of providing intensive, home-based services was $4,767 per family served, over $700,000 in total (McDonald and Associates 1990). Unfortunately, data on the costs of nonplacement services provided to the control group were not available, but it is reasonable to assume that these were considerably lower than the cost of intensive, in-home services. Thus, it is quite likely that the total costs for cases in the family preservation program exceeded the costs of services to control cases.

On balance, evidence for the cost effectiveness of family preservation programs is scant and the results of available studies are mixed.

THE PREVENTION OF CHILD ABUSE AND NEGLECT

We look briefly at studies of other programs aimed at preventing or treating child maltreatment.[26] A number of approaches have been developed in an effort to prevent maltreatment in families thought to be at high risk of harming their children or in families in which children have been harmed in the past.[27] There is little evidence that such programs are successful in reducing the incidence (or recurrence) of child abuse and neglect (Kaufman and Zigler 1992). While some studies of programs aimed at preventing child abuse and neglect have reported positive outcomes, much of this research is methodologically flawed. Studies often provide insufficient information on characteristics of clients, maltreatment, and interventions (Blythe 1983) and lack adequate controls for threats to internal validity (Daro 1988).

Cohn and Daro (1987) reviewed four studies on 88 federally funded demonstration projects conducted between 1974 and 1982.[28] These programs served families at "high risk" of child maltreatment and those who had been the subject of substantiated reports of maltreatment. Some projects focused on specific subgroups, including families in which there had been sexual abuse, substance abuse, maltreatment of adolescents, or child neglect. Each of the studies compared groups who received different services, but clients were not randomly assigned. Two studies reported rates of subsequent maltreatment during treatment that ranged from 44 to 47%; a third found that severe maltreatment occurred during treatment in 30% of families in the study; data on maltreatment rates were not available in the fourth study. In the two largest studies, over half of the families were judged by caseworkers as likely to abuse or neglect their children following termination.

Lutzker and Rice (1984) conducted a comparison group study of the effects of Project 12-ways, an in-home services program, on the recurrence of child abuse and neglect. Families were referred to the project by state child protective services units in southern Illinois. Families in the program had significantly fewer incidents of child abuse and neglect than a random sample of other child protective services cases in the same geographic area, but the comparability of groups prior to service is unknown.

Olds and Kitzman's (1990) review of randomized trials of prenatal and postnatal home-visitation programs for economically disadvantaged women and children included three studies that examined program effects on child abuse and neglect. These included Gray, Cutler, Dean, and Kempe's (1979) study of a Denver program that combined intensive pediatric consultation with weekly home visits by public health nurses and paraprofessionals from infancy through the first two years of a child's life. The second study compared a Greensboro, North Carolina, program of early and extended contact between mothers and newborns and nine home visits by paraprofessionals during the first 3 months of the children's lives with a no-treatment control (Siegel, Bauman, Schaefer, Saunders, and Ingram 1980). The third trial tested the effects of nurse home visiting during the prenatal period in Elmira, New York (Olds, Henderson, Chamberlin, and Tatlebaum 1986; Olds and Henderson 1989). In all three of these studies there were no statistically significant differences between program and control cases in rates of child maltreatment.[29]

Barth, Hacking, and Ash (1988) evaluated a home-visiting program for women who had been identified by community professionals as at risk of child abuse. Fifty women were referred to the project during pregnancy or after childbirth and were randomly assigned to program or control groups. Experimental services involved six months of home visiting by paraprofessional women and linkage to formal and informal community resources; women in the control group received "traditional community services." Although the program resulted in some advantages for the experimental group,[30] there were no significant differences between experimental and control groups in the number of reports or substantiated reports of child abuse.[31]

The National Academy of Sciences Panel on Research on Child Abuse and Neglect concluded that

Evaluations of home visitation programs, school-based programs for the prevention of child sexual abuse and violence, and other community-based child maltreatment prevention programs are quite limited. Many evaluations are compromised by serious methodological problems, and many promising preventive interventions do not systematically include child maltreatment as a program outcome. Children and families who are most at risk for child maltreatment may not participate in the interventions, and those that do may not be sufficiently motivated to change or will have difficulty in implementing skills in their social context, especially if they live in violent neighborhoods (Panel on Research on Child Abuse and Neglect 1993:14).

Thus far, the prevention and effective treatment of child abuse and neglect appear to be elusive goals. Although a variety of strategies have been tried, there is little evidence of the effectiveness of any particular approach. Kaufman and Zigler (1992) suggest that the equivocal findings of research in this area may be explained by preoccupation with simple main effects (does the program work or not?), rather than identifying conditions under which certain approaches may be effective.

Several controlled studies have examined the effects of family support programs on parents' knowledge of child development, parenting skills, and stressors that may contribute to child abuse and neglect. Siegel et al. (1980) found no significant differences between experimental and control groups in maternal attachment or health care utilization. Taylor and Beauchamp (1988) conducted a randomized trial of a four-week program of postnatal visiting of first-time mothers by student nurse volunteers. Subjects were not screened for potential for abuse; 30 mothers participated in the study. Dependent measures were collected by research staff who were blind to group assignments. At 3 months postpartum, mothers in the experimental group demonstrated greater knowledge of child development, more democratic views of child rearing, and more liberal attitudes toward discipline. They provided their infants with more verbal stimulation and generated a greater number of solutions to child-rearing problems. Larson (1980) conducted a study in which 80 pregnant women were randomly assigned to three groups: (1) a prenatal home visit, postpartum hospital visit, home visits for the infants' first six weeks, and additional visits throughout the first year; (2) home visits during the child's sixth through fifteenth weeks; and (3) no visits. Children in the first group had significantly lower accident rates and were more likely to receive immunizations than those in the other two groups.

SUMMARY AND CONCLUSIONS

The results of nonexperimental studies can be misleading—and nowhere is this more apparent than in the evaluation of family preservation programs. In addition, early studies of family preservation programs involved samples that were so small that it would have been quite difficult to detect significant program effects. Further, information about the nature of interventions was often incomplete. In response to these problems, recent evaluations have used larger samples and increasingly more sophisticated methods—including the use of comparison or control groups; systematic collection of data on family problems, services, and outcomes; and attempts to understand factors related to outcomes for families. However, there are few large, well-controlled studies of family preservation programs. Problems of sample size and questions about the nature of services provided and the comparability of groups remain, even in recent experiments.

As to the effects of intensive in-home services on placement and maltreatment, many of the programs studied did not focus on populations that had high rates of placement or maltreatment, and thus these rates in both experimental and control groups were low. Hence, the possibility of detecting effects on placement or maltreatment was low. It is not surprising then that few studies have demonstrated program effects in these areas or that, in the studies that have found such effects, they tend to be small and short-lived. It should also be noted that the approaches that have been tried tend to focus on the parent or the family and often ignore conditions in the community or larger social environment that may contribute to child maltreatment.

Our review suggests that family preservation programs have very modest effects on family and child functioning. Researchers have found few significant differences between program and comparison groups in levels of child and family functioning after services have been provided, and the results of available studies are conflicting. We suggest that it is not realistic to expect dramatic results in this area, given the number and magnitude of the problems faced by many child welfare clients and the short-term nature of family preservation services.

Many questions remain. For example, little attention has been paid to investigation of differential effects of family preservation programs for subgroups of families, the relative effectiveness of different approaches, or contextual factors that may affect outcomes (including community characteristics, availability of community services, and follow-up or aftercare services). We attempted to address some of these questions in the study reported in this book, but there is much that remains to be done.

NOTES

1. Studies that did not employ comparison or control groups include Bartsch and Kawamura (1993); Wheeler et al. (1993); Berry (1992); Kinney et al.

(1991); Smith (1991); Fondacaro and Tighe (1990); Thieman et al. (1990); Bribitzer and Verdieck (1988); Van Meter (1986); Hinckley and Ellis (1985); Landsman (1985); Leeds (1984); Florida Office of the Inspector General (1982); and Kinney et al. (1977). Studies that employed nonequivalent comparison group designs include Bergquist et al. (1993); Reid, Kagan, and Schlosberg (1988); and Pearson and King (1987). Previous reviews of this literature have been provided by McDonald and Associates (1992); Nelson and Landsman (1992); Rossi (1991); Fraser, Pecora, and Haapala (1991); Davis (1988); Frankel (1988); Jones (1985); Stein (1985); and Magura (1981).

Studies of programs designed to prevent placement of status offenders (Nugent, Carpenter, and Parks 1993) or delinquent and emotionally disturbed children (Cunningham, Homer, Bass, and Brown 1993) have also relied on non-experimental designs.

2. To create the comparison groups, one child who was designated "at imminent risk of placement" within each Families First case was matched with a child who had exited foster care within 90 days of the date the Families First case was initiated. The pairs of children were also matched on age, county of residence, type of referral, and prior involvement with protective services.

3. The Michigan Families First program began in 17 counties in 1988 and was quickly expanded to the rest of the state. During that time, the number of new foster care placements in that state increased steadily from 6,490 in 1988 to 8,299 in 1991, followed by a decrease to 7,632 new placements in 1992. The foster care caseload in Michigan grew from 15,878 in 1988 to 17,124 in 1992 (Michigan Department of Social Services 1993).

4. This analysis shows a slight increase in the rate of foster care placements per 1,000 children (under age 18) in the counties in which Families First began. In fiscal 1987, children in these counties were placed in out-of-home care for the first time at a rate of 2.5 per 1,000; the rates were 2.8 in 1988, 2.6 in 1989, 2.8 in 1990, and 3.1 in 1991. A similar rise in placement rates was found in the rest of the state (Schwartz et al. forthcoming).

5. See Hartman (1993), Berry (1992), Pecora et al. (1992), Kinney et al. (1991).

6. Our interviews with child protective services workers in Illinois suggest that this practice is viewed as advocacy on behalf of the client.

7. Other reviews of this literature are Jones (1985), Stein (1985), Frankel (1988), Fraser et al. (1991), Rossi (1991), Wells and Beigel (1991), and Nelson and Landsman (1992).

8. Data on informal placements with relatives and friends and on placements outside the project county were not available.

9. The authors describe another study, involving an A-B-A reversal design that focused on the numbers of substitute care placements in Jackson County, Oregon, before, during, and after installation of a social learning treatment program. Although the authors suggest that placements declined during the 9-month period in which the program was in operation, the results are not convincing, since placement was a fairly low-incident event among the target group in this county (only 58 placements were recorded during the entire 49-month study period).

10. The "less difficult" group included families with fewer than three reports of abuse, no serious housing or transportation problems, and children with conduct problems. Those in the "more difficult" group had three or more prior reports; serious problems with employment, transportation, and housing; and "major problems outside of their relationship with their child" (Szykula and Fleischman 1985:281).

11. Our review of these studies is adapted from Schuerman, Rzepnicki, Littell, and Budde (1992).

12. The overflow group consisted of 26 of the 38 families that were referred to the family preservation program but not served because program staff had full caseloads. They received traditional child welfare or mental health services. Twelve of the 38 families were referred to the program early on and could not be traced. The remaining 26 cases were tracked for one year or until a child at risk was placed, whichever came first (Pecora et al. 1991).

13. Of the cases that did not participate, slightly more than half (51%) were asked not to participate by their worker (for reasons that are not entirely clear), 24% refused to participate, 20% did not have the opportunity to participate because of research administration problems, and 5% were excluded for treatment reasons (Pecora, Fraser, and Haapala 1991).

14. During the second year of the study, *imminent risk* was defined as the expectation (based on statements from the referral source) that action would be taken to remove the child(ren) within two weeks unless intensive services were provided. The authors reported that many caseworkers found this definition too stringent and confusing.

15. Placements that terminated within 8 weeks of random assignment were not included in analyses of placement rates; in these cases, children were considered to be reunified with their parents during the intensive service period. A child-level analysis showed that 18% of children in the project group and 17% of children in the control group were placed between 2 and 8 months after random assignment.

16. Control group children tended to be placed more quickly than those who received intensive in-home services. Rossi (1991) has termed this the "moratorium effect" of family preservation programs in delaying, but not necessarily preventing placement.

17. For control group cases, termination was defined as "6 weeks after referral to FPS or actual termination of community services, whichever came first" (Feldman 1991:69).

18. Differences between groups were computed at termination and at 1, 2, 3, 6, 9, and 12 months posttermination.

19. Types of placements included homes of relatives, foster homes, emergency and runaway shelters, residential centers, detention, independent living, mental health in-patient facilities, and teaching family homes.

20. The project also accepted some referrals from schools, hospitals, mental health clinics, and other community agencies. Compared with families referred by DCS, cases that were referred by other sources were seen by the in-home services workers as having less severe problems at referral (William Meezan, personal communication, November 5, 1993).

21. For example, in a review of 11 programs in six states, Nelson, Emlen, Landsman, and Hutchinson (1988) found that the risk of placement was higher for children with prior group or institutional placements, families with more severe problems, families with problems related to adolescence, and families who were not motivated to receive services. McDonald and Associates (1990) found that placement rates were higher for families on public assistance, families with a disabled caretaker, and families who had subsequent investigations of abuse or neglect or children at high risk of neglect. Compared with other children, the risk of placement was greater among younger children, disabled children, children who had been placed previously, and children who were court

dependents (McDonald and Associates 1990). Fraser et al. (1991) reported that placement rates were higher when parents requested placement, were openly hostile to their children, or had poor verbal discipline skills, and when children had intensive intervention histories, drug involvement, truancy, delinquency, oppositional behaviors, or mental illness. Feldman (1991) found that placements were more likely among minorities, families with poor parenting skills, and children with behavioral or emotional problems. In Iowa, placement was more likely among families with "multiple functioning problems," low incomes, and children with delinquency problems (Thieman et al. 1990). Haapala (1983) and others have found that younger children are more likely to be placed than older children. Reid et al. (1988) compared 31 families with a child in placement with a matched sample of 55 intact families. The placed cases included a higher proportion of children whose problems were numerous and serious, adolescents (who were placed because their behavioral problems were more numerous and were seen as a threat to the community), and families with fewer resources who used services less, made less progress, and were less satisfied with the agency's efforts on their behalf. Parents in the placed group were more likely to see the child as the problem and were reluctant to acknowledge family problems, compared with intact families. See also Nelson and Landsman (1992), Nelson (1991), and Yuan and Struckman-Johnson (1991).

22. For example, McDonald and Associates (1990) found that placement was more likely among families who received less intensive family preservation services. Nelson et al. (1988) reported that placement rates were lower in programs that offered more focused, shorter-term, office-based services to families with fewer risk factors (versus more comprehensive, in-home services for families with more risk factors). Nelson and Landsman (1992) found that placement was less likely when caretakers participated in most or all treatment sessions. The provision of paraprofessional services was correlated with reduced placement rates among child neglect cases, while reduced placement rates were related to the receipt of marital counseling in cases of physical abuse.

23. See Wells and Whittington (1993), Berry (1992), Fraser et al. (1991), McDonald and Associates (1990), Mitchell et al. (1989), and Jones (1985). Other studies have compared measures of functioning for clients who received home-based services and those with children in foster care (e.g., Wald, Carlsmith, and Leiderman 1988); however, interpretation of the findings is complicated by the fact that initial differences between these groups are many.

24. Some cases were referred from the Los Angeles County Department of Children's Services (DCS) while others came from other agencies. Workers reported significant improvements in all six domains of family functioning for non-DCS referrals, while changes were observed in four domains for DCS cases (William Meezan, personal communication, November 5, 1993).

25. For examples of these types of cost estimates, see Bartsch and Kawamura (1993), Bergquist, Szwejda, and Pope (1993), Kinney et al. (1991), Hinckley and Ellis (1985), and Florida Office of the Inspector General (1982).

26. We confine this review to studies that concern the physical abuse and neglect of children. There is an extensive literature on the prevention and treatment of sexual abuse, which is not considered here.

27. For a discussion of various approaches to the prevention of child abuse and neglect, see Willis, Holden, and Rosenberg (1992) and Daro (1993).

28. The studies reviewed included Berkeley Planning Associates' evaluation of 11 demonstration programs conducted between 1974 and 1977 with a sample

of over 1,600 families; Abt Associates' study of 488 families served by 20 demonstration and treatment projects between 1977 and 1981; White's evaluation of 29 service improvement grants conducted between 1978 and 1981 with a sample of 165 families; and Berkeley Planning Associates' evaluation of 19 demonstration projects that served 1,000 families between 1978 and 1982 (Cohn and Daro 1987).

29.   Gray et al. (1979) found no program effects on reported or verified incidents of child maltreatment or the number of accidents that children had. However, children in the experimental group were less likely to be hospitalized for serious injuries; apparently none of the 50 children in the program suffered serious injury, while 5 of the 50 children in the control group were hospitalized for serious injury and one for failure-to-thrive. Siegel et al. (1980) found no differences between groups in child abuse or neglect. Olds et al. (1986) found that the incidence of child maltreatment was 10% in the control group compared with 5% in the treatment group, a nonsignificant difference. Differences between program and control cases were greater among poor, teenage, single parents (within this subgroup, child maltreatment occurred in 19% of control cases versus 4% of those in the treatment group; $p = .07$).

30.   Mothers in the experimental group reported better prenatal eating habits and less discomfort during childbirth. Children in the experimental group were not as easily distracted as controls; in addition, they received better medical care, had fewer emergency room visits, and were less likely to be removed from the home by a police officer or social worker or cared for by a neighbor because the mother was not available. There were no significant differences between groups in measures of maternal anxiety, mastery, or child abuse potential; informal or formal support; number of prenatal visits; birth outcomes including pregnancy problems, hospital stay, birth weight, and maternal worries; or children's activity level or illnesses.

31.   Reports of maltreatment were filed during or after services in 5 of the 24 cases in the home-visiting program and in 5 of the 26 control cases. Reports were substantiated in two (8%) of the program cases and 3 (12%) of the control cases.

Chapter 3

The Evaluation of Family First

As plans for the Family First program developed, the Illinois Child Welfare Advisory Committee (CWAC), a group representing the private agencies, urged DCFS to conduct a rigorous evaluation of its effects. Members of a CWAC subcommittee on research on family preservation services argued that the results of previous evaluations in this area were not convincing and that the child welfare field needed solid evidence of effects. DCFS decided to take up this challenge and in August 1988 issued a request for proposals for an evaluation of the Family First placement prevention program. In the RFP and in subsequent discussions, DCFS staff indicated that they would only consider proposals that included plans for a randomized experiment to test the effects of the program.

In January 1989, DCFS contracted with the Chapin Hall Center for Children to evaluate the Family First placement prevention program. Our evaluation was conducted during the first four years of the Family First program. The study was designed to describe the kinds of families served and the nature of the services provided and to assess the effects of the program on out-of-home placement of children and other outcomes. Qualitative and quantitative data were gathered from multiple sources to describe the program, the families served, the workers who provided services, the types and amounts of services provided, and case outcomes. The study included the largest randomized experiment conducted to date on a family preservation program and a longitudinal survey of a subsample of clients. In this chapter we describe the study's design and methods.

During the first half of 1989, evaluation activities focused on understanding and describing the process of program development and implementation, refining the evaluation design, and developing protocols for data collection. In this initial phase, we talked with DCFS and private agency staff at all levels (from executive directors to direct service staff) about the goals of the new family preservation program and how this program fit with existing services. These conversations also included discussion of the purpose and methods of the evaluation. Similar interviews were conducted throughout the course of the evaluation.

The study employed the three-tiered design shown in Figure 3.1. This design was based on DCFS's RFP, Chapin Hall's proposal, input from the CWAC subcommittee on family preservation research, and considerable feedback from DCFS and private agency staff.

The first tier of the study was primarily descriptive and included over 6,500 families referred to the program from its inception until December 31, 1992. Information on these cases was gathered from the state's computerized administrative data files and from forms completed by private agency Family First workers. Data from these sources were used to describe initial allegations, the kinds of problems that the families experienced, types and amounts of services provided, and case dispositions. Family First workers also completed a series of structured, self-administered questionnaires that provided information on worker characteristics and attitudes toward the program. In addition, we conducted a series of conversations with service providers and DCFS staff exploring issues in program implementation and administration,

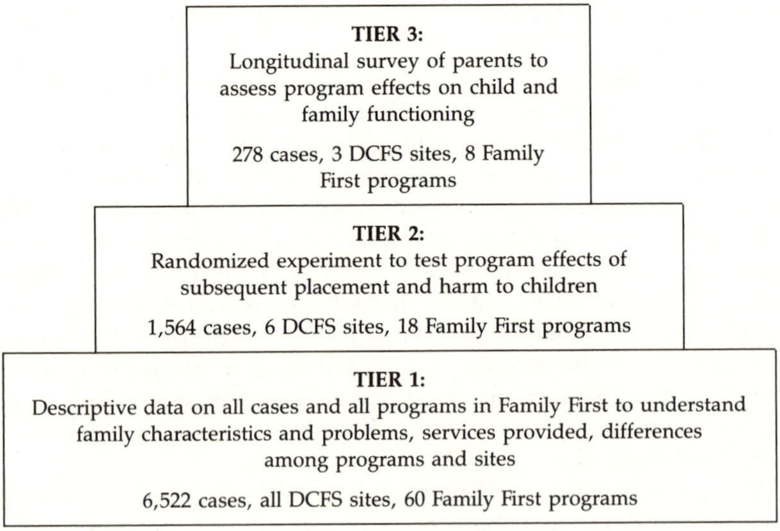

TIER 3:
Longitudinal survey of parents to assess program effects on child and family functioning

278 cases, 3 DCFS sites, 8 Family First programs

TIER 2:
Randomized experiment to test program effects of subsequent placement and harm to children

1,564 cases, 6 DCFS sites, 18 Family First programs

TIER 1:
Descriptive data on all cases and all programs in Family First to understand family characteristics and problems, services provided, differences among programs and sites

6,522 cases, all DCFS sites, 60 Family First programs

Figure 3.1.   Three-tiered design of the Illinois Family First placement prevention evaluation.

interorganizational relationships, the nature of families' problems, service delivery processes, and nature of the work with families.

The second tier was a randomized experiment in six sites comparing the effects of family preservation services with regular child welfare services. Sites selected for inclusion in the experiment were those that had large numbers of cases, programs that were well-established, and public agency staff that agreed to participate in the experiment. Experimental sites were also chosen to provide geographic and demographic diversity. Data comparable to information gathered on the treatment group in the first tier (on family problems, types and amounts of services provided, and case dispositions) were obtained on cases in the regular services group through telephone interviews with DCFS staff.

The third tier of the evaluation involved a series of interviews with a sample of parents in both the experimental and control groups in three experimental sites. The purpose of these interviews was to gather data on the effects of the program on child and family well-being over time and to obtain information on clients' experiences and views of the services they received.

Sources and types of data available for the Family First evaluation are described in Table 3.1.

We turn now to a more detailed discussion of evaluation activities and methods within each tier.

TIER 1: UNDERSTANDING THE FAMILY FIRST PROGRAM

At the broadest level, we aimed to describe the goals and implementation of the Family First program, the types of clients it served, the services provided, and the characteristics and views of direct service staff. In addition, descriptive data obtained in the first tier supported analyses of similarities and differences in various features of the program across sites and over time.

Discussions with DCFS and Private Agency Staff

We conducted extensive, guided discussions with DCFS and Family First staff throughout the evaluation. These conversations served to identify important policy, implementation, and practice issues in Family First. They also provided data on workers' views of the strengths and limitations of the program, the kinds of families that may be most likely to benefit from these services, and the kinds of outcomes that are reasonable to expect. The conversations also provided opportunities to discuss the evaluation, data collection methods, and preliminary findings.

Table 3.1: Sources of Data for the Evaluation of the Family First Placement Prevention Program

Form or type of data	Description	Content	Evaluation usage
Qualitative interviews	Semistructured and unstructured interviews were conducted by evaluation staff with service providers, program supervisors, and administrators in private child welfare agencies and DCFS.	Discussion of issues in program implementation and administration, program strengths and limitations, goals of the program, kinds of clients that are more or less likely to benefit, case management and intervention processes.	Documentation of program implementation and service delivery processes. Identification and analysis of various policy and practice issues.
Administrative records (CANTS and CYCIS files)	DCFS computerized records.	CANTS: Dates of reports of maltreatment, types of maltreatment, and results of DCFS investigations of alleged maltreatment. MARS/CYCIS: types and dates of out-of-home placements, service history (types and dates of services provided to children and families).	Analysis of chronicity and types of maltreatment and placement history prior to referral. Analysis of outcomes of subsequent maltreatment, placement, duration and types of placements, and case closing.
Service summary forms	Questionnaires completed by Family First workers on each family served by the Family First program. One form was completed approximately 90 days after services begin. If Family First services were extended beyond 104 days, another ("extension") form was completed when the family left Family First.	Case and service characteristics, including household composition, family problems, court involvement, service objectives, types and amounts of services provided, types of intervention techniques used, family members' involvement and cooperation with services, case disposition, out-of-home place-	Descriptions of family and service characteristics, case disposition, and workers' views of case outcomes. Analysis of relationships among case characteristics, services, and outcomes.

56

	For "regular services" cases, service summary data were gathered by evaluation staff in structured telephone interviews with the DCFS caseworker responsible for the case. These interviews were conducted at approximately 30 and 90 days after random assignment.	ments, workers' ratings of the achievement of case objectives, and perceived "success."	Analysis of worker characteristics and attitudes toward the program.
Worker surveys	Family First workers and supervisors completed a one-time survey that focused on demographic characteristics, educational attainment, and prior experience. In addition, attitudinal questionnaires were completed annually (in 1990, 1991, and 1992) by Family First caseworkers and supervisors.	One-time survey: workers' education and experience, demographic characteristics. Annual surveys: attitudes toward the program (views of the types of clients that are most appropriate for the program, views of program philosophy and administration), relationships with other agencies, factors related to staff turnover, salary levels, and burn-out.	
Parent surveys	Structured interviews conducted by evaluation staff with a sample of parents in the Family First and "regular services" groups in three sites.	Measures of family and child functioning; housing and economic conditions, physical care of children, children's behavior, school adjustment, stressful life events, self-efficacy, parental coping skills, sources of social support, service utilization.	Analysis of program effects on measures of child and family functioning; parents' views of the program and their relationship with caseworkers; levels of personal efficacy, social support, and formal service utilization.

57

These discussions were conducted by a staff of liaison-interviewers, most of whom were master's level social workers or graduate students in social work. Each liaison worked with a set of private agencies and DCFS regional offices, conducting interviews and helping agency staff understand the evaluation and its data collection requirements. There was some tension in the liaison role between the need to develop open lines of communication with agency staff and the need to obtain data forms from workers (which workers sometimes resented).

Over the course of the study, the evaluation team developed a series of semistructured discussion guides. These began with fairly general questions about the nature and purpose of Family First. Over time, the guides focused on more specific aspects of the program and particular issues in service delivery. (A summary of topics covered in these discussions is provided in Table 3.2). When a series of discussions was conducted with various staff in a single agency, we typically spoke with administrators and supervisors before talking with line staff.[1] Sometimes the discussions were audiotaped, but more often our liaisons took copious notes.

Our discussions with staff began in the spring of 1989 with interviews with key DCFS administrators and regional staff. At the same time, we interviewed all of the private agency executive directors, program supervisors, and line staff in the 31 original Family First program sites. The purpose of these initial discussions was to understand various stakeholders' perspectives on the program. We were particularly interested in the extent to which the program was seen as a departure from existing child welfare programs, issues in initial implementation, and the development of relationships between DCFS and the provider agencies. We also sought views on the kinds of families that might benefit most from these services and the kinds of outcomes that would be reasonable to expect.[2] A second round of discussions with all private agency supervisors and line staff began in the fall of 1989, when the programs had had some experience in serving cases. These conversations focused on the processes of referral and "hand back" (i.e., returning cases to DCFS), experiences with clients, aftercare plans, and the developing relationships between the public and private agencies. When 33 new program sites were added to the Family First program in the spring of 1990, we conducted similar discussions with executive directors, program supervisors, and line staff in these agencies.

In 1990, we conducted interviews with direct service staff that focused on the processes and nature of their work with families, from engagement through termination.[3] These discussions were conducted in all agencies and they formed the basis for a series of interviews that followed, each of which explored more specific aspects of practice in Family

First. In the spring of 1991 we conducted interviews regarding the processes of assessment and case planning with workers in 28 agencies. We selected articulate workers for these discussions. We were particularly interested in the extent to which workers relied on information from previous DCFS investigations of child abuse or neglect complaints, the kinds of additional information they wanted, and how they obtained additional information. We wondered how case objectives were set, when and by whom; how important these were to workers; and how workers assessed families' progress in relation to case objectives.[4] Next, we held discussions with 20 Family First workers in experimental sites on the nature of their interventions with families. These interviews focused on the activities of workers and the strategies they used after initial case plans were completed. Workers were asked to talk about the principles that guide their work, how they see their roles in working with families, how they think about and use the 90-day "limit" on services, the specific intervention activities and strategies they use, how they establish and handle linkages with other service providers, and decisions regarding continuation and termination of services.[5] After we analyzed data obtained in these interviews, it became apparent that the meanings of several important concepts were not clear. In particular, many workers said that they engaged in crisis intervention, advocacy, empowerment, and counseling, but they did not define these terms (and we did not probe for clarification). Since these activities are thought to be central to family preservation practice, we conducted nine interviews with selected workers in experimental sites in order to find out what these terms meant to them. One of our hypotheses was that these terms have different meanings to different workers.

We also talked about the program with line staff and supervisors in DCFS. One issue we pursued with DCFS staff was that of targeting. The primary purpose of these discussions was to determine whether investigators consider intensive, in-home services as an alternative to placement. Secondarily, we hoped to develop a useful conceptualization of the reasons workers give for placement or referral to family preservation services.[6]

Considerable attention has been paid to the training and professional development of line staff in Family First (and in family preservation programs nationwide). Problems in hiring and retaining family preservation workers and supervisors are well documented.[7] We have followed and chronicled the department's efforts to provide training for Family First workers and supervisors. In the spring of 1992, we conducted interviews with nine direct service workers in experimental sites in order to elicit their views about the kinds of experiences that are most helpful in preparing them for family preservation work.

Table 3.2: Semistructured Interviews with Family First Staff

Topic	Contents	Sample	Dates
Program development	Goals for Family First, views of program strengths and limitations, status of program implementation	Executive directors, program directors, supervisors, direct service staff in the initial 31 Family First agencies	Spring 1989
Program implementation	Processes of referral and "hand back" (i.e., returning cases to DCFS), experiences with clients, aftercare plans, relationships between the public and private agencies	Program supervisors and direct service staff in the initial 31 Family First agencies	Fall 1989
Program development and implementation	Goals for Family First, views of program's strengths and limitations, processes of referral and hand back, experiences with clients, aftercare plans, relationships between the public and private agencies	Executive directors, program directors, supervisors, direct service staff in 33 new Family First agencies	Spring 1990
Nature of work with families	Processes of service delivery, including engagement, assessment, case planning, intervention methods, and termination	Direct service staff in all 60 Family First agencies (total of 276 interviews)	1990

Assessment and case planning	Sources of information for problem identification and case assessment; how case objectives are established; importance of case objectives; involvement of DCFS, other professionals, and family members in case planning; assessment of progress in cases	Direct service staff in 28 Family First agencies	Spring 1991
Intervention with families: principles and strategies	Workers' roles, guiding principles, specific intervention strategies and activities, linkages to other services, the use of the 90-day limit, decisions regarding termination and continuation of family preservation services	Twenty-one direct service staff in 18 Family First agencies in experimental sites (staff were selected for participation in these interviews by their supervisors)	
Meanings of key concepts	Crisis intervention, advocacy, empowerment, and counseling	Nine direct service staff in 9 Family First agencies in experimental sites	Spring 1992
Staff development	Preparation for family preservation work, nature of in-service training and supervision, training needs	Nine direct service staff in 9 Family First agencies in experimental sites	Spring 1992
Final interviews	Current views of the program and its goals, types of cases that are most appropriate for the program, relationships with DCFS, and thoughts on the evaluation	Direct service staff and supervisors in all Family First agencies	Spring 1991, Summer 1992

From the beginning of the Family First program, we conducted qualitative interviews with DCFS staff and private agency staff on child fatality cases in the program. These cases were identified to us by public or
private agency staff or through administrative data. We interviewed the
workers involved in these cases to document the circumstances leading
to the death and the responses of DCFS and the providers. Separate
interviews were conducted with the Family First worker or supervisor,
the DCFS Family First coordinator or liaison, and the DCFS investigator.

As data collection for the evaluation neared an end, we conducted a
final round of interviews with staff in the private agencies and DCFS
regional offices. The purpose of these interviews was to bring closure to
the series of discussions that had begun three to four years earlier.[8] We
solicited current views of the program, comments on preliminary evaluation findings, and suggestions for further work on the evaluation.

In all, we conducted over 650 informal interviews over four years. In
general, we found that DCFS and Family First staff were more than
willing to talk about their work and their views of Family First. We
sensed that most workers enjoyed our interest in their work. Many told
us that the interviews provided a rare opportunity for them to reflect on
their work; some said the interviews were cathartic. Some workers were
suspicious, particularly at the beginning of the project, about what we
were up to and whether we would be making judgments about their job
performance. Inevitably there was some tension between service providers and the evaluation. This was due at least in part to differences in
perspectives: Most service providers expressed a firm belief in the program (at least initially), while the evaluation raised questions about it.
The interviews deepened our understanding of the problems faced by
Family First clients, the nature of services provided to them, and the
tremendous constraints under which DCFS and Family First staff operated. In general, we used information gleaned from these conversations
informally, as background or contextual material, which often suggested
valuable directions for further research and different ways of analyzing
or interpreting our data.

Data on Case Characteristics, Services
Provided, and Outcomes

Data on individual families and their problems, services provided by
Family First, and outcomes came from DCFS administrative data and
Chapin Hall forms (see Table 3.1). Lists of cases referred to the Family
First program were provided to us by DCFS regional staff and Family
First agencies on a monthly basis.[9] These referral logs contained identi-
fying information that we used to locate cases in the DCFS administra-

tive data files. In all, 6,522 families were identified as having received Family First services between December 1, 1988, and December 31, 1992.[10]

Administrative Data. DCFS provides portions of its computer files to Chapin Hall on a quarterly basis. Data come from the DCFS Child Abuse and Neglect Tracking System (CANTS), the Management and Accounting Reporting System (MARS), and the Child and Youth Centered Information System (CYCIS). These systems gave us important information about nearly all of the families and children in our study. The CANTS system provided information on the allegations and findings of the investigation of child maltreatment that preceded referral to Family First. This file also gave us information on reports of child abuse and neglect following referral.[11] MARS/CYCIS data provided information on DCFS case openings and closings, amounts and types of services provided to families, children's living arrangements, and out-of-home placements.[12] The DCFS data files were prepared for analysis by the Chapin Hall computing staff, under the direction of Robert Goerge.[13]

Service Summary Data. Service summary forms were developed by Chapin Hall to collect additional data on household composition, family problems, service and intervention characteristics, client cooperation with services, court involvement, formal and informal placements, and the disposition of the case.[14] The forms were to be completed by Family First caseworkers 90 days after referral or at case termination, whichever came first.[15] If the case remained in the Family First program beyond 104 days, a second service summary form—called an extension form—was completed at case termination.[16]

As indicated above, we tracked the completion of forms and periodically notified providers of missing service summary forms. When we received the forms, they were entered into a computerized database that contained automated error-checking routines. Data entry staff identified answers that were not codeable or were not consistent with other information on the case. Forms that were missing information or that included inconsistent information were given to our agency liaisons, who contacted providers to retrieve additional information. Agency liaisons also provided training and assistance to providers on the completion of these forms.

The service summary forms went through two major revisions. An early version of the form was used in the first six months of the program. This version did not include an extension form. After initial experience with this form and based on feedback from providers, the form was revised and an extension form added. The second version of the form was in use from July 1, 1989, until July 1, 1991. The form was revised again to include more specific questions on worker contacts with various family members, the extent and nature of substance abuse and housing problems, and uses of cash assistance in Family First. The third version of the form was used in experimental sites only from July 1, 1991, until December 31, 1992.

Due to resource constraints, the collection of service summary data on Family First cases in nonexperimental sites was curtailed in the summer of 1991. Agencies in nonexperimental sites were expected to provide us with data on all cases referred prior to April 1, 1991. We received 90-day service summaries on 3,467 (93%) of the 3,714 families referred before that date.[17] Agencies in experimental sites continued to provide service summary data on cases referred through the end of the experiment (April 30, 1992). Overall, 90-day service summary data were provided for 4,276 (66%) of the 6,522 families served between December 1, 1988 and December 31, 1992.[18]

Data on Worker Characteristics and Attitudes

A total of 608 agency staff workers served Family First clients during the period of our evaluation. Each direct service worker and supervisor was asked to complete a form on his or her demographic characteristics and educational and work experience (the "one-time survey"). Each January in 1990, 1991, and 1992, Family First caseworkers and supervisors were also asked to complete self-administered questionnaires on their views of the Family First program and its clients (the "annual survey").[19] Adapted from the Family-Based Services Inventory (Nelson, Landsman, and Hutchinson 1986) and the Human Services Survey (Maslach and Jackson 1981a), these questionnaires were designed to gather information on working conditions within Family First programs, the philosophy and emphasis of agency programs, relationships with other agencies, workers' views of the kinds of clients that are most and least likely to succeed in these programs, factors related to staff turnover, and burnout. The supervisor version of the annual survey instrument also included questions about program administration and funding. Supervisors who provided direct services to families were asked to complete both the worker and supervisor forms.

Identifying and keeping track of Family First workers turned out to be more difficult than tracking clients in the program. Our evaluation activities were largely focused on obtaining data on clients and we developed systematic procedures for doing this, procedures that became fairly well integrated and routinized within DCFS offices and Family First agencies. We were less successful in establishing systematic procedures for collecting data on workers. Each quarter, we sent the agencies a list of Family

First staff that we knew of and asked them to add termination dates for those who had left, along with the names and hire dates for new staff. It appeared that many agencies did not have accurate information on when workers were hired or when they left. In addition, the collection of data on workers was a relatively low priority for the agencies. Because the bulk of the worker surveys were completed in the winter months, we missed some staff who worked in these agencies for short periods of time over the spring, summer, and fall. Our own methods of organizing and storing information on workers were also less sophisticated than our system for tracking clients.[20]

The overall response rates for the one-time survey of workers was 79%.[21] Response rates from the annual workers surveys were 76% in 1990, 72% in 1991, and 68% in 1992.[22] For annual surveys of supervisors, response rates were 74% in 1990, 67% in 1991, and 50% in 1992.[23]

TIER 2: ASSESSING THE EFFECTS OF THE PROGRAM

The evaluation included a large-scale randomized experiment to test the effects of the Family First program. In selected sites around the state, families thought to be in need of the services were randomly assigned to Family First or to the regular services of DCFS.

As is often the case in implementing randomized experiments in social programs, considerable discussion with staff at all levels was required. Numerous discussions with DCFS staff at the central office and regional level were held to consider ethical and legal issues involved in such a study, alternative research designs, and the kind of information needed to understand program effects on clients. Many DCFS staff had come to believe in the benefits of family preservation services and raised ethical objections to the denial of these services to the control group. We argued that the benefits of the program had not been demonstrated, so it was not known that the control group would be deprived of a useful benefit. Further, resources were inadequate to provide Family First services to all eligible families. Rationing of services would take place and random assignment was a justifiable rationing procedure. Other concerns were that the experiment would abrogate the judgment of workers regarding service needs. Two steps were taken to address this issue: First, workers were allowed to make a certain number of "exceptions" to random assignment so that they could ensure that families received intensive services under special circumstances (these exceptions are discussed in greater detail below). Second, the random assignment procedure was constructed so that the probability of assignment to Family

First was 0.6 for each case, so workers had a better than fifty-fifty chance that a referred case would be assigned to Family First.

DCFS implemented the randomized study in six sites during April 1990. A seventh site was added in January 1991. The criteria for site selection were sufficient numbers of referrals to Family First, the presence of "good" family preservation programs (in the opinion of DCFS administrators and in our view), willingness of DCFS regional staff to

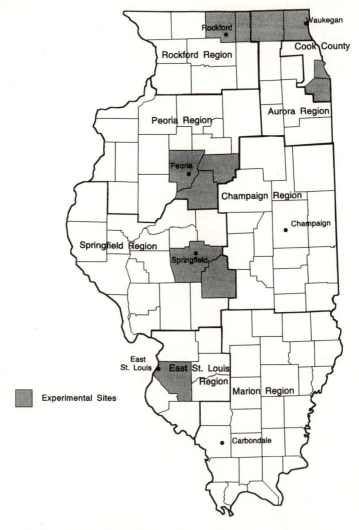

Figure 3.2. Location of experiment sites.
Note: The Rockford site was dropped from analysis of experimental data.

submit cases to random assignment, and geographic diversity among sites. The sites chosen were Chicago East, Chicago South, East St. Louis, Lake Villa/Waukegan, Peoria, Rockford, and Springfield. The location of sites is shown in Figure 3.2.

We needed a system for random assignment that could be implemented in all sites, could be used easily by workers seeking to refer families, and was relatively tamper-proof. We recognized that there are powerful incentives to bypass any randomization procedure, so we devised various mechanisms to prevent manipulation of the system and to detect manipulation when it did occur.

After a decision was made by a DCFS child protection investigator or caseworker to refer a case to a Family First placement prevention program in one of the experimental sites, the investigator or caseworker called an 800 number at DCFS headquarters in the state capital, Springfield, where a supervisor ran a computerized case assignment program. The Springfield supervisor entered identifying information about the case and the worker into the computer. The computer program used a random number generator to assign the case to Family First or to regular services. The case assignment was recorded in the computer along with the identifying information. Once a case was assigned to a group, the assignment could not be changed (the program would not allow a case to be entered a second time).

The Springfield supervisor sent an electronic copy of the case assignments to Chapin Hall every two weeks. We also received lists of referrals from the private agency Family First programs and from DCFS referring offices.[24] By comparing these lists and carefully tracking cases in the service system, we were able to identify deviations from the random assignment procedures. On occasion, the courts or DCFS circumvented or violated the random assignment. These cases were not included in the experiment.

Assignment to the experiment continued until April 30, 1992.[25] Table 3.3 shows the number of cases in the experiment by site. The Rockford site was deleted from the analysis for reasons explained below. We next describe the remaining sites.

The Experimental Sites

Chicago East. The Chicago East site was composed of the center of the city, running roughly from North Avenue south to 75th Street and from Lake Michigan to Western Avenue. It includes the central business district (the Loop), the area just north of the Loop, and the near south side. It includes many of the city's large high-rise public housing projects and a number of other poor neighborhoods. The population of the

Table 3.3: Cases in the Experiment

	Cases referred to Family First in experimental sites											
	Cases randomly assigned[a]									Exceptions[a]		
	Cases in the experiment											
	Family First		Regular services			Violations 1[b]		Violations 2[c]				
Region	N	Percentage of total assigned	N	Percentage of total assigned	Subtotal	N	Percentage of total assigned	N	Percentage of total assigned	Total assigned	N	Percentage of grand total	Grand total
Chicago East	389	58.1	231	34.5	620	42	6.3	8	1.2	670	84	11.1	754
Chicago South	274	61.0	141	31.4	415	25	5.6	9	2.0	449	91	16.9	540
East St. Louis	59	60.8	31	32.0	90	6	6.2	1	1.0	97	42	30.2	139
Lake Villa/Waukegan	85	52.5	61	37.7	146	12	7.4	4	2.5	162	37	18.6	199
Peoria	112	59.9	63	33.7	175	9	4.8	3	1.6	187	51	21.4	238
Rockford	50	61.7	15	18.5	65	15	18.5	1	1.2	81	16	16.5	97
Springfield	76	54.3	42	30.0	118	14	10.0	8	5.7	140	20	12.5	160
Total	1045	58.5	584	32.7	1,629	123	6.9	34	1.9	1,786	341	16.0	2,127
Revised total (excluding Rockford)	995	58.4	569	33.4	1,564	108	6.3	33	1.9	1,705	325	16.0	2,030

[a] This does not include forty-two cases that were found to be ineligible for random assignment (because they had received Family First in the past) and five cases that were referred to nonexperimental agencies after random assignment.

[b] Includes 74 cases in which DCFS switched assignment from regular services to Family First and forty-nine cases in which the courts switched assignment from regular services to Family First.

[c] Includes thirty-four cases that were randomly assigned to Family First, but never received Family First services.

[d] Exceptions include thirty-five cases in which DCFS referred to Family First prior to random assignment (and followed the protocol for exceptions), 235 cases in which DCFS referred to Family First but failed to randomly assign and did not follow the protocol, and 71 cases that were court ordered to Family First. This does not include 16 cases that were referred from nonexperimental sites to programs in experimental sites.

area in 1990 was approximately 480,000, mostly minorities.[26] About 55% were African-Americans, 28% white, and the rest were other minorities. Seventeen percent were classified as of Hispanic origin.[27] Poverty rates in 1989 for the neighborhoods in the site ranged from 10% in the Loop to 72% in Oakland, an area on the near South Side next to the lake, the area with the highest poverty rate in Chicago.

Chicago South. The Chicago South site contains the southern part of the city and the southern suburbs in Cook County. The portion of Chicago contained in the site has about 550,000 residents, of whom 81% are African-American and 15% white. Six percent of the residents of this part of Chicago are of Hispanic origin. Many of these communities are poor. Riverdale at the far southern edge of the city has a large housing project and a poverty rate of 63%. The area also contains a number of middle-class communities, for example, Beverly, with a poverty rate of 4%. The suburbs included in the site include some of the poorest suburbs of Chicago (for example, Ford Heights, with a poverty rate of 49%), as well as a number of quite affluent communities.

Lake Villa/Waukegan. This site includes Lake and McHenry Counties, north of Chicago. The area includes distant suburbs of Chicago as well as more rural areas. The total population of the two counties in 1990 was about 700,000. Ninety percent of the population was white, 5% African-American, and 6% was of Hispanic origin. About 3% of the families lived below the poverty line.

Peoria. The Peoria site, in the north-central part of the state, included Peoria, Tazewell, and Woodford counties. Total population of the three counties was 339,172, of whom 113,504 lived in the city of Peoria. About 91% of the population was white, 7% African-American, and only 1% was of Hispanic origin. Nine percent of the families were below the poverty line.

East St. Louis. The East St. Louis site included all of St. Clair County. In 1990, the county had a population of 262,852, of whom 40,944 lived in the city of East St. Louis. The county as a whole is 72% white and 27% African-American. Fourteen percent of its families were below the poverty line. However, the city of East St. Louis is one of the poorest communities in the state. Forty percent of the families in the city were in poverty. Its population is 99% African-American.

Springfield. The Springfield site, containing Sangamon and Christian counties, had a population in 1990 of 212,804, of whom 105,227 lived in Springfield, the state capital. Ninety-two percent of the population of the site was white, 7% African-American. Less than 1% were of Hispanic origin. Seven percent of the families in the site were living below the poverty line in 1989.

Exceptions and Violations in the Experiment

Some families in the experimental sites were referred to Family First without going through the random assignment procedure. We call these cases "exceptions." Exceptions may cause difficulties in specifying the population to which the experimental results can be generalized. We would like to generalize to the whole population including those represented by the exceptions. Because the exceptions were excluded, families in the experiment may not be fully representative of the population.

DCFS allotted a certain number of legitimate exceptions to random assignment each year in each experimental site. The purpose of this was to provide referring staff with a way to ensure that Family First services would be provided under special circumstances. The two Chicago sites were each permitted to make 8 exceptions a year (for a total of 16 in each site during the experiment), the other five sites were permitted 4 exceptions a year (for a total of 8 in each site, except in Rockford, where the experiment lasted about one year). Thus the number of legitimate exceptions was not to exceed 68. The procedure for making exceptions included obtaining approval from a designated regional staff person prior to random assignment. Table 3.3 shows that most regions made many more exceptions than they were allowed. Overall, 16% of those eligible for random assignment were exceptions. Although this was considerably higher than we had hoped, we do not believe it materially affected our ability to draw conclusions from the study. We discuss the reasons for this below.

Violations of group assignments (that is, putting a case into the "wrong" group after it was randomly assigned) were not supposed to be allowed, unless these occurred through court orders. There were 49 court-ordered violations. DCFS staff violated assignments in 108 cases. Violations are of greater concern than exceptions, since they threaten the "internal validity" of the experiment by altering the initial equality of the experimental groups. The vast majority of violations involved providing Family First services to families that were randomly assigned to the control group. Half (15) of the 30 cases assigned to the regular services group in Rockford were violations (i.e., they were reassigned to Family First). Thus, for most purposes, Rockford was dropped from further analysis of experimental data. Once Rockford was dropped from the analysis, there were 141 violations (8.3% of the 1,705 cases that were randomly assigned in other sites) and 325 exceptions (16% of the 2,030 cases referred for Family First services in other experimental sites during the period of random assignment).

Analyses were conducted to compare the risks of placement and subsequent maltreatment for cases in the Family First, regular services, exceptions, and violations groups. Differences between groups were not significant.[28] We believe it is unlikely that exceptions and violations had a substantial effect on the results of the experiment at least in regard to comparisons of the risk of placement or subsequent harm among cases in the experimental and control groups.

Data Collection on Family First Cases

As noted above, we continued to collect service summary data in experimental sites until December 31, 1992, eight months after assignment of cases in the experiment ended. Data completion rates for Family First cases in the experiment are presented in Table 3.4.

Data Collection on DCFS Regular Services Cases

Families who were randomly assigned to the regular services of DCFS could receive any service other than Family First placement prevention services. This could include casework and counseling services from pub-

Table 3.4: Service Summary Response Rates for Family First in the Experiment, by Site

Site	Number of cases referred	Ninety-day forms available for analysis[a]		Number of cases requiring extension forms	Extension forms received		Families with some service summary data (90 day or extension form)[a]	
		N	%		N	%	N	%
Chicago East	389	345	88.7	182	171	94.0	346	89.0
Chicago South	274	241	88.0	142	128	90.1	245	89.4
East St. Louis	59	51	86.4	17	15	88.2	53	89.8
Lake Villa/ Waukegan	85	85	100.0	30	30	100.0	85	100.0
Peoria	112	111	99.1	41	40	97.6	111	99.1
Springfield	76	72	94.7	32	32	100.0	72	94.7
Total	995	905	91.0	444	416	93.7	912	91.7

[a] Excludes cases with substantial amounts of missing data or irreconcilable discrepancies in the data provided.

Table 3.5: Service Summary Response Rates for Regular Services Cases, by Site

Site	Number of regular services cases	Number of cases that were never opened for DCFS services		Cases eligible for further data collection	Thirty-day interviews available for analysis[a]		Ninety-day interviews available for analysis[a]		Cases with service summary data[b]	
		N	%		N	%	N	%	N	%
Chicago East	231	35	15.2	196	112	57.1	187	95.4	200	86.6
Chicago South	141	26	18.4	115	58	50.4	103	89.6	118	83.7
East St. Louis	31	2	6.5	29	21	72.4	28	96.6	30	96.8
Lake Villa/ Waukegan	61	25	41.0	36	27	75.0	35	97.2	58	95.1
Peoria	63	20	31.8	43	30	69.8	40	93.0	63	100.0
Springfield	42	3	7.1	39	32	82.1	37	94.9	41	97.6
Total	569	111	19.5	458	280	61.1	430	93.9	510	89.6

[a] Excludes cases with substantial amounts of missing data or irreconcilable discrepancies in the data provided.
[b] Includes data on the characteristics and problems faced by cases that were not opened for services.

lic or private agencies. Some regular services cases (20%) were not opened for services, some were served primarily by DCFS follow-up workers, others were referred to regular in-home services programs and family stabilization programs in private agencies, and some cases involving placement were served in Family First reunification programs. Thus, "regular services" included any service that would have been available to families in the absence of intensive placement prevention programs.

Data on regular service cases were to be collected through telephone interviews with the DCFS worker responsible for the case at approximately 30 and 90 days after the case was assigned to the control group.[29] The 30-day interview was intended to be a brief contact with the worker designed for the purposes of locating the case within the system, learning about initial plans for the cases, and introducing the study. If the case was opened for services, additional information—on service plans and court involvement—was obtained in the 30-day interview. The 90-day telephone interview was intended to collect data parallel to that collected at 90 days on families referred to the Family First placement prevention program. Information on family characteristics, services, and outcomes was obtained during the 90-day interview.

Response rates for regular services cases are shown in Table 3.5. Thirty-day interviews were completed for 61% of the cases that were opened for services in DCFS (some cases had not been assigned to a caseworker or could not be located at 30 days). Ninety-day interviews were completed on 94% of the regular services cases that were opened in DCFS. Interview data on family problems and characteristics were available for 90% of all regular services cases, including those that were not opened for services.

TIER 3: INTERVIEWS WITH PARENTS

Our study included a series of interviews with parents in the Family First and regular services groups in selected experimental sites. These interviews were designed to provide data on the effects of the program on child and family functioning over time. This component of our evaluation is unique; we know of no other large-scale randomized experiment on family preservation programs that has included a longitudinal study of parents.

The parent interviews elicited clients' perspectives on what happened before referral for child welfare services and provided measurements of child and family well-being. We collected data on current conditions in the home, economic conditions, the health and development of children, and parental coping skills. In addition, we obtained information from parents on their experiences with services (including their views of the services that they received and thoughts about other services that might be helpful), their relationships with caseworkers, sources of formal and informal support, and significant events in their lives.

We developed a structured interview guide for use in this survey. This instrument was adapted from several widely used research tools. Questions on family and child functioning and views of services were adapted from the Magura and Moses (1986) Parent Outcome Interview, which was developed especially for child welfare service evaluations and has been used in several states. Information on family problems and services provided was obtained within nine life domains related to potential risks to children. The inventory of informal social support was based on Barrera's (1981) Social Support Interview Schedule.[30] An inventory of stressful life circumstances was developed from Cochrane and Robertson's (1973) Life Events Inventory.

The sites selected for this survey were Chicago East, Lake Villa/Waukegan (a suburban area north of Chicago), and Peoria (in the center of the state), all sites that were participating in the experiment. We selected sites that had sufficient numbers of cases in the experiment and "good" family preservation programs (in the eyes of DCFS administrators and in our view). We also chose sites that provided some geographic diversity. Originally, we had hoped to include East St. Louis in this component of the evaluation (since that site contained a particularly strong program), but there were relatively few cases in the experiment there.

We elected to begin the survey in the Chicago East site because of the large number of cases in the experiment there and because we suspected that any difficulties that we would encounter in locating and interviewing clients would be most severe in that region.[31] Our proximity to this region was also an important factor, since this endeavor was new and we wanted to be close to initial locating and interviewing efforts. Interviews with parents were pilot-tested in the Chicago East region in the spring of 1991, followed by a full-scale survey in that region in the summer and fall of 1991. Chapin Hall conducted the pilot test and first wave of interviews in Chicago East. A second wave of interviews with the same sample of parents in Chicago East and an initial wave of interviews with new samples in the Lake Villa/Waukegan and Peoria sites were conducted by NORC (the National Opinion Research Center) in the spring of 1992 under a subcontract with Chapin Hall. A final wave of interviews was conducted by NORC in all three sites in the spring of 1993.[32]

Cases in the Chicago East sample include a random sample of 75

(61%) of the 123 cases that were randomly assigned to Family First between September 1, 1990, and March 31, 1991, and a random sample of 75 (95%) of the 79 cases randomly assigned to regular services during that time. Since the numbers of cases in the Lake Villa/Waukegan and Peoria sites were smaller than those in Chicago, we included all cases randomly assigned between September 1, 1990, and October 1, 1991, in the parent survey in these two sites. The Lake Villa/Waukegan sample included 55 Family First cases and 47 regular services cases. The Peoria sample included 58 Family First cases and 39 cases in the regular services group. In each case, the respondent was the adult (usually a primary caretaker) in the family who was most involved in DCFS or Family First services on or after the date of random assignment. Cases in which the random assignment was violated were removed from the sample, as were cases that received services in nonexperimental sites and those in which the primary caregiver died before the interview study began.[33]

Interviewers had an average of five years of experience in conducting in-person, structured social surveys. Two-day training sessions for interviewers were conducted in June 1991 and again in February 1992. This training focused on techniques for locating respondents, administering the informed-consent procedures, gaining cooperation, administering the interview, using probes for specific questions, and following administrative procedures. Included in this training were examples of difficult situations that the interviewer might encounter, role plays, and practice interviews. A one-day training session was held in February 1993, to reacquaint interviewers with the project prior to the final wave of interviews.

Efforts to locate families in the sample were more difficult than expected. Address information was obtained from DCFS staff in all sites. Additional locating information was obtained from several state agencies' computer files. Despite this, interviewers had difficulty in locating DCFS clients and found that some of these families move frequently without leaving forwarding addresses. Once in the field, interviewers attempted to locate respondents by asking neighbors about the whereabouts of families that were hard to find. In our first interviews with parents we obtained information for our later locating efforts, including names, addresses, and phone numbers of friends and relatives who would know where respondents were. However, by the time of the second interview, some families had moved and their whereabouts were not known to friends and family members. We expected to have fewer problems locating families outside Chicago. However, this was not the case. Families in the other two sites were just as mobile and tended to move greater distances (to another suburb, for instance), while families in Chicago typically stayed in the same area. Several steps were taken to improve our locating efforts in the final round of interviews. We obtained updated address information from DCFS administrative data, DCFS caseworkers, the post office, and voter registration records.

Parents were informed of their selection for the survey by mail. At that time, parents had an opportunity to refuse to participate by returning a card. Interviewers attempted to contact those who did not refuse to participate. At the initial contact, the interviewer requested the parent's participation in the survey and administered a formal informed consent procedure. This procedure was repeated in each wave of interviews.[34]

Very few parents refused to participate in the study.[35] Most parents seemed to enjoy the opportunity to discuss their situation and their experiences with services. The interviews took approximately 90 minutes, although interviewers spent an average of 10 hours on each case (much of this time was spent locating families, preparing for interviews, and reviewing the interviews to make sure they were complete).

In the spring of 1992, the wrong family member was interviewed in eight cases. This was often the father or a surrogate parent, who had been less involved in services than the mother. A new screening protocol was added in the final round of interviews in order to select the correct respondent, that is, the person in the household who had the most contact with DCFS or Family First services after the date of random assignment. In spite of this precaution, 7 invalid interviews were conducted in the final wave. Most of these cases were parents with the same name as the correct respondent who had also been involved with DCFS but were not related to the correct respondent (most of these invalid cases were located through voter registration records). All invalid interviews were dropped from analysis and are not counted in valid response rates.

Response rates for the three waves of interviews in Chicago were 67, 56, and 75% (Table 3.6). Response rates for the first round of interviews in Lake Villa/Waukegan and Peoria were 64 and 67%, respectively, although response rates were higher for Family First than regular services cases in these sites.[36] The differential response rates for program and control cases in Lake Villa/Waukegan and Peoria and the low numbers of completed cases in the control groups in these regions are of some concern. This problem is largely due to the fact that many cases in the regular services groups in the Lake Villa/Waukegan and Peoria sites were never opened for services and thus had no ongoing contact with DCFS. In the final round of interviews, we took steps to correct the underrepresentation of cases in the control group in the Lake Villa/Waukegan and Peoria sites; interviewers in these sites were asked to concentrate on finding cases in the control group. These efforts ap-

Table 3.6: Parent Survey Response Rates, by Year Site, and Group

Site	Group	Original sample	Adjusted sample size[a]	1991 Valid interviews (N)	1991 Valid response rate (%)	1992 Valid interviews (N)	1992 Valid response rate (%)	1993 Valid interviews (N)	1993 Valid response rate (%)
Chicago East	Family First	75	71	48	68	41	58	54	76
	Regular services	75	69	46	67	38	55	51	74
	Subtotal	150	140	94	67	79	56	105	75
Lake Villa/ Waukegan	Family First	55	52	—	—	39	75	41	79
	Regular services	47	45	—	—	23	51	29	64
	Subtotal	102	97	—	—	62	64	70	72
Peoria	Family First	58	55	—	—	38	69	45	82
	Regular services	39	37	—	—	24	65	34	92
	Subtotal	97	93	—	—	62	67	79	85
Total		349	329	—	—	203	62	254	77

[a] Excludes seventeen cases in which the random assignment was violated, two cases served in nonexperimental sites, and one case in which the primary caregiver died prior to the survey. Includes one case in the Chicago regular services group in which the primary caregiver participated in the first two interviews and died before the final round of interviews.

peared to be most successful in the Peoria site. Response rates in the final wave were 72% in Lake Villa/Waukegan and 85% in Peoria. Almost half (49%) of respondents in Chicago participated in all three waves; two-thirds participated in at least two interviews, 16% were interviewed only once, and 17% were not interviewed at all (see Appendix E, Table E.5). In Lake Villa/Waukegan, 54% participated in both waves,[37] 29% were interviewed once, and 18% were never interviewed. In Peoria, 64% of the parents were interviewed in both waves, 25% were interviewed only once, and 11% were not interviewed.

Administrative data and information collected from the caseworkers allowed us to compare families interviewed and those selected for the sample but not interviewed. Very few differences between respondents and nonrespondents were found in either the experimental or control group.[38]

The range in the time between referral and first interview in Chicago East was 97 to 417 days; the median was approximately 7 months (see Table 3.7). The median times between referral and second and third interviews in Chicago East were 16 months and 28 months, respectively. The range between referral and the first interviews in Lake Villa/Waukegan was 208 days to 585 days; the median was about 13 months. For first interviews in Peoria, the range was 154 days to 589 days; again, the median was approximately 13 months. The median time between referral and second interviews was 25 months in Lake Villa/Waukegan and 26 months in Peoria. As can be seen, the time between referral and first interviews in Lake Villa/Waukegan and Peoria was similar to the time between referral and second interviews in Chicago East; the time to second interviews in Lake Villa/Waukegan and Peoria was similar to the time to the third interviews in Chicago East. Hence, in some analyses across sites we compared first interviews in Lake Villa/Waukegan and Peoria with second interviews in Chicago East and second interviews in Lake Villa/Waukegan and Peoria with third interviews in Chicago East.

Table 3.7: Number of Days between Random Assignment and Interview, by Year and Site

Site	1991			1992			1993		
	Min.	Max.	Median	Min.	Max.	Median	Min.	Max.	Median
Chicago East	97	417	225	349	598	486	719	970	848
Lake Villa/ Waukegan	—	—	—	208	585	395	565	913	759
Peoria	—	—	—	154	589	401	532	927	788

Interviewers attempted to review completed survey forms prior to leaving the respondents' residences, to make sure that all questions were asked and answered. Chapin Hall or NORC obtained independent verification that interviews were conducted on a random sample of 10% of the cases (verification was obtained from respondents by telephone). Data were entered into a computerized database and edited with automated error-checking routines that were developed and tested in the first wave of the Chicago East survey. Cases that failed the edit (because of missing or inconsistent data) were returned to the interviewers for retrieval of missing information.

LIMITATIONS OF THE STUDY

All research studies have limitations and ours is no exception. We discuss some of those limitations in Chapter 7. We mention here one problem that occurs in all research: We could not look at everything. As to outcomes, we examined a number of variables representing the outcomes that are most salient in the family preservation field, but many more could be and have been proposed. We also examined a number of other variables to understand their effects on outcome (e.g., types of family problems, family composition, kinds of services provided) but many more could have been included. In addition, some variables were indirect indicators of the reality that we would have liked to observe (for example, we would like to know how many children experience abuse or neglect but we must depend on official reports to the child abuse hotline and reports from workers and these are likely to underestimate harm). Our resources and those of DCFS and the private agencies were limited so there are many things that we would have liked to examine that we could not. In spite of its limitations, this is the largest and most comprehensive study of the effects of family preservation programs conducted to date.

NOTES

1. We found that staff seemed more comfortable talking with us about their work if we were not planning to talk with their supervisors immediately afterward!

2. For a summary of material gleaned from this initial round of interviews, see Schuerman, Rzepnicki, Littell, and Jones (1989).

3. Information gathered in these interviews is summarized in Littell and Howard (1990).

    4.   For an analysis of data from interviews on assessment and case planning, see Rzepnicki and Budde (1991).
    5.   These interviews formed the basis of a report on intervention with families in Family First (Littell, Howard, Rzepnicki, Budde, and Pellowe 1992) and a paper on clinical issues in the termination of family preservation services (Pellowe 1992).
    6.   Our colleague Stephen Budde is pursuing this issue through analysis of interviews with child protection staff about their decisions to take custody of children and decisions to refer families to Family First.
    7.   See Schuerman, Rzepnicki, and Littell (1990).
    8.   In nonexperimental sites, these interviews were conducted during the spring of 1991. In experimental sites, they occurred the following year.
    9.   All DCFS regions and the Family First providers in experimental sites were expected to provide referral information to the evaluation through December 31, 1992. Referral information from service providers in nonexperimental sites was collected through April 1, 1991.
    10.   This is an unduplicated count of families referred to the program. Some families were referred to and served by the Family First program several times. We believe that the actual number of families who received Family First services during this period is somewhat higher than the figure reported here, since we did not receive complete referral information from the Aurora, Champaign, Marion, and Peoria regions.
    11.   CANTS data were available on 6,255 (96%) of the 6,522 families referred to Family First in the first four years of the program (prior to January 1, 1993).
    12.   Data on placements were available for 6,456 (99%) of the families referred during the first four years of the program. Data on case openings and closings were available for 6,238 (96%).
    13.   John Van Voorhis, Paul Whitenier, Eboni Howard, Bong Joo Lee, and Ted Chen contributed to the preparation of administrative data files for our analyses.
    14.   Copies of the service summary forms and all other instruments used in this study are available from the authors.
    15.   The median duration between referral and completion of 90-day service summary forms was 98 days (based on an analysis of data on the 3,467 families referred to Family First before April 1, 1991).
    16.   Some cases remained in Family First beyond 90 days because additional time was needed to transfer the case back to DCFS. If the family left the program within 104 days (which provided a two-week window for the transfer), the Family First worker reported all services provided within this 104-day period on the 90-day service summary form. When case transfer took longer than two weeks, Family First agencies usually provided additional services to the family after 90 days; thus, the additional (extension) form was required.
    17.   For 90-day forms, response rates ranged from 86% in the Chicago North region to 99% in the Champaign and Peoria regions (see Appendix E, Table E.1). Extension forms were required for 1,034 of the families referred during this period; we received extension forms for 84% (870). Overall, service summary data of some type (90-day or extension form) were available for 95% of the cases referred before April 1, 1991.
    18.   These are unduplicated counts of families served in the program. Since some families were served more than once in Family First and we obtained service summary data on each case opening, multiple service summary forms

are available for some families. Service summary data are available on 4,331 (64%) of the 6,748 case openings in the program.

19. In 1992, the survey was limited to staff in experimental sites.

20. For example, we maintained only one computer record per worker. This included information on the worker's most recent agency and position, not previous positions within the agency or in other Family First agencies. In contrast, we opened a new record for clients every time the case was served in Family First; this provided a cumulative record of services to families in the program.

21. Overall, we received one-time survey forms for 479 (79%) of 608 Family First staff (see Appendix E, Table E.2). Response rates were 73% for homemakers (130 of 178), 81% for caseworkers (256 of 318), and 83% for supervisors (93 of 112).

22. The survey of workers was completed by 104 (76%) of the 137 staff working in Family First programs in 1990, 230 (72%) of the 318 staff in 1991, and 82 (68%) of the 120 workers (in experimental sites only) in 1992 (see Appendix E, Table E.3).

23. The supervisor survey was completed by 42 (74%) of the 57 supervisors in 1990, 56 (67%) of 84 supervisors in 1992, and 13 (50%) of 26 supervisors (in experimental sites only) in 1992 (see Appendix E, Table E.4).

24. Information on referrals made through April 30, 1992, in all experimental sites is available for this analysis.

25. Actual start and end dates for random assignment in each site were as follows: Chicago East and Chicago South: April 23, 1990, to April 30, 1992; East St. Louis: April 16, 1990, to April 1, 1992; Lake Villa/Waukegan: April 16, 1990, to April 2, 1992; Peoria: April 9, 1990, to April 24, 1992; Rockford: January 1, 1991, to April 30, 1992; Springfield: April 2, 1990, to March 6, 1992.

26. Data are from the 1990 census. For the Chicago sites, data are approximations derived from information on neighborhoods contained in each site. Neighborhood boundaries do not match site boundaries exactly.

27. In the census, persons of "Hispanic origin" may be of any race.

28. At six months after referral, the risk of placement was .20 for Family First cases, .17 for those in the regular services group, .19 for exceptions, and .18 for violations. At one year, the risks were .27, .21, .24, and .22, respectively. At 18 months, the risks were .31, .26, .27, and .25. Six months after referral, the risk of subsequent maltreatment was .17 for Family First cases, .15 for regular services cases, .19 for exceptions, and .13 for violations; at one year, these figures were .25, .22, .24, and .19; at 18 months, the risks were .32, .28, .30, and .21. There were also no significant differences between groups when violations cases were limited to the first group shown in Table 3.3 (i.e., cases that were originally assigned to regular services).

29. The median duration between random assignment and the 30-day interview was 49.5 days; the median duration between random assignment and the 90-day interview was 134 days.

30. Sandra Beeman assisted in adapting this instrument for use in this study. At the time, Ms. Beeman was a doctoral student at the University of Chicago School of Social Service Administration. She is now assistant professor at the University of Minnesota School of Social Work.

31. Since the Chicago DCFS offices are much larger and more bureaucratic than those in other sites, we expected to have greater difficulty obtaining accu-

rate information about clients' addresses. We also anticipated difficulties inter-viewing clients in the city's high-rise public housing projects.

32.   DCFS funded the pilot test and the first and second waves of interviews in the Chicago East region. Two waves in the Lake Villa/Waukegan and Peoria sites and the final wave of interviews in Chicago were funded by the U.S. Department of Health and Human Services (HHS) Administration for Children and Families (ACF).

33.   The identification of many of the violations of the random assignment procedure (discussed earlier in this chapter) occurred after the selection of the interview sample. Nine regular services cases (6 in Chicago East, 2 in Lake Villa/Waukegan, and 1 in Peoria) received Family First services. Eight cases were randomly assigned to Family First but never received these services (2 in Chi-cago, 3 in Aurora, and 3 in Peoria) . One Family First case in Chicago and one regular service case in Peoria received services in other sites. In one Chicago East Family First case, the primary caregiver died before the first wave of interviews. These cases were dropped from the sample. Thus, 329 cases remained in the Parent Survey. In one of the cases that remained (a regular service case in Chicago), the primary caregiver participated in the first two waves of interviews but died between the second and third wave; this case is included in the sample and in analysis of data from the first two waves.

34.   The informed-consent procedure and the interview study were approved by the University of Chicago School of Social Service Administration Institution-al Review Board.

35.   Thirteen parents refused to participate in the interviews conducted in the spring of 1992 (this is 6% of the 233 families that were located in that wave). Eighteen refused to participate in the spring of 1993 (6% of the 277 families located). In both years most of these refusals were in the Peoria region.

36.   In Lake Villa/Waukegan valid interviews were obtained on 76% of Family First cases and 54% of regular services cases in the sample. In Peoria, valid response rates were 69% for Family First cases and 62% for regular services cases.

37.   Due to difficulties locating regular services cases in the initial round of interviews in Lake Villa/Waukegan, Family First cases were more likely to partic-ipate in both waves in this site (65% of Family First cases were interviewed in both waves, compared with 40% of those in the regular services group).

38.   For example, data provided by workers on family characteristics, major problems, prior court contact, and services were available for 76 (81%) of the 94 families who participated in the first round of interviews and 34 (74%) of the 46 families in the Chicago East sample who were not interviewed at that time. Administrative data on founded reports of abuse and neglect and out-of-home placements were also available for all of the families in the Chicago East sample. On all but one measure, respondents and nonrespondents were found to be similar. In the regular service group, workers reported poverty as a major prob-lem significantly less often for respondents than for nonrespondents (29 vs. 55%, Chi-square = 4.053, d.f. = 1, p = 0.044).

PART II

Chapter 4

The Families[1]

Donna and Jon Potter were reported to child protective services after they took their children for a routine medical exam. Their doctor observed what appeared to be rope burns on 5-month-old Alicia's neck. The investigator who visited the home found both girls left in the care of their 8-year-old brother, Alex. The worker observed opened bottles of wine and marijuana around the house, within easy reach of the children. The house was heavily infested with cockroaches. Because she was unable to locate the parents (Alex didn't know where they were or when they would return), the report of maltreatment was substantiated on the basis of "inadequate supervision" and referred to Family First.

This was the first report of child neglect against the Potter family. Eight-year-old Alex was enrolled in a special education class for developmentally delayed children. He was unable to tie his shoes and did not know his last name. His mother, Donna, lacked confidence in dealing with him and the two girls; she relied on Jon to make decisions regarding the care and discipline of the children. Donna and Jon owed $1,400 in back rent on their public housing apartment and eviction was imminent. The housing authority had recently notified the family that it would no longer be entitled to public housing. Both parents were out looking for a new apartment when the investigator found the children alone.

Jasmine Morrisey, a 24-year-old African-American woman, lived with her four children in a rambling apartment on the south side of Chicago. She was referred to Family First after being reported by her boyfriend for child abuse. The investigator found that Jasmine's 6-year-old son, Mac, had welts on his back and arms. His mother did not deny that she had hit him, saying that he "was a bad seed, the spitting image of his father." Jasmine used corporal punishment only when disciplining Mac and not her other boys ages 4, 2, and 1. While she was warm and attentive to her younger children, this affection was not shown toward Mac. Instead, she was usually angry and verbally abusive. Mac expressed sadness that his father wasn't involved in his life, like the father of his brothers (his mother's boyfriend). Mac got along well with his brothers, but school was another story; he was sent to the principal's office for fighting with classmates on an average of twice a week. Jasmine's mother lived close by. She and Jasmine's brother visited often and occasionally provided the Morrisey family with money to buy household furnishings. The apartment was very sparsely furnished; only two beds were available for the four children and they had no kitchen table or comfortable chairs.

The Potter and Morrisey families were typical referrals to Family First in that their situations presented severe problems, yet the protective service investigator did not seriously consider removal of the children from their homes. The investigator referred them because their environmental and parenting problems required prompt attention. Most, if not all, families who received program services had multiple service needs. In this chapter we describe the families and the circumstances in which they lived.

DEMOGRAPHIC AND HOUSEHOLD CHARACTERISTICS

Here we report on the characteristics of cases in the experiment and provide some information about all of the cases served in Family First during the time we studied the program. Thus we refer to "experimental" cases and to "statewide" data.[2] Results of our analyses of statewide data are presented when they deviate significantly from findings in the experimental sites.

Although families were randomly assigned to experimental and control groups, we examined the data for possible between-group differences produced by chance or resulting from violations in the experiment. In most of our analyses, the Family First and regular service groups did not differ significantly on demographic or household characteristics. Significant differences are reported below. We also report differences among the DCFS regions.

Much of the data in this chapter come from forms completed by Family First workers or interviews with workers responsible for regular service cases. Data on age and gender of family members and on household composition were taken from a household composition table completed by workers. Workers were asked to list family members and all other persons residing at the same location, together with their ages, gender, and relationship to the primary caretaker. In the following, *household* refers to the collection of persons living at a particular location, sometimes including extended family or unrelated individuals and occasionally including more than one family unit.

Age and Ethnicity

We collected information on age and gender of the primary caretaker in 1,341 families in the experiment. The primary caretaker (identified by the caseworker) was almost always the mother (96% of the families).[3] They were, on average, 28 years old. Statewide age and gender of the primary caretaker in 2,974 Family First cases did not deviate significantly from those in the experimental sites.

One of the criteria for referral of a family to the program was the presence of an "involved" child (a child who was found to have been abused or neglected) age 12 or under. As a result, the children in the household were relatively young.[4] The average age of the youngest child across all regions was 3 and 54% of the youngest children were 1 year old or less. There was significant regional variation. In East St. Louis, for example, the average age of the youngest child was 1 while in Peoria it was 4 years old. Average age of the oldest child in the household for the entire sample in the experiment was 8, with little regional variation. Half the children were boys and half girls.

Statewide ($N = 3,472$), 50% of Family First families were white, 43% African-American, 6% Latino, and less than 1% other (including Asian and Native American families).[5] In the experimental sites, however, the sample ($N = 1,509$) was primarily African-American (72%), with almost one-quarter of the families (24%) white, 3% Latino, and less than 1%

Table 4.1: Ethnicity of Clients in the Experiment, by Site[a]

	African-American		Latino		White		Other[b]	
	N	%	N	%	N	%	N	%
Chicago East	555	92	21	3	28	5	—	—
Chicago South	349	87	11	3	39	10	1	0
East St. Louis	75	86	—	—	12	14	—	—
Lake Villa/Waukegan	39	29	16	12	78	57	3	2
Peoria	37	22	—	—	131	78	—	—
Springfield	32	28	2	2	79	69	1	1
Total (1,509 families)	1087	72	50	3	367	24	5	0

[a] Row percentages are reported in this table.
[b] Asian families are included in the Other category.

other. Approximately 90% of families served in the experiment in Chicago East, Chicago South, and East St. Louis regions were African-American. The majority of families in Peoria, Springfield, and Lake Villa/Waukegan regions were white (Table 4.1). There were no significant differences between experimental groups in ethnicity in any region except in Chicago South, where 91% of the Family First cases were African-American compared to 80% of the regular service cases ($p = 0.007$).

Household Composition

At the time of referral to Family First, 97% of the cases in the experiment had at least one child in the household. Hence, there were a few families in which there were no children in the home at referral: In about 2% of the families, children were informally placed with other relatives or with the other parent and in 1% of the cases, all the children were formally placed in substitute care at the time of referral. Seventeen percent of the households had one child, 29% two children, 24% three, 15% four, and 16% had five or more children.

In the experimental sites, 51% of the households were single-parent families (primary caretaker and children only),[6] 24% were two-parent families (couple and children only), 21% included extended family members (with one or two parents), and 4% were composed of other combinations of adults and children. A grandparent was present in one-third of the households with extended family; other configurations of kin occurred much less frequently. These data did not deviate significantly from those obtained statewide. Table 4.2 shows, however, that household composition varied across regions. Lake Villa/Waukegan had the fewest single-parent families (40%) and Chicago East had the most (57%). Two-parent families were most common in the Springfield (37%), Lake Villa/Waukegan (36%), and Peoria (35%) regions and least common in Chicago East (16%).

A comparison of the experimental and regular service groups found significant differences in household composition ($p < 0.001$). Fifty-six percent of Family First cases were single-parent families compared to 43% of the regular services cases, and 17% of Family First households included extended family compared to 27% of regular service households. At the regional level, significant differences between the experimental and regular service groups were found in the two Chicago regions, where the Family First group had a larger proportion of single-parent households and smaller proportions of two-parent and extended family households than the regular services group.[7] A possible explana-

Table 4.2: Household Composition at Referral of Clients in the Experiment, by Site

	Chicago East		Chicago South		East St. Louis		Lake Villa/ Waukegan		Peoria		Springfield		Total	
	N	%	N	%	N	%	N	%	N	%	N	%	N	%
Single-parent family	308	57	179	50	38	48	56	40	84	49	52	46	717	51
Two-parent family	87	16	75	21	15	19	51	36	60	35	41	37	329	24
Primary caretaker and extended family	120	22	85	24	25	31	26	18	20	12	15	13	291	21
Other	23	4	16	5	2	3	8	6	9	5	4	4	62	4
Total (1,399 families)	538	38	355	25	80	6	141	10	173	12	112	8	1,399	100

tion for this is that workers in the two groups defined household differently.[8]

Two-parent families (without extended kin) were more likely among white families (45%) than African-American families (16%), and single-parent families (only the primary caretaker and the children) were more likely among African-American (56%) than white (41%) families. African-American households were more likely than white families to include a primary caretaker and extended family (22 and 8%, respectively).

Income

Although income information for the entire sample was not available, parents who were interviewed in the Chicago East, Peoria, and Lake Villa/Waukegan regions reported their household income. Twenty-three of the 254 respondents either refused to answer or did not know their annual income. Overall, families were poor; 52% reported annual incomes under $5,000 and less than a quarter reported receiving more than $10,000. Chicago East families were the poorest (72% under $5,000 and 7% over $10,000); Lake Villa /Waukegan families the most prosperous (30% under $5,000, 42% over $10,000, and 25% over $20,000). Very few families in any site reported income over $40,000 (2% overall). Unfortunately, data on income sources, including public assistance, were not available.

REPORTS OF ABUSE AND NEGLECT

DCFS computerized data were examined to determine the number and types of child maltreatment allegations prior to program referral. We found that families were generally new to the child welfare system. Of the families for whom we have data in the experimental sites (N = 1,525), two-thirds had no reports of maltreatment prior to the incident that led to the current referral.[9] Seventeen percent had one prior report, 7% two, 4% three, and 6% four or more. One of the criteria for referral was three or fewer reports, a requirement that was violated in a few cases. There is some variation at the regional level in the proportion of cases that were new to the child welfare system, ranging from a low of 63% of the families in the Chicago East region to a high of 78% in Peoria. No significant differences were found between experimental groups.

Reports of maltreatment that led to program referral often included more than one allegation. In 64% of the families in the experiment the

Table 4.3: Type of Allegation Present in Experimental Cases, by Site (%)[a]

	Chicago East	Chicago South	East St. Louis	Lake Villa/ Waukegan	Peoria	Springfield	Total
Physical injury (priority 1)[b]	1	4	2	1	3	2	2
Physical injury (priority 2)[c]	13	17	21	21	25	29	18
Risk of physical injury[d]	15	19	16	22	42	31	21
Sexual abuse[e]	2	3	3	9	4	5	4
Substance misuse	26	20	29	14	2	7	20
Inadequate supervision[f]	27	29	13	24	22	22	25
Inadequate food[g]	11	6	9	4	2	5	7
Medical neglect[h]	15	12	24	10	15	4	13
Environmental neglect[i]	7	6	8	7	12	13	8
Inadequate shelter	5	4	19	3	2	3	5
Other[j]	2	2	2	3	1	1	2
Total number of families	610	403	89	139	170	114	1,525

[a] Column percentages are reported in this table. Physical injury, substance misuse, and mental injury may be due to either abuse or neglect. A case may have had more than one allegation.

[b] Includes death, brain damage, subdural hematomas, internal injuries, wounds, torture.

[c] Includes burns/scalding, bone fractures, poison, cuts/bruises/welts, human bites, tying/confinement, sprains/dislocation.

[d] Circumstances lead a reasonable person to believe that a child is in danger of being injured or harmed, although no definable harm has yet resulted. Includes incidents of domestic violence.

[e] Includes sexually transmitted disease, sexual penetration, sexual exploitation, sexual molestation.

[f] Includes lock-out.

[g] Includes malnutrition.

[h] Includes failure to thrive.

[i] The child's body, clothing, or living conditions are unsanitary to the point of threatening the child's health.

[j] Includes mental injury, abandonment/desertion, educational neglect, inadequate clothing.

finding was neglect, in 27% abuse, and in 9% of the families the finding was a combination of abuse and neglect, although there was significant regional variation. Statewide ($N = 3,472$) half of the families (51%) had confirmed allegations for neglect only, 31% for abuse only, and 10% for both. For 8% of the families, the allegations were unsubstantiated. African-American families were more likely to be reported for neglect (73%) than abuse (20%) prior to referral to Family First (the remainder were reported for both). Among white families, 39% were reported for neglect and 48% for abuse.

Using the DCFS categories, Table 4.3 shows that the most commonly reported allegations were inadequate supervision (25%), risk of physical injury (21%), physical injury (20%), and substance misuse (20%). Allegations of substance misuse (which usually means that a baby tested positive for drugs at birth) were highest in East St. Louis (29%) and Cook County (Chicago East, 26%, and Chicago South, 20%), perhaps reflecting a higher incidence of substance-affected infants in these areas. East St. Louis also had the highest proportion of medical neglect (24%) and inadequate shelter (19%) allegations, reflecting the material deprivation common in that region. There were only two significant differences between the two experimental groups in types of allegations: the categories "risk of physical injury" in Peoria (48% of the Family First cases compared to 32% of the regular service cases, $p = 0.051$) and "sex abuse" in Lake Villa/Waukegan (4% of the Family First cases compared to 15% of the regular service cases, $p = 0.017$).

FAMILY PROBLEMS AS VIEWED BY THE
FAMILY FIRST CASEWORKERS

As the stories of the Potter and Morrisey families illustrate, program families faced multiple and often severe hardships. We collected data on family problems from their Family First caseworkers and from a sample of parents in the experimental sites who were interviewed.

For each case, workers selected up to five of the most serious problems identified during the course of service from a list of 35 problems. Problems identified most often were drug abuse, emotional problems of the parent, inadequate supervision, poverty, homelessness, child discipline, and marital/adult relationship problems (Table 4.4). There was significant regional variation in the extent to which different types of problems were identified. Caseworkers in Chicago reported the highest percentages of cases with drug abuse: About half the cases in Chicago East and Chicago South involved serious drug abuse, most often cocaine (over one-third of all cases). Downstate, Peoria and Springfield reported the fewest families with drug problems (12 and 14%, respectively).

In East St. Louis, we observed a pattern of problems associated with severe poverty. For example, homelessness (39%), deficits in physical care of children (35%), and acute health problems of children (22%) were most often identified in the East St. Louis region. Peoria presents a very different picture. A number of psychological and relationship problems were reported most frequently: emotional problems of the parent (39%), child discipline problems (37%), child behavior problems (32%), and marital/relationship problems (31%). Drug abuse (12%), poverty/financial need (15%), homelessness (13%), and child acute health problems (5%) were all identified less often than in most of the other regions.

Data reported by Springfield caseworkers resembled data from Peoria in some respects. Marital/relationship problems were reported for about one-third (32%) of the families, while drug problems (14%) and acute child health problems (6%) were infrequent. Unlike Peoria caseworkers, however, Springfield caseworkers identified poverty/financial need as a major family problem for nearly half the cases (48%).

These patterns may be explained in several ways. The results may suggest real differences in the types of problems families bring to the Family First program in different geographic areas. In this sample, families from blighted urban areas display the effects of environmental stresses and poverty-related problems. This should not be interpreted to mean that psychological or family conflict–related harms occur less often in those areas—only that environmental stresses are proportionately more important. Alternatively, caseworkers in different sites may have been predisposed to identify certain types of problems. Their perceptions of resource availability or their orientation toward their clients and the work they do could produce biases. We have some limited evidence that this happened. There were some differences in the problems identified by caseworkers in the Family First and regular service groups. Homelessness was identified as a problem more frequently for Family First clients than regular service clients in four of the six regions. Worker bias is unlikely to provide a complete explanation of these differences; we suspect that program characteristics also contributed. For example, lower caseloads and additional resources (e.g., cash assistance) in Family First meant that caseworkers had more opportunities to take action on tough problems like homelessness, which may have led them to identify the problem more often than regular service workers. In every region, between-group differences were observed in one to three of the top eight problem areas (although differences were not found in any region for drug abuse and marital/relationship problems).

Table 4.4: Major Problems Reported by Family First Workers in the Experiment, by Site[a]

	Chicago South (N = 236) (%)	Chicago East (N = 337) (%)	East St. Louis (N = 51) (%)	Lake Villa / Waukegan (N = 81) (%)	Peoria (N = 111) (%)	Springfield (N = 71) (%)	Total (N = 887) (%)	Significance between regions (p value)
Adult criminal offense	7	5	2	16	11	8	7	0.005
Alcohol abuse	21	17	6	27	23	15	19	0.03
Behavior problem of child	14	16	10	15	32	25	18	<0.001
Child care skill deficit: physical care	22	11	35	16	25	10	18	<0.001
Child care skill deficit: discipline	20	14	25	28	37	14	21	<0.001
Child relationship problem with peers or siblings	3	2	0	1	4	7	3	—
Chronic mental illness of parent	5	2	2	14	3	1	4	<0.001
Cultural conflicts	1	2	4	5	1	1	2	—
Dangerous housing	12	14	12	7	3	7	11	0.02
Death of a family member	6	4	4	4	3	3	4	—
Desertion, unresolved divorce, or separation	6	2	2	7	7	8	5	—
Domestic violence	9	10	14	11	19	17	12	—
Drug abuse	48	50	39	21	12	14	39	<0.001
Emotional problem of child	5	5	4	4	13	14	7	0.006
Emotional problems of parent	30	23	20	38	39	32	29	0.003

								p
Health problems: child	17	18	22	9	5	6	14	<0.001
Health problems: parent	2	3	2	2	5	1	2	—
Homelessness	25	16	39	20	13	30	21	<0.001
Housekeeping problems	20	20	12	11	14	15	18	—
Juvenile delinquency	1	1	2	2	2	0	1	—
Marital/adult relationship problems	15	14	14	22	31	32	18	<0.001
Parent/child conflict	9	7	8	7	24	14	10	<0.001
Physical development problem of child	9	9	8	14	9	4	9	—
Physical development problem of parent	2	2	0	2	2	0	2	—
Poverty or financial need	25	19	25	28	15	48	24	<0.001
Retardation or learning problem of child	4	3	2	1	5	1	3	—
Retardation or learning problem of parent	3	2	2	2	4	4	3	—
School problems: behavioral	5	4	4	2	5	1	4	—
School problems: academic	6	3	2	1	3	1	3	—
School problems: truancy	7	11	4	0	5	4	7	0.01
Sexual abuse	3	4	8	9	8	8	5	—
Social isolation	6	2	6	4	4	8	4	—
Supervision of child inadequate	28	25	31	26	20	34	26	—
Teenage pregnancy or marriage	6	3	2	2	1	4	3	—
Unemployment/underemployment	17	6	6	14	5	25	11	<0.001

ᵃ The numbers and percentages in this table refer to families.

95

The casework perspective on problems represents an incomplete picture of family difficulties, due to the variety of factors likely to influence a caseworker's selection of problems to address. We sought to improve the picture by finding out directly from clients how they viewed their own situations.

CLIENT VIEWS

In our interviews with a sample of primary caretakers we attempted to piece together the story of how they came to be involved with the child welfare system. We asked them to recall family problems at the time of referral and the major events that occurred in their lives during the last year. In the interest of obtaining a more comprehensive picture of family characteristics, we asked about perceptions of self-efficacy and informal social supports. It was clear to us that despite the adverse circumstances families endured, they also had important personal and environmental resources. Kendra Fillmore, who lived in a town in central Illinois, is an example.

> A 22-year-old African-American woman, Kendra was investigated by protective services for neglect after leaving her three young children, ages 4 years, 3 years, and 6 months, alone in the apartment while she went out with friends. Her aunt, who lived downstairs, had agreed to look in often on the children. However, she became angry and phoned the hotline when Kendra was gone for over six hours. The investigator confirmed the allegation of inadequate supervision and referred Kendra to Family First.
>
> Kendra grew up in a household with her mother and six brothers. The family was on welfare during most of her adolescence. They moved frequently (mostly from one public housing complex to another in the same community) and she attended five different high schools. Kendra was the only one of her siblings in special education classes. Her family called her "the slow one." She had two children while in high school. Both fathers of her children got in trouble with the law and were sent to prison. In twelfth grade she was arrested for burglary and was also sent to prison. Kendra's mother cared for her two young granddaughters for the two years her daughter was in jail. After Kendra's release, her mother "forced her to move out so she would grow up and take some responsibility for herself and her children." A few days before her last child was born, Kendra moved into the apartment above her aunt. She told her Family First caseworker that life has been "mighty tough" since her son was born.
>
> Friction between Kendra, her mother, and aunt was a big problem after the move to her own place. Her mother and aunt liked to keep an eye on her. But much of what they had to say was critical of her parenting style, continually accusing her of spoiling the children.

At the time of referral to Family First, Kendra did not typically use physical punishment (which had been used with her) and her caseworker thought she was firm and consistent. She was very affectionate with her children and took delight in preparing a pancake breakfast that they enjoyed, several times a week. Despite the conflict with her mom and aunt, Kendra relied heavily on their assistance and support, including their willingness to look after the kids when she needed to go out.

Kendra viewed her family as both her biggest asset and her biggest problem. It was clear to her early on that what she really needed was some distance (but not too much) from her mother and aunt, so she could establish her own household. The support they could offer her was vital for the continued good care of her children—but the relationships required more positive communication between the generations for them to be beneficial to her.

In the Lake Villa/Waukegan and Peoria sites, the initial parent interviews were conducted many months after families had been referred to the program. We were concerned that difficulties recalling events that occurred so long ago would substantially decrease the validity of the data we obtained. For this reason, questions about problems at the time of referral were asked of the Chicago East sample only. Interviews that addressed the family's situation at the time of referral were completed with 94 primary caretakers in the Chicago East region, 48 in Family First and 46 in the regular services group. We report here on the parents' descriptions of their problems at the time of referral. In Chapter 6, we describe changes in those descriptions over time. Few differences were observed in background characteristics of Family First and regular service clients who were interviewed. Nearly all respondents were female (99%) and African-American (95%). They averaged 29 years of age. Only 5% of the primary caretakers were adolescents, 54% were single adults. Nearly one-third of the households (30%) were multigenerational. A comparison of families in the Family First and regular service groups who were interviewed suggests that Family First clients in the Chicago East area may have been worse off in two respects. A significantly larger percentage of Family First cases were reported for severe physical injury of a child (24% compared to 4% of the regular service respondents, $p = 0.006$) and had been investigated more than once prior to referral (58% of Family First clients interviewed compared to 20% of the regular service cases interviewed, $p < 0.001$).

Problems at Referral

In eight domains of functioning, parents were asked about the presence or absence of a number of specific problems at the time they were referred for services. There were no significant differences in problems reported by Family First and regular services clients.

Three-quarters of the families said parental coping was a problem. A similar proportion reported difficulties with housing, and economic problems were reported by about half of the sample (52%). These were followed by child discipline problems (45%) and difficulties with the physical care of children (40%). Of parents who had school-aged children ($N = 41$), the majority experienced child conduct problems (63%) and 39% had children with academic problems. Thirty-eight percent of respondents with children over age 3 observed symptomatic behavior in their children, such as nightmares, bedwetting, and unusual or extreme fears.

When parental perceptions of problems were compared to worker views for this sample, there were some striking similarities, despite differences in the way the question was posed and in the problem categories. Caseworkers for parents who were interviewed in the Chicago East region most often identified drug abuse (52% of the families), poverty (30%), supervision (25%), and child discipline (18%) as among the most serious problems facing the family during the time services were provided.

Major Life Events

We were also interested in learning about stressful events that had taken place in the lives of the families, events that may not have been identified specifically as problems, but nonetheless required coping. For some families, major life events or their cumulative effects could be expected to lead to maladaptive coping, including the abuse or neglect of children. Although our research did not test this hypothesis, we believed that information concerning major life events would be useful in describing the program families and in achieving a more complete understanding of their personal and environmental difficulties.

Our scale was based on Cochrane and Robertson's (1973) Life Events Inventory, a modified version of the widely used Holmes and Rahe (1967) scale. We adapted the scale to the child welfare population by removing or rewording a few items that were not likely to be relevant. Parents did not provide details of the events they listed or the meanings attributed to the events. In each of the three rounds of interviews, we asked respondents to select, from a list of 55 events, those that they or someone in their household had experienced during the last year.

Table 4.5 shows the percentage of families who experienced each type of event as reported in the first interview. We present data for the com-

Table 4.5: Percentage of Families Who Experienced Major Life Events: First Interviews

Life events	Chicago (N = 94)		Lake Villa/ Waukegan (N = 62)		Peoria (N = 62)	
	N	%	N	%	N	%
Unemployment	27	29	26	47	31	50
Trouble at work	4	4	5	8	9	15
Job/responsibility change	0	0	7	12	11	18
New job	3	3	9	15	12	19
Start job	3	3	4	7	4	7
Retirement	0	0	0	0	0	0
Start school/training	6	6	5	8	17	27
Moved	29	31	19	31	23	37
Purchased home	1	1	3	5	1	2
Quarreled with neighbor	3	3	4	7	5	8
Income change substantially	13	14	13	21	30	48
In debt beyond repayment	4	4	5	8	9	15
On/off welfare	17	18	14	23	22	36
Trouble with welfare	19	20	0	0	7	12
Money problem	56	60	22	36	29	47
Foreclosure	0	0	2	3	0	0
Convicted of minor violation	1	1	1	2	7	11
Appeared in court	37	39	29	47	22	36
Probation/parole	3	3	12	19	8	13
Arrested	14	15	12	19	9	15
Jail sentence	2	2	5	8	4	7
Family member in prison	3	3	2	3	6	10
Family member in physical fight	6	6	6	10	13	21
Family member substance misuse	8	9	6	10	5	8
Family member attempted suicide	0	0	1	2	2	3
Victim of crime	16	17	6	10	5	8
Family member died	17	18	8	13	14	23
Close friend died	16	17	3	5	11	18
Family member seriously ill	13	14	7	11	19	31
New family member: birth/marriage	31	33	12	19	9	15
New family member: not birth/marriage	6	7	2	3	6	10
Adopted/took in child	2	2	2	3	1	2
Drug/alcohol problem	10	11	11	18	8	13
Serious social life restriction	3	3	4	7	10	16
Period of homelessness	5	5	2	3	6	10
Serious physical illness/injury	5	5	7	12	11	18
Pregnancy	21	22	13	21	13	21
Miscarriage	3	3	0	0	1	2
Abortion	1	1	2	3	1	2
Marriage	0	0	3	5	5	8

(*continued*)

Table 4.5: *(Continued)*

Life events	Chicago (N = 94)		Lake Villa/ Waukegan (N = 62)		Peoria (N = 62)	
	N	%	N	%	N	%
Increased argument with partner	6	6	6	10	11	18
Increased argument with family members	4	4	5	8	6	10
Trouble with relatives	6	6	7	11	14	23
Child left home	5	5	7	11	9	15
Changed child care arrangement	7	7	5	8	12	19
Lost custody of child	11	12	5	8	7	12
Child behavior problems	10	11	15	24	14	23
Death of partner	0	0	1	2	0	0
Divorce	0	0	4	7	10	16
Marital separation/breakup	1	1	6	10	13	21
Breakup with boy-/girlfriend	9	10	3	5	12	19
Extramarital sexual affair	0	0	3	5	3	5
Marital reconciliation	0	0	1	2	1	2
Sexual relationship problem	1	1	3	5	4	7
Custody/visitation problem	4	4	6	10	8	13

bined sample in the three sites where parents were interviewed. (On only one item at one site—Chicago East—was a significant difference found between the experimental and control groups; changes in housing were reported by 44% of the Family First respondents compared to 17% of the regular services parents, $p = 0.006$.) The major life events identified by the most families again reflected their material deprivation and environmental stresses. Those events included money problems, unemployment, court appearances, and changes in housing. Money problems were mentioned by the majority of Chicago East respondents (60%), almost half (47%) of those in Peoria, and about one-third (35%) of the respondents in the Lake Villa/Waukegan sites. But only 29% of the Chicago East respondents reported that they or someone in their families had become unemployed in the last year compared to approximately half of the families in the other two sites (47% in Lake Villa/Waukegan and 50% in Peoria). The percentage of parents reporting court appearances (40% overall) reflected, in part, court involvement in child welfare case decision-making. A number of families who were interviewed had recently moved: Approximately one-third of the respondents in all three sites experienced a change in housing in the previous year. The median numbers of major life events reported in each site were 4 in Chicago East, 5 in Lake Villa/Waukegan, and 7 in Peoria.

Informal Social Support

The literature suggests that social support frequently counters environmental stressors and is associated with responsive, caring maternal behavior (Crnic, Ragozin, Greenberg, Robinson, and Basham 1983; Crockenberg 1981). Furthermore, it appears to facilitate the maintenance of self-esteem (Cohen and McKay 1984) and protect against maternal depression (Cutrona and Troutman 1986) in stressful situations. Therefore, we considered it to be important to examine some of the environmental supports families used to help them cope with the difficult circumstances of their lives. In our discussions with program workers it appeared that many clients in the Family First program had others around them who helped them through tough times.

We asked parents to identify the types of concrete and psychological support they received from family and friends (Tables 6.14 and 6.15). They reported each type that was available and whether it had been received in the past month. We did not determine levels of support prior to referral or during most of the time they had been in the program. Here we focus on data from the first interview conducted after termination of Family First services.

In Chicago East, 92% of the Family First respondents reported receiving at least one kind of informal social support. Each type of assistance was received by nearly half to almost three-quarters of the parents. The one exception was advice about things other than raising children; in this domain just over one-quarter of the respondents reported having received assistance. Twenty-three percent indicated that their child-rearing style had been criticized by friends or family members (Table 6.14).

Downstate, too, the vast majority of families reported having received informal support in the past month. Ninety-five percent of the parents in Peoria and 85% of those in the Lake Villa/Waukegan region reported receiving at least one type of support. The proportion of Family First cases receiving each type of support in the Lake Villa/Waukegan region was similar to or slightly less than that reported by parents in the other two regions (Table 6.15). In Peoria most types of support were available to and received by more families than in the other two regions. Two-thirds or more of the Peoria respondents had gone out with others socially (84%), had received physical assistance (74%), or had someone listen to their problems in the last month (66%). Just over 60% had received general praise or help with child care; more than half had received general and child-rearing advice or material assistance. These parents, however, also reported more unsupportive communication than was the case in Chicago; 42% said that they had been criticized for the way they were raising their children. Our interview data in all three regions provide evidence that Family First parents typically had others around them who provided a variety of concrete and psychological support while some experienced strained relationships.

Personal Efficacy

Parenting behavior is influenced by knowledge and skills, personal and environmental stresses, the assistance of family and friends, community support, and the child's temperament. A mediating factor that also appears to contribute to the quality of parenting is the parent's perception of self-efficacy, perceived control over life and over her child's behavior. A concept from social learning theory, self-efficacy

Table 4.6: Percentage of Parents Who Agreed with Statements about Personal Efficacy, by Site and Group[a]

	Agree or strongly agree (%)					
			Lake Villa/ Waukegan			
	Chicago East				Peoria	
Statements on personal efficacy	Family First	Regular services	Family First	Regular services	Family First	Regular services
I can do things as well as most people I know	95	100	94	100	94	100
I feel like what happens in my life is mostly determined by powerful people	48	42	45	57	27	46
I often feel helpless in dealing with the problems in my life	50	39	47	39	33	39
What I do can make things better for my children	95	95	97	100	97	100
When I get what I want it's usually because I'm lucky	48	50	20	35	27	38
I feel I do not have much to be proud of	25	13	11	13	5	17
Most of the things that happen to me are under my control	78	71	78	91	78	75
Total N of cases[b]	40	38	36	23	37	24

[a] None of the differences between the Family First and regular services groups were statistically significant.

[b] Since some cases were missing data on specific items, percentages are based on the number of cases with valid data on each item, not on the total number of cases.

is based on the conviction that when people experience success in their dealings with others, they come to believe that events are largely controllable (Bandura 1982). The literature suggests that a mother's response to her child is influenced, in part, by her perceptions of self-efficacy (Bugental and Shennum 1984; Dix and Grusec 1985; Donovan and Leavitt 1992; Manusco and Hardin 1985). For this reason, we wanted respondents to provide some insight into their self-perceptions.

In the second interviews in Chicago East and the first interviews in Lake Villa/Waukegan and Peoria, parents were asked seven questions addressing their self-confidence, control over what happens to them, and their ability to effect change (Table 4.6). We describe here the responses of the Family First group (differences between experimental groups are addressed in Chapter 6).

The parents we interviewed responded confidently regarding their ability to do things as well as others and make things better for their children (approximately 96% of the Family First parents agreed with these statements). Although one-quarter of the Family First parents in Chicago East said they did not have much to be proud of, fewer parents in Lake Villa/Waukegan and Peoria agreed with this statement (11 and 5%, respectively). Approximately three-quarters of the parents said that most of the things that happened to them were under their control, although between one-quarter and one-half felt that what happened in their lives was mostly determined by powerful people. Between one-third and one-half also said that they felt helpless in dealing with their problems. About half (48%) of the parents interviewed in Chicago East, one-quarter (27%) of Peoria parents, and one-fifth of Lake Villa/Waukegan parents felt that when they got what they wanted it was usually due to luck.

In each region, the questions were repeated in the subsequent interviews. Parents reported little or no change in views. The data suggest that the parents had a generally positive and efficacious view of themselves: They were confident in their abilities to take control of their lives and improve the future of their children. Many expressed vulnerability to external forces (especially in Chicago and Lake Villa/Waukegan sites), a realistic perception for many, given the nature of their problems and their involvement in the child welfare system.

SUMMARY

The families referred to Family First were most often poor, female-headed, single-parent households. Primary caretakers were generally under the age of 30. Over half the households had three or more children and about the same proportion had a child 1 year old or younger. Almost three-quarters of the families in the experiment were African-American, compared to 43% served statewide.

Families tended to be new to the child welfare system, although they suffered from a range of severe environmental and personal difficulties. Nearly two-thirds of them were referred following an allegation of neglect. Regional differences were found in the types of family problems identified most often by caseworkers. For example, drug abuse, a major problem for about half the families in Chicago, was identified far less frequently in most other parts of the state. The variations we found may have been the result of a number of factors, including actual differences in families, perceptions of resource availability, and worker bias.

Between one-half and three-quarters of the respondents who were interviewed in our parent survey said they had emotional, housing, and financial problems at the time of referral. These families also identified a number of major life changes that had occurred over the last year and that were often tied to these life areas.

Despite the multiple and severe stresses they faced, families often appeared to be quite resilient. They reported having personal resources and an array of environmental supports. In the next chapter, we look at the services they received.

NOTES

1.   Analysis of data for this chapter was performed by Amy Chak and Lucinda Fox.

2.   Efforts were made to obtain service summary data on all cases referred to the program through March 31, 1991, after which data collection continued in the experimental sites only.

3.   In some two-parent families the father was listed as the primary caretaker. In a very small number of cases, the worker specified the maternal grandmother as the primary caretaker, usually because the natural mother was absent or the natural mother was a teenager.

4.   These data come from the service summaries. All children in the household under 18 years old were included. The following issues should be considered when interpreting the data. First, the number of children per household may be undercounted if a worker included in a household only those who directly received Family First services, usually the primary caretaker and his or her children. Second, *children* includes teenage mothers (if the grandmother was listed as the primary caretaker of the grandchild) and their siblings. This inclusion slightly increases the average age of the oldest child.

5.   Data are from DCFS computer files. The family's ethnicity is based on the ethnicity of the youngest female caretaker in the family.

6.   The service summary data we obtained on individuals in a household

depended on each worker's interpretation of *household*. Some households that should have been categorized as having extended family may have been placed in the single-parent household category.

7. In the Chicago East region, 62% of the Family First households were single-parent, 15% were two-parent, 17% included extended family, and 6% were other. In the regular services group, 49% of the households were single-parent, 18% were two-parent, 32% included extended family, and 2% were other. (The difference between Family First and regular service groups is significant at 0.001.) In the Chicago South region, single-parent households constituted 55% of the Family First group; two-parent 19%; extended family households, 21%; and 6% other. The regular services group was composed of 42% single-parent households; 26% two-parent; 30% included extended family, and 2% other. (The difference between Family First and regular service groups is significant at 0.015.)

8. Because regular service workers were interviewed to obtain case information, they had opportunities to request clarification from the interviewer. Family First workers completed the data collection forms on their own.

9. Data on prior reports come from the computerized DCFS investigation records.

Chapter 5

Services Provided and Issues in Implementation[1]

Kendra Fillmore was referred to Family First after an investigation confirmed that she had left her three young children alone in their apartment while she went out with friends. Family First provided concrete resources throughout the 90-day period, including transportation for medical appointments, groceries, formula, diapers, cockroach treatment, and cash assistance for overdue rent. The caseworker helped Kendra get a stalled application for SSI benefits approved, resolved a paperwork problem that had kept the oldest child out of a Head Start program, and assisted Kendra in filing charges against a man who had hit her over the head with a tire iron. The caseworker also provided parent training. She worked with Kendra's mother and aunt to help them become less verbally abusive and more supportive of her. Ultimately, one of the most successful interventions was to convince the public housing authority to move Kendra up on the waiting list for subsidized housing, which she got into at about the time Family First services ended three and a half months later.

This chapter describes the services provided in the Family First program in the experimental sites and compares them to services provided to the control group. We also describe the Family First workers, their attitudes about the program, and the techniques and activities in which they engaged. The picture is rounded out by presenting client views of service as elicited through our interviews with a sample of primary caretakers. The final section of the chapter addresses issues in program implementation.

MODEL OF SERVICE

As indicated in Chapter 1, the Illinois approach to family preservation services encouraged providers to develop their own programs within guidelines on caseload size, initial response time, and time limits of service. No specific model was imposed. Training on the multisystems approach to service was provided to Family First staff throughout the state, although agencies received little assistance in integrating the multisystems perspective into their programs. This led to a variety of interpretations by providers about the extent to which they were expected to design their own approaches. Because we found differences between what was done in Chicago and downstate, in this chapter we will frequently compare Chicago and downstate experimental sites.

The multisystems approach (Cimmarusti 1989) is based on the work of Salvadore Minuchin (1974), Breunlin et al. (1992), and others (Boyd-Franklin 1989; Aponte and Van Deusen 1981; Hartman and Laird 1983; Minuchin and Fishman 1981). The systems considered to be most relevant to family preservation efforts are the nuclear family and kin, the community, and the family preservation intervention agents (the caseworker, supervisor, case aides, and other agency personnel); intervention is expected to address each level. It is claimed that the multisystems approach to family preservation is distinguished from other approaches in that it balances the tension between child protection and family "empowerment." By engaging family members in a collaborative process of planning and implementing services, family and individual competencies are strengthened, increasing child safety (Cimmarusti 1992). This approach also emphasizes that the demands and services of others (family members, the court, social service agencies, etc.) be coordinated for the purpose of achieving case goals. The focus of all effort is the removal of barriers (at all levels) to preserving the family unit as opposed to a focus on psychopathology or personal deficits. Finally, "joining," a kind of therapeutic alliance, is central to this approach. Cimmarusti (1992) describes it as the foundation for all casework activities. He suggests that joining is accomplished by the worker accommodating family interests, by encouraging and facilitating the participation of family members in identifying problems and searching for solutions, and by exerting leadership when necessary.

Training was carried out by both DCFS and the provider agencies. During fiscal year 1992, for example, DCFS provided four days of core training on the Family First program and the multisystem perspective, 15 days on the assessment and treatment of substance abuse, and eight days on parenting skills. Sessions were repeated periodically for new workers. Private agencies usually supplemented the training provided by the state by offering workshops that addressed other issues faced by their workers. Nearly all workers with whom we spoke wanted additional training on how to work with substance-abusing caretakers, finding these families to be the most difficult and observing that they represented a large percentage of the caseload.

The overall effect of training was evident in the vocabulary workers used to describe the character of their relationship with families. For example, they often spoke of the importance of "joining" a family as a prerequisite to therapeutic change. They spoke of the importance of helping families deal with other agencies and professionals. They described their efforts to advocate for and support client efforts to obtain resources and services as a major focus of their work. The application of other principles, such as focusing on family strengths, was described infrequently.

SERVICES RECEIVED BY FAMILY FIRST
AND REGULAR SERVICE FAMILIES

The data on the amount and types of services provided come from three sources: service summaries completed by private agency Family First workers, interviews with DCFS workers responsible for the regular service cases, and interviews with a sample of parents in the experimental sites.

Amount of Service

The median length of Family First service for the experimental group was 108 days. This is probably an underestimate. Most cases that were still open at the point of data collection and not included in the analysis had been open for at least 150 days. The distribution of lengths of Family First services is shown in Table 5.1 by experimental site. Overall, 8% of Family First cases were closed within 30 days, 4% were closed in the next month, 28% were closed between 60 and 93 days after referral, 19% were closed between 94 and 120 days after referral, and 40% were served for more than 120 days. Although initially planned as a 90-day program, modifications were made during the first year to grant extensions to cases that Family First staff thought needed additional intensive services.

There is substantial evidence that the Family First program provided both a wider range and far more intensive service than cases in the regular service group. Overall, experimental group workers reported a mean of 3.8 concrete services and 3.2 counseling services per case, while regular services workers reported a mean of 0.8 concrete services and 0.8 counseling services. The number of hours spent in face-to-face contact with each family was also reported by workers in both groups. Table 5.1 shows the distribution of hours for caseworkers and homemakers dur-

Table 5.1: Characteristics of Services Provided by Experimental Site and Group

Site	Family First cases			Regular services cases		
	Mean total hours of contact within the first 90 days of services[b]	Mean number of concrete services provided within 90 days	Proportion of cases that terminated in family first within 108 days	Mean total hours of contact within the first 90 days of services[b]	Mean number of concrete services provided within 90 days	Proportion of cases closed in DCFS within 108 days
Chicago East	89.8	3.8	42.7	4.3	0.6	27.3
Chicago South	130.9	4.1	36.7	3.6	0.7	29.1
East St. Louis	89.0	5.8	67.3	67.1	1.6	9.7
Lake Villa/ Waukegan	54.4	3.4	69.9	6.1	0.5	50.8
Peoria	77.1	3.5	64.0	10.7	0.4	33.3
Springfield	35.0	2.7	59.7	16.4	2.4	45.2
Total	91.4	3.8	49.6	10.1	0.8	31.3
Median	70.3	4.0	108 days	2.5	0.0	c
Valid N[a]	897	903	845	474	507	569

[a] The valid N is the number of cases with available data from a specific source. It is the basis upon which percentages are calculated. Data on service characteristics are derived from the Chapin Hall Service Summary form and client tracking system and from DCFS administrative data.

[b] Includes hours of in-person contact with caseworkers/therapists and parent aides/homemakers during the first ninety days of services.

[c] Since many regular services cases (69%) were still open in DCFS as of March 31, 1993, we did not calculate the median number of days that regular services cases were open in DCFS.

ing the first 90 days of service for Family First and regular service cases in the experimental sites. Family First caseworkers recorded an overall mean of 91 hours in the first 90 days of service, ranging from a low of 35 hours in the Springfield site to a high of 131 in the Chicago South sites. For the regular services group, an overall mean of 10 hours was reported. Again regional differences were evident with regular services workers reporting a low of 4 hours in Chicago South to a high of 67 hours[2] in East St. Louis. Throughout the study, the data on hours of contact were problematic. It appears that in many cases the information provided was a very rough estimate. The estimates are particularly problematic for the regular service group since a case may have been served by workers other than the worker completing the interview.

A comparison of our findings with other recent evaluations of family preservation programs suggests that families in Illinois received services that were at least as intensive as services provided in those programs. Families in the Homebuilders program in Utah received an average of 23 hours of in-person contact with workers over a 60-day period; those in the Washington program received 21 hours of in-person contact over 30 days (Pecora et al. 1992). In California, families received an average of 32 hours of direct contact with workers over an average of 7 weeks (McDonald and Associates 1990). In New Jersey, families received a median of 31 hours of face-to-face contact with workers over a median of 6 weeks (Feldman 1991). Of course, these comparisons should be viewed cautiously, given differences in data collection strategies and problems with data quality, such as those noted above.

Service Planning

Interviews were conducted with service staff from 28 agencies across the state to obtain an understanding of how family problems, problem-solving activities, and case objectives were formulated into service plans for Family First clients. Workers described their activities with specific families and talked more generally about how they approached their cases. They also provided insight into the obstacles they faced in planning and serving families in the program.

The allegations that led to a referral to family preservation services usually played a key role in case planning. They pointed to child safety issues and medical problems, which nearly all Family First workers identified as top priorities. Allegations were frequently reflected in the service plan as problems to be addressed in intervention.

When basic living needs, such as housing, food, and clothing, were extreme at the point of referral, they often became the focal point of initial work with clients. Since both clients and workers viewed concrete needs as important problems that Family First could address, there was generally agreement and cooperation in solving these problems. Other problems, such as substance abuse were often not as readily acknowledged by primary caretakers.

While caseworkers addressed family resource deficits, many believed that underlying psychological or interpersonal problems required attention in order to achieve meaningful and lasting improvements in family functioning. Some workers told us that they tried to meet the family's concrete needs first and then addressed emotional needs and issues. They found it frustrating when clients did not view these other problems as important and did not want to work on them. In fact, client acknowledgment of problems other than resource deficits was sometimes viewed as an important goal by workers. Clients who did not agree with this goal were sometimes perceived to be "in denial." Our examination of service summary data found that workers viewed lack of acknowledgment of problems by the primary caretaker to be the number one reason for case failure (51% of the cases that workers viewed as unsuccessful).[3] If substance abuse was not uncovered and addressed early, improvements in other areas were unlikely.

Case objectives were usually derived from the problems identified by the worker. For the most part, caseworkers did not ascribe the same importance to setting goals that they did to problem identification and assessment. Some caseworkers indicated that attention must be paid to the interests of other parties, including DCFS and the courts. Priority was given to establishing safer conditions in the home that would reduce the need for court involvement or authoritative involvement by DCFS, and to linking the family to ongoing but less intensive support services. Continued service was frequently viewed as necessary to maintain child safety and to address issues for which there was little time in the Family First program. Case objectives often reflected process concerns (e.g., expectations regarding client participation in services) rather than outcomes (e.g., desirable changes in conditions of the home or caretaker behavior).

We examined the content of problem-solving objectives that workers listed in the service summaries for 1,043 cases in the experiment. Workers were asked to list a maximum of five of the most important case objectives. A coding scheme with 36 categories was developed based on an examination of the first hundred cases in the study. Two independent coders were trained to apply the scheme to the list of objectives.[4] Results of the analysis (Table 5.2) indicate that cases most commonly had objectives that addressed substance abuse treatment (44% of the Family First cases), housing (31%), physical health or medical care (31%), supervision of children (26%), and general parenting skills (24%). Approximately one-fifth of the families in both groups (22% of Family First cases and

Table 5.2: Types of Case Objectives Identified, by Experimental Group

	Percentage of cases	
Case objectives	Family First (N = 715)	Regular services (N = 328)
Problems and services		
Housing**	31	11
Economic/financial**	13	5
Employment	1	2
Education/GED	3	1
Clothing	1	2
Transportation	1	1
Food	6	8
Physical health/medical care	31	26
Mental health	10	7
Homemaker/housekeeping	7	6
Supervision**	26	14
Discipline and emotional care of child	17	22
Child's school adjustment**	8	2
Child's behavior	2	1
Drug/Alcohol	44	40
Adult relationships	5	4
Sexual abuse	3	3
Intellectual capacity	1	—
General parenting skills**	24	40
Unspecified behavior change	7	2
Unspecified environmental change	7	6
Cooperation/acknowledgment of problem**	7	16
Child protection	4	6
Unspecified assessment/counseling	18	22
Child's living arrangement		
Maintain family unit**	3	6
Return child home	—	3
Place child with relative	—	2
Place child in foster care	—	2
Other living arrangement	—	1
Case management		
Parent-child visits**	1	10
Involve or locate family member	—	—
Monitor services or behavior**	1	7
Legal assistance	1	1
Court appearance	1	3
Other	4	3

** Difference between Family First and regular service significant at $p \leq 0.01$.

18% of regular service cases) had an objective concerning the discipline and emotional care of the child. Unspecified assessment, treatment, or counseling services were also listed for approximately one-fifth of the cases in both groups. Differences between the experimental groups favoring the Family First cases were found with respect to the proportion of families with housing or supervision objectives. Objectives that addressed general parenting skills, client cooperation or acknowledgment of a problem, or case management activities (specifying parent-child visits and case monitoring) were identified for significantly more regular service cases. As we expected, objectives identified for most families roughly corresponded to the problem categories frequently identified by workers: drug abuse, parent emotional problems, supervision, poverty, parenting skill deficits in the area of discipline, and homelessness.

Types of Service

Caseworkers reported types of services provided to each case by selecting from a checklist of 30 services on the service summary form. No services of any kind were provided to 51% of the regular service cases that were opened for services in DCFS compared to only 3% of the

Table 5.3: Concrete Services Provided in Family First and Regular Service Groups

	Percentage of cases receiving service	
	Family First (N = 903)	Regular service (N = 507)
Babysitter (less than 24 hours at a time, in or out of home)	13	2
Caretaker/respite care (more than 24 hours at a time, in or out of home)	4	1
Chore service/cleaning	8	1
Clothing	30	7
Day care (out of home)	8	5
Educational services/GED	8	2
Employment (job finding)	5	1
Financial assistance	57	7
Food	46	7
Furniture/household goods	33	4
Homemaker	19	8
Language translation*	1	0
Legal aid/immigration assistance	3	0
Medical or dental care	26	8
Move to new housing	21	3
Nursing services (in-home)*	2	2
Recreational activities	6	0
Toys/recreational equipment	10	2
Transportation	67	11
Utility benefits	17	1

* Nonsignificant difference between groups. For all other types of service, significant differences between groups were found ($p < 0.05$).

Table 5.4:   Counseling Services Provided in Family First and
Regular Service Groups

	Percentage of cases receiving service	
	Family First *(N = 903)*	*Regular service* *(N = 507)*
Advocacy services	50	5
Crisis intervention	48	4
Drug or alcohol treatment	37	15
Parent education/training	49	16
Job training/counseling	4	1
Psychiatric treatment	5	3
Marital counseling	10	2
Family counseling	43	8
Individual counseling	62	13
Group counseling	9	2

Family First cases. There were significant differences ($p \leq 0.02$) between the experimental and control groups in every region and no significant differences for Family First cases across regions. As shown in Tables 5.3 and 5.4, compared with regular services cases, larger proportions of Family First clients were provided with most types of services.

We found that 89% of the Family First cases received at least one concrete service (resources such as food, clothing, housing, and financial assistance) compared to less than one-third (31%) of the regular service families. Springfield was the only region in which there was no significant difference between the experimental groups in the percentage of cases that received concrete services (78% of the Family First cases compared to 65% of the regular service cases). There was, however, significant variation across regions for Family First cases, ranging from a low of 78% in Springfield to a high of 96% in East St. Louis ($p < 0.001$). Other concrete resources provided to at least half the Family First clients were transportation and financial assistance. While the largest proportion of regular service clients also received help with transportation, no more than 11% of them received any type of concrete service.[5]

Workers were asked specifically about cash assistance they provided to families. They provided cash assistance to about three-quarters (74%) of the Family First cases and only 7% of the regular service cases.[6] Significantly more Family First cases in Chicago received money than in the downstate regions (78 vs. 66%, $p = 0.006$). Overall, 44% of the families who received cash assistance from the program received $200 or less, 25% received between $200 and $400, and 30% received over $400. The money was used most often for furniture, food, clothing, transportation, rent payments, and utility bills.[7]

Ninety-three percent of the Family First cases received at least one counseling service (such as verbal and behavioral therapies aimed at changing the client's functioning) compared to 37% of those in the regular services group. Individual counseling was provided to 62% of Family First clients and 13% of regular services clients. Workers reported that advocacy services, parent education, and crisis intervention were provided to approximately half of the Family First families, while far fewer regular services families received these services.

Our data on services provided to the Family First and regular services groups are not strictly comparable. Families in the regular service group may have received services from sources other than DCFS without the knowledge of the DCFS worker. In addition, services might have been provided by a previous worker and not recorded. This was less likely to happen in the Family First sample because workers spent a considerable amount of time with the families.

We were able to compare service summary data provided by Family First workers with parent reports of services received for the Chicago East region. Services reported as received by the greatest percentage of parents (transportation, household goods, food, drug treatment, family counseling, clothing, financial assistance, and individual counseling) were, for the most part, also identified by caseworkers. However, receipt of these services was reported by between one-quarter and one-third of the program families—far less than reported by workers. A possible explanation for the discrepancy is that parents did not distinguish among services the same way as their workers. Problems in recall may also have been a factor, particularly when the parent interview occurred several months after termination of service, as sometimes happened. When asked whether they received help with the problems for which they were referred, significantly more Family First than regular service parents said that they had (69 vs. 26%, $p < 0.001$).

Regardless of source of information, differences between the experimental and regular service groups appear to confirm that Family First clients received much more in the way of services than regular service cases.[8] And it should be noted that the median size of the caseload reported by DCFS workers for the regular service cases was 50, 10 times that of Family First workers.[9]

Major Techniques and Strategies

In order to obtain a more comprehensive picture of the approaches workers used, for each case we asked workers to select from a list of 50 items up to five techniques they used most. Although there was significant variation across sites, techniques identified most often by Family

First workers were accompanying the client to other agencies (35% of the families), examination of current behavior (28%), examination of past life experiences and their effects on current behavior (26%), building structure and a daily routine in the client's home (24%), and teaching child management skills (24%) (Table 5.5). We grouped techniques into larger categories of similar techniques. The data suggest that workers most often focused on psychological functioning of their clients (58% of the cases overall); this emphasis was most common everywhere but East St. Louis, where a problem-solving focus predominated. A problem-solving focus was mentioned as a major emphasis for approximately half the cases in the other sites. Skills building (48%) was commonly listed as a focus, as was structuring interventions (including structuring of the casework session, 48%). Workers less often reported an emphasis on individual behavior (23%), characterized by the application of behavior modification techniques. Focus on the family was a major emphasis for only about one-third (32%) of the cases overall.[10] Workers, however, reported it as a major emphasis from a high of 50% of the cases in Chicago East to a low of 11% in East St. Louis. Providing information (most often on child development) was viewed as central activity for only one-fifth of the cases. The monitoring of parent and child behavior was rarely considered to be a technique of major import. It appears that the measurement of client progress is not viewed as a critical part of casework practice. In addition, the provision of concrete services was not viewed as a major focus of work in any site, yet we know that nearly all families received concrete assistance through the Family First program. As noted earlier, however, workers viewed the provision of tangible resources as a necessary, but only first step in the therapeutic enterprise. Concrete assistance for many clients may also have been provided swiftly and therefore did not require a great time investment on the part of the workers.

Family Involvement in Services:
The Workers' Views

Workers were asked a number of questions about the participation of family members in planning and carrying out interventions. Overall, they reported that primary caretakers were usually cooperative (54% of the cases), as were other adults (57%) and children (74%). More than a third of the primary caretakers (40%) fully participated in the development of their service plans, half were reported to agree with the plans that were implemented, and 44% usually completed their tasks. There were significant differences across sites in the extent to which family members were involved in services, with Lake Villa/Waukegan workers

Table 5.5: Major Techniques Used by Workers in Family First Cases, by Experimental Site (%)[a]

	Chicago South (N = 226)	Chicago East (N = 325)	East St. Louis (N = 47)	Lake Villa/ Waukegan (N = 79)	Peoria (N = 103)	Springfield (N = 70)	Total (N = 850)
Focus on structure**	54	50	53	32	36	50	48
Building structure/daily routine	24	27	28	18	19	19	24
De-escalating (providing structure during crisis)*	7	5	9	5	10	17	7
Structuring interview: focus client on goals, problems**	27	19	15	10	13	24	20
Structuring treatment situation**	3	7	11	1	1	0	4
Focus on problem-solving	47	50	60	43	55	49	50
Analysis of obstacles to task achievement	18	16	19	10	24	9	16
Contract setting/negotiation	6	10	13	5	8	9	8
Exploration**	12	5	11	8	15	9	9
Generating alternative actions, planning details of problem-solving steps	14	15	21	13	21	14	16
Homework assignments (tasks)**	2	6	9	11	11	10	7
Seeking verbal reports of between-session experiences	3	7	4	4	7	6	5
Focus on individual psychological functioning***	61	53	32	54	79	63	58
Encouraging catharsis /ventilation***	6	5	6	4	19	0	6
Examining client's current behavior and its consequences***	27	26	13	25	47	31	28
Examining client's past life experiences and their effects**	26	21	13	38	31	34	26
Examining patterns of client behavior, how they affect goal achievement**	26	17	13	16	31	19	21
Analysis of transference**	3	0	0	0	4	0	1
Focus on individual behavior**	25	17	30	33	19	36	23
Behavioral contracting*	6	2	4	4	7	11	5
Teaching cognitive self-control	3	4	2	1	1	3	3
Reinforcement*	9	6	4	13	1	11	7
Simulation (modeling, role playing, behavioral rehearsal)**	4	2	11	11	2	4	4
Systematic desensitization	0	0	0	0	0	0	0
Teaching use of time-out*	4	3	13	10	7	7	5
Teaching use of token system	1	2	0	0	3	1	2

Technique							
Focus on the family***	50	23	11	23	28	43	32
Clarifying family roles***	37	18	9	22	15	27	23
Clarifying family rules**	10	4	2	3	9	10	6
Use of family process*	5	2	0	1	8	4	3
Family sculpture	2	1	0	0	1	0	1
Reframing***	8	1	0	0	3	14	4
Focus on skills	50	49	57	37	47	40	48
Anger management skills	11	10	9	4	12	11	10
Assertiveness skills**	2	6	13	1	2	3	4
Child management*	27	22	38	27	20	14	24
Communication skills	9	11	9	6	12	4	10
Negotiation skills	0	0	0	0	1	1	0
Problem-solving skills	6	11	11	6	10	4	9
Relaxation skills	0	1	0	0	0	3	1
Social skills**	2	5	0	0	0	0	2
Provision of information***	17	17	38	32	10	30	20
Provide information on child development**	14	10	30	15	10	21	14
Provide literature	0	0	2	3	0	3	1
Provide resource information***	3	7	6	18	1	9	6
Monitoring	8	7	9	10	7	7	8
Daily journal use by client	4	3	4	0	1	0	3
Repeated use of scales of questionnaires	0	0	2	0	0	1	0
Tracking child behavior	1	3	0	1	2	6	2
Tracking parent behavior or affect*	4	2	2	9	5	0	3
Other techniques[b]							
Accompanying client to other agencies/resources**	35	37	49	47	24	21	35
Advice, direction or instruction***	19	27	9	28	5	23	21
Providing concrete resources*	12	17	17	19	13	30	16
Encouraging and building hope*	12	18	19	27	23	13	18
Use of group process	1	0	0	0	0	0	0
Recreation or activity therapy	0	0	0	0	1	0	0
Self-disclosure of practitioner	0	1	2	3	3	0	1
Values clarification**	6	1	0	0	5	0	3

[a] Asterisks indicate significant differences among sites: *, $p < 0.05$; **, $p < 0.01$; ***, $p < 0.001$.
[b] Techniques categorized as *Other techniques* cannot be grouped together conceptually.

consistently reporting the lowest levels of participation and cooperation.[11] There were also consistent differences between the experimental
groups favoring the Family First program. For example, smaller percentages of Family First parents compared to regular service parents rarely
kept appointments (14 vs. 21%), rarely completed tasks (23 vs. 33%), and
failed to participate in the development of their service plans (12 vs.
21%).

Extended Family Participation in Services. The multisystems training
emphasized the importance of involving family members in services.
Our interviews suggested that workers were reluctant to involve extended family members in the development of initial service plans. Kin
were more likely to be involved in efforts to gather information concerning problem conditions, to provide support for the caretaker, and to
arrange child care and shelter.

Workers noted that it was difficult to know who and how many family
members to involve in planning sessions. They feared that the inclusion
of many people would be overwhelming because it would bring in complicated family dynamics that could not be managed in time-limited
services. Service planning with one person, the primary caretaker, was
seen by some workers as being clearer and more straightforward. Many
caseworkers expressed concerns about the negative impact of extended
family members on clients and on the intervention. Family members
were sometimes viewed as a destructive force—intrusive and judgmental
—from which clients needed to separate. Alternatively they were often
seen as colluding with clients, for example, by taking care of children
when parents wanted to get high or by financially supporting parents
who spent money on drugs. Some workers believed that clients with
less family support had more incentive to participate in Family First
services. They also told us that clients often preferred that family
members not be contacted. Most workers did not press to involve kin,
agreeing with clients who wanted to separate from negative family
influences.

The Casework Relationship: The Parents' Views

We also obtained information about the relationship between the
caseworker and parents from our interviews with primary caretakers in
the Chicago East, Lake Villa/Waukegan, and Peoria regions. Parents
were asked a number of questions regarding the quality of their contacts with their caseworkers. Parents rated various aspects of caseworker activity on a scale of "never" to "always." Parents who reported
they did not have a caseworker between the time of referral and

the time of the first interview were excluded from this analysis. Fifteen percent of regular services cases in Chicago East, 21% of Family First and 28% of regular services cases in Lake Villa/Waukegan, and 35% of Family First and 25% of regular services cases in Peoria reported that they had no caseworker.[12] Our client tracking system indicates that all of the Family First cases had been served by a Family First provider.

Overall, Family First caseworkers were evaluated positively by the respondents in all three sites. Activities and attitudes that approximately three-quarters of the parents said were always a part of the casework relationship were feeling they had a worker who was concerned about them as people, who explained what was going on, and who was "straight" with them (Table 5.6). The positive items on which the fewest caseworkers scored highly were fighting for or sticking up for their clients with other agencies (48%) and letting clients know when they were not working hard enough on their problems (35%). Most items related to the worker's skills or professionalism were scored slightly lower than items that described the worker's empathy, worker's availability, and the client's level of comfort or trust toward the worker.

Termination and Continuation of Services

One aspect of the Family First program that was most difficult for workers to accept was the expectation that they provide brief services to multiproblem families who, in their assessment, required long-term help (this issue is raised later in the chapter). In fact, only half of the cases were closed in Family First within 108 days of referral. Our service summary data show that workers found ways to maintain some service or monitoring following Family First. Forty-eight percent of the cases terminated from the program were scheduled to remain open in DCFS and one-third were expected to receive continued supervision of the court. One-half of the cases had a plan for aftercare, most frequently identified as monitoring services (49% of the cases with an aftercare plan) or substance abuse treatment (22% of the cases with an aftercare plan). There were significant regional variations, with the Chicago regions reporting the highest percentage of cases with continued court supervision (42% for Chicago South and 39% for Chicago East) and the lowest percentage of cases with plans for aftercare (47% for Chicago South and 42% for Chicago East). The issue of how to think about and structure ongoing services to families received little attention from the state, despite the large numbers of families who

Table 5.6: Parents' View of the Relationship with Their Caseworkers, by Site[a,b]

	Chicago East		Lake Villa/Waukegan		Peoria	
	Family First N = 48	Regular services N = 38	Family First N = 30	Regular services N = 17	Family First N = 24	Regular services N = 17
Worker's empathy						
Did you feel that your caseworker was concerned about you as a person?	79*	55*	60	29	79	67
Did you feel that your caseworker understood your opinions, even if she/he didn't always agree with you?	65	50	57	35	63	41
Did your caseworker make you feel everything wrong was your own fault?	10	8	20	24	8	6
Did your caseworker assure you that progress could be made in solving your problem?	73	58	53	41	83	59
Did your caseworker ask how you felt about your problems and the kinds of help you wanted?	65**	34**	50	47	79	56
Worker's availability						
Did your caseworker visit you or keep in touch with you?	67**	32**	63*	24*	92	69
Was your caseworker available when you needed her/him?	69**	39**	67*	24*	79*	41*
Worker's skills or professionalism						
Did your caseworker explain to you what she/he was trying to do and why she/he was doing it?	77	66	73	59	75	88

122

Did your caseworker try to help you better understand your own feelings and behavior?	63**	32**	47	24	65	33
Did your caseworker fight for you or stick up for you with other agencies or people?	64**	33**	61	23	69	33
Did you feel that your caseworker was well organized and competent?	77	58	57	41	71	71
Did your caseworker help you to talk about issues that were not easy to talk about?	58*	34*	50	29	50	35
Did your caseworker help you see your good points as well as your problem areas?	69**	39**	38	18	61	35
Worker's expectations						
Did your caseworker let you know when she/he thought you weren't working hard enough on your problems?	50**	24**	31	29	13	12
Client's level of comfort (trust) toward worker						
Did you feel comfortable talking with your caseworker?	75	63	57	59	75	56
Did you feel you could depend on your caseworker when you ran into a problem?	71**	37**	67	47	65	53
Did you feel your caseworker was open or "straight" with you?	75	63	67*	24*	75	71

[a] Parents who reported they did not have a caseworker between the time of referral and the time of interview were excluded from the analysis. In Chicago East, this was 15% (seven) of the regular services group; in Lake Villa/Waukegan, 21% (nine) of the Family First group and 28% (seven) of the regular services group; in Peoria, 35% (fourteen) of the Family First group and 25% (six) of the regular services group.

[b] Asterisks indicate significant differences between groups: *, $p < .05$; **, $p < .01$. In Chicago East, Family First parents rated ten out of seventeen items significantly more positively. In Lake Villa/Waukegan, Family First parents rated three out of seventeen items significantly more positively. In Peoria, the differences between Family First and regular services groups were statistically significant for only one item.

[c] Since some cases were missing data on specific items, percentages are based on the number of cases with valid data on each item, not on the total number of cases.

123

continued to receive services following their involvement in the Family First program.

THE FAMILY FIRST WORKERS AND
THEIR WORK ENVIRONMENT

Given the difficult cases served by the child welfare system and the special demands placed on family preservation workers, staff must be especially skilled and motivated to perform their jobs well. If they are not, dissatisfaction and burnout are likely to cause them to resign. Of course, clients suffer from the discontinuity caused by the replacement of workers. The high rate of worker turnover in child welfare services has been widely recognized as a significant problem affecting the quality of services to families. Because human services work can be so stressful, a body of research has evolved that examine factors related to levels of job satisfaction and worker burnout. Of particular importance are organizational factors and characteristics of the jobs that can create stress in the first place (Karger 1981; Pecora, Briar, and Zlotnik 1989; Cohen 1992).

In our surveys of workers we attempted to elicit information on job characteristics and work conditions, in addition to demographic data and attitudes about the Family First Program. Most of the data come from survey instruments completed by workers and their supervisors as described in Chapter 3. A one-time survey provided demographic information on supervisors, caseworkers, and homemakers. Survey results are reported for the experimental sites only, but significant deviations from statewide data are described. We also examine differences in demographic characteristics for workers who started at various points in the course of the program. Our annual surveys provided information regarding staff attitudes toward the Family First program and their work environment. These instruments were completed by staff in 1990, 1991, and 1992. We focus on the results of the 1992 survey and note significant differences in responses over time when they occur.

In many of the analyses we divide the staff into three categories: supervisors, caseworkers, and homemakers. These are somewhat arbitrary terms. Persons we have categorized as supervisors include individuals with titles such as clinical director, program director, and program coordinator, as well as supervisor. Staff we have classified as caseworkers were often called therapists, case coordinators, and case managers. Homemakers were called case aides, parent aides, or home intervention specialists. In a few agencies where we understand that caseworkers or case managers functioned primarily as homemakers, we have included them in our homemaker category.

Worker Characteristics

Family First staff in the experimental sites were mostly women (71% of the supervisors, 67% of the caseworkers, and 94% of the homemakers) and under the age of 40 (52% of supervisors, 80% of caseworkers, and 69% of homemakers). Caseworkers and homemakers were more likely to be in their twenties (39% of each). Thirty-nine percent of the staff were white, 57% African-American, 4% Latino, and 1% other. The experimental sites had a larger percentage of minority staff than the state as a whole.[13] With respect to education, the vast majority of supervisors (83%) but only slightly more than one-third of caseworkers (39%) held master's degrees. Approximately one-half (51%) of the homemakers had received some education beyond the high school level. The distribution of staff characteristics did not vary significantly by the date of hire.

Annual salary for full-time employees was reported in intervals. Our 1992 survey in the experimental sites found that 38% of the caseworkers ($N = 60$) reported making less than $20,000, 52% reported $20,000 to $25,000, and 10% reported $25,000 to $30,000. All full-time homemakers ($N = 20$) reported annual salaries between $10,000 and $20,000. Two supervisors reported their annual salaries; both were over $30,000.

Job Conditions

In our annual survey of workers we asked for perceptions of job characteristics and organizational environment. Hackman and Oldham's model of internal work motivation (1980) provides some guidance for interpreting responses to this set of questions. The model describes the connection between job design, critical aspects of the individual worker's psychology, and motivation to perform a job well. Research has pointed to five core job characteristics: skill variety, task identity, and task significance contribute to experienced meaningfulness of the work; autonomy contributes to experienced responsibility for outcomes; and feedback contributes to knowledge of the results of one's work (Hackman and Lawler 1971; Hackman and Oldham 1976; Turner and Lawrence 1965, as cited in Hackman and Oldham 1980). Although our data do not provide a test of these relationships, the worker survey contains questions on some of these dimensions thought to be related to worker motivation, performance, and staff retention.

Here we report 1992 annual survey results for the final year it was administered in the experimental sites for 82 staff who worked directly with families (including supervisors who carried cases, caseworkers, and homemakers). Findings that depart significantly from the previous two surveys are noted. Although some staff participated in more than one round of this survey (48 workers completed it in two different years and 18 completed the survey in all three years), it should be remembered that the respondents at the three points were not all the same people. Hence, differences do not necessarily reflect changes in individuals.

Table 5.7: Opinion about the Job in the Family First Program, 1992 Annual Survey in Experimental Sites

	Strongly agree or mostly agree (%)
Job condition	
The chances for promotion were good.	45
I never seemed to have enough time to get everything done on my job.	55
The pay was good.	41
The job security was good.	87
My fringe benefits were good.	81
The physical surroundings were pleasant.	81
I had enough time to get the job done.	52
I was free from conflicting demands.	59
The hours were good.	85
Promotions were handled fairly.	82
I had too much work to do everything well.	26
I was clear about what my job responsibilities were.	96
Job autonomy	
I had the freedom to decide what I did on my job.	92
I decided the speed with which I worked.	72
It was my responsibility to decide how my job got done.	77
I decided who I worked with on the job.	3
Personal development	
I had the opportunity to develop my own special abilities.	91
The work was interesting.	96
I was given a chance to do the things I do best.	95
I could see the results of my work.	85
The work I do is very important.	96
My work values were in conflict with what I had to do on the job.	12
Personal relationship	
The people I worked with took a personal interest in me.	90
To satisfy some people on my job, I had to upset others.	11
The people I worked with were friendly.	96

Table 5.8: Workers' Opinions of Staff Development and Program Management 1992 Annual Survey, Experimental Sites

	Never or sometimes (%)	Often or always (%)
In-service training was adequate and helpful.	39	61
Supervision was adequate and helpful.	16	84
The program had too many meetings.	85	15
Staff meetings were productive.	30	70
Active client cases were regularly reviewed by agency supervisors.	13	87
If there was no progress in a case, it was usually because the right intervention had not been hit upon.	78	22
Caseloads were too high to fully implement the home-based approach.	98	3
Statistical information generated about the program was shared with the workers.	38	62
Paperwork was too heavy.	51	49

Work Environment. Family First staff were asked about their agreement with a number of statements regarding working conditions. Results are presented in Table 5.7. The responses generally reflected a positive view of job conditions, the degree of autonomy on the job, opportunities for personal development, and personal relationships on the job. Positive items with which workers were most likely to disagree were the chances for promotion were "good" and "the pay was good." Workers generally disagreed with negative items. Three gross measures of task identity ("I was clear about what my job responsibilities were"), skill variety ("The work was interesting"), and task significance ("The work I do is very important") were items with which 96% of the respondents strongly or mostly agreed. As an indication of feedback received on the job, 85% of the workers reported agreement with the statement that they could see the results of their work. The issue of feedback was also addressed in questions that solicited worker opinions about supervision (Table 5.8). Large percentages of respondents reported that supervision was adequate and helpful (84%) and that cases were regularly reviewed by supervisors (87%). Workers were relatively less positive about in-service training and about the degree to which statistical information was shared with workers. Not surprisingly, almost one-half of the workers believed that often "paperwork was too heavy." Overall, findings suggest that workers' attitudes toward their jobs were fairly stable across the three surveys.

Job Satisfaction and Burnout. Job satisfaction and burnout are often viewed as two sides of the same coin. Burnout refers to a group of symptoms related to job stress and includes emotional exhaustion, lack of a sense of personal accomplishment, and depersonalization of clients (Maslach and Jackson 1981b). It represents a withdrawal of commitment and emotional detachment indicative of low job motivation. A sizable body of research in the last twenty years has documented the problem of worker burnout and its sources in social work and child welfare (see, for example Arches 1991; Cherniss 1980; Freudenberger 1977; Gillespie and Cohen 1984; Harrison 1980; Jayaratne and Chess 1984; Jayaratne, Chess, and Kunkel 1986; Jayaratne, Tripodi, and Chess 1983; Maslach 1978, 1982; McCullock and O'Brien 1986). A national survey of social workers in child welfare, community mental health, and family service workers found similarities across the three practice arenas in levels of satisfaction and burnout (Jayaratne and Chess 1984). A global measure of job satisfaction indicated high levels of satisfaction regardless of field of practice (35% were very satisfied and 49% were somewhat satisfied). Child welfare workers, however, reported an environment that was worse on three dimensions: role conflict, value conflict, and challenge. The authors interpreted the lack of challenging work to be the result of a restrictive environment that minimizes choices rather than an indication that the clients present nonchallenging situations.

Our results were similar to those in the national study: 39% of our respondents rated their job satisfaction as very high while 52% rated themselves as somewhat satisfied and 9% as not satisfied. Homemakers tended to be more satisfied than either supervisors or caseworkers (49% were very satisfied compared to 34% of the caseworkers and 29% of the supervisors, p = 0.03). There was little change in job satisfaction over time.

A burnout scale was included in the survey. Staff indicated their level of agreement with a series of 17 statements, for example, "I can easily understand how my clients feel about things" and "Many clients cannot be helped no matter what I do." Negative items were reversed and average responses for each worker were computed. These scores could range from 1 (high burnout) to 4 (low burnout).

Average scores for supervisors (2.50), caseworkers (2.51), and homemakers (2.90) were very close to each other and in the middle of the range (differences were not significant in an analysis of variance). Regional variation in scores was not significant. An examination of responses to individual items on the scale presents a fuller picture of staff attitudes toward work. More than half (52%) of the respondents reported that their personal values differed with those of their clients. About one-fifth (21%)

indicated that they had difficulty in getting useful feedback from clients; a slightly smaller percentage (18%) stated that they had become more callous toward people since taking their job. A full third (34%) of the Family First staff reported feeling "burned out" from their work.

Staff Morale. Staff were asked to rate the level of morale in their agency during the last year (low, average, high, or very high) and whether the morale was declining, remaining stable, or increasing. About 62% of respondents reported that morale was average or low, a slightly higher percentage than was reported in the previous year (53%)

Table 5.9: Workers' Assessments of Importance of Characteristics of Family Preservation Programs (Percentage of Workers in Experimental Sites, 1992 Annual Survey)

	Not important or slightly important	Moderately important	Extremely important
Delivery of concrete services like moving, cleaning, grocery shopping with clients.	14	25	61
Asking clients to identify and prioritize their own treatment goals.	4	33	63
Workers are available 24 hours a day for emergency visits or calls.	10	40	50
Referring family to other counseling services.	11	38	51
Services are routinely provided in the home.	6	26	68
Services are routinely provided during evenings and weekends.	37	47	16
Client appointments are at the convenience of the families.	29	39	33
Initial contact with clients is routinely made within 24 hours of the referral.	8	15	78
Using a family-centered vs. a child-centered approach.	2	32	66
Working with multiproblem families.	12	33	54
Services are brief in duration, lasting no more than 90 days.	38	43	19
Services are intense, provided two or three times a week for 1 to 4 hours per time.	1	24	74
The philosophy of service providers is that most children are better off in their own homes.	1	26	73
Service providers teach families to take initiative in service planning and act on their own behalf.	6	21	73
Services are focused on goal-oriented case plans.	5	27	68

or the year before (51%). Half of the respondents thought that morale was remaining stable, 30% thought it was getting worse, and 20% thought it was getting better.

In sum, while staff attitudes were fairly positive about work conditions, overall they were less than enthusiastic about their work. We expected that low caseloads and increased resources would contribute to higher levels of job satisfaction. However, when compared to a national survey of social workers in child welfare, community mental health services, and family services, Family First workers experienced similar levels of contentment. It is possible that unmeasured factors, like the difficulty of the cases or perception of safety when working in clients' homes, made working in this program particularly difficult.

Characteristics of the Work

Family First staff assessed the importance of various characteristics of family preservation programs (Table 5.9). The characteristics thought to be extremely important to approximately three-quarters of the respondents were initial contact with families within 24 hours, intensive services, a philosophy of service that most children are better off in their own homes, and teaching families to take initiative in service planning. Items identified as important by the fewest respondents were making appointments at the convenience of families, brief time limits (90 days or less), and services routinely provided during evenings and weekends. Ratings of program characteristics did not vary across surveys in the three years, with the single exception of 24-hour availability. More respondents viewed this characteristic to be extremely important in the 1991 survey than in the other two years (60% in 1991 compared to 40% in 1990 and 50% in 1992, $p = 0.01$). The reason for this shift is unclear and may merely be a statistical artifact.

Staff Turnover

One test of program stability is the degree to which staff are retained over time. We collected information on dates of hire and termination of employment and examined rates of turnover for the three-year period from 1989 through 1991.[14] Tables 5.10 through 5.12 indicate that turnover rates were highest for casework staff, with about one-quarter to over one-third of workers leaving the program during each of the three years. This finding was not surprising, given the demands of the work and levels of job satisfaction.

Table 5.10: Family First Supervisor Turnover in Experimental Sites

Year	Staffing changes			
	Number of hires	*Number of departures*	*Number remaining at year's end*	*Turnover rate (%)[a]*
1989	24	3	21	13
1990	7	2	26	7
1991	2	3	25	11

[a] Number of departures divided by number of staff retained from previous year and new hires.

Table 5.11: Family First Caseworker Turnover in Experimental Sites

Year	Staffing Changes			
	Number of hires	*Number of departures*	*Number remaining at year's end*	*Turnover rate (%)[a]*
1989	43	15	28	35
1990	62	25	65	28
1991	23	21	67	24

[a] Number of departures divided by number of staff retained from previous year and new hires.

Table 5.12: Family First Homemaker Turnover in Experimental Sites

Year	Staffing changes			
	Number of hires	*Number of departures*	*Number remaining at year's end*	*Turnover rate (%)[a]*
1989	27	4	23	15
1990	32	13	42	24
1991	9	8	43	16

[a] Number of departures divided by number of staff retained from previous year and new hires.

ISSUES IN PROGRAM IMPLEMENTATION

While there has long been collaboration between DCFS and the private sector, in Family First private agency case responsibility for cases increased to a level not previously seen. Collaboration of this sort raises important questions about the delineation of roles and conditions required for effective, harmonious work.

Our interviews with staff and administrators uncovered a number of issues in program implementation. There were many tensions in the relationship between DCFS and the provider agencies. Because the state encouraged program flexibility, there was a general lack of clarity regarding how the program was to be carried out with clients who had extremely difficult and complex problems. Workers also faced difficulties in striking a balance between their roles as social control agents and helpers. We discuss here the sources of strain and the strategies agency personnel used to manage them.

Conflicts in Program Goals and Philosophy

The public-private partnership was complicated by a fundamental difference in agency missions. The overriding goal of the state child welfare agency is the protection of children, while private providers tend to be most concerned with improvements in parental and family functioning (although certainly not at the expense of children's safety). Much of the time these goals were complementary. But in some situations they led to disagreements over important case decisions regarding appropriate service strategies.

For some private agencies this conflict resulted in continuous monitoring and (often unwelcome) supervision of their work by DCFS. This was most likely to happen in agencies that were inexperienced in serving DCFS clients and that had no track record in working with protective service families. DCFS expressed this concern in criticisms of the agencies' lack of training or experience in assessing risk of harm and in cautions about the possibility that focusing on parents could compromise children's safety. Some private agency staff believed that DCFS distrusted them and therefore referred families whose problems did not pose an immediate or significant risk to the child. However, many Family First liaisons (local DCFS staff responsible for overseeing the Family First program) were perceived by service providers to be accessible and supportive, without being too intrusive. Exceptions to this view were most common among workers who felt that they were monitored too closely.

Family First staff rated several dimensions of their relationship with DCFS. About 89% found their DCFS liaisons to be helpful and 11% not helpful in understanding and planning their work. There was little difference between Cook County and downstate respondents in ratings of helpfulness. There were substantial regional differences in the extent to which they frequently talked with DCFS workers about cases (39% overall). Significantly more Cook County respondents than downstate respondents said that they rarely or never discussed cases with DCFS staff (36 vs. 14%, $p = 0.03$). Finally, workers were asked to rate their working relationships with DCFS. Overall, 26% said the relationship was excellent, 72% good or fair, and 3% poor. Significantly fewer Family First staff in Cook County than downstate rated relationships with DCFS as excellent (16 vs. 38%, $p = 0.025$). There was no significant change over time in these ratings.

Because private agency line staff generally recognized the validity of the child protection goal, they often struggled to balance this against their interest in improved family functioning. Difficulties with the state child welfare system sometimes arose over the use of authority with families and the type and amount of pressure to place on families to conform to a particular view of their problems and appropriate remedies.

The Use of Authority in Planning and Implementing Services

Families typically entered the Family First program under coercive circumstances. The referral was usually made following a protective service investigation in which an allegation of child maltreatment had been confirmed and the family was required to receive services (this condition was sometimes strengthened by a petition for court supervision). An original criterion for program eligibility was the judgment that a child was at risk of imminent placement. Although this criterion was not maintained, families were under threat (either real or perceived) of child removal as a consequence of nonparticipation in services. Thus, families were obliged to comply with service plans and intensive monitoring, but the manner in which the Family First workers handled this authority varied considerably.

Many discussions of brief treatment approaches and family preservation models underscore the importance of client participation. Involving clients in service planning and implementation is seen as a way to encourage self-determination and develop problem-solving skills. Workers expressed discomfort with the conflict between the value of client self-determination and the involuntary status of protective service clients.

Although most Family First workers indicated that client priorities were an important part of their work together, not surprisingly caseworkers often found other factors more important in their own selection of problems on which to focus. The relative weight given to client interests varied depending on whether these interests were related to the allegations, the presence of other severe problems, and the value that workers placed on involving clients in the process.

Joint Case Planning with DCFS

Family First workers attempted to separate their role from that of DCFS in order to establish a productive relationship with their clients. They did not involve DCFS staff in planning case activities, but they recognized the importance of representing DCFS interests in the service plan. These interests often coincided with the Family First worker's own interest in child safety. Workers were troubled, however, by DCFS's occasional insistence that the Family First worker maintain a narrow focus on the allegation that had led to the referral of the family.

Workers also told us that there was sometimes pressure from DCFS to achieve goals as soon as possible. They worried that clients may have been threatened into compliance by DCFS staff or that they (Family First workers) would feel pressured into doing things for clients so that goals would be rapidly achieved. Workers believed that such actions would foster hostility and dependency rather than motivation and cooperation.

The Role of the Court

In some cases, the court was asked, by either DCFS or Family First workers, to order parents to cooperate with the Family First program. In some regions, the court was automatically involved in cases with certain kinds of problems, for example, in cases where substance abuse was related to the allegation. Court orders included such elements as problems, goals, strategies to be implemented, and the consequences for noncompliance. Workers sometimes felt constrained by court involvement in the same way they felt limited by DCFS. They had a variety of ways to deal with the restrictions imposed on their work.

At times the court mandate became the basis of the service plan. This strategy was most likely to be successful when parents accepted the mandate because they agreed with the problems and goals or because they wanted to avoid the consequences of noncompliance (e.g., foster care placement of their children). Workers suggested that this approach did not work with clients who did not acknowledge problems as defined by the authorities, had little confidence in the proposed solutions, or who believed that they would not be subject to the consequences described. Some caseworkers proceeded only after reshaping the mandate of the court to overlap with client interests.

In the Chicago regions there was some debate between DCFS and the private providers regarding the role of the court in Family First cases. The private agencies wanted court involvement to provide them additional authority on cases by issuing orders of protection or supervision. Frequent requests for court involvement became a source of tension between the public and private sector for two reasons. Such requests meant additional time for the investigator if the case went to court, and they undermined the investigator's prerogative in deciding which cases really needed court involvement. Our service summary data show that court orders were obtained for 45% of the Chicago region cases after referral to the program. Fifty-seven percent of these cases had orders of protection or supervision, 50% had orders for temporary custody, and 11% had been ordered to receive Family First services.

There was significantly less court involvement downstate and less disagreement about how the court should be used. In sites where court involvement was less common, DCFS was generally supportive when private agencies sought court assistance in securing family cooperation. Court orders were obtained following referral to Family First for 31% of the downstate cases. Of the cases with court orders, 36% had orders of protection or supervision and 26% had temporary custody orders. Compared to Chicago, significantly more downstate cases involved court orders for Family First services (11 vs. 24%, $p = 0.004$).

Findings from a comparison of the Family First and regular service groups indicate that in four out of six regions (Chicago South, Chicago East, Lake Villa/Waukegan, and East St. Louis), court orders were obtained for significantly more Family First cases than regular services cases (Table 5.13).

Role of Crisis Intervention

Much of the family preservation literature and early training efforts in Illinois identified crisis intervention as the fundamental approach workers should use. Crisis intervention was selected because of the widely shared belief that families are thrown into a state of crisis when subjected to a protective service investigation. The crisis theory literature suggests that a unique opportunity for change may be present when a family is in a state of crisis. The objective of intervention is to move toward restoring equilibrium to the family unit by seizing this oppor-

Table 5.13: Number and Percentage of Cases Involved with the Court during Service, by Experimental Site[a]

	Family First		Regular services	
	N	%	N	%
Chicago South	240	48	100	37
Chicago East***	335	43	186	24
Peoria	111	25	52	27
Lake Villa/Waukegan*	83	33	54	15
Springfield	71	23	39	21
East St. Louis*	51	53	27	30
Total***	891	40	458	26

[a] Asterisks indicate significant differences between Family
First and regular services: ***, $p < .001$; *, $p < .05$.

tunity and actively working with the family to resolve its immediate
problems (see discussion of crisis intervention in Chapter 1).

For most families, there is little evidence that the investigation or the
threat of placement precipitated a crisis and, in our interviews, workers
rarely identified family crisis or crisis intervention as concepts guiding
their practice. Despite this, between half and three-quarters of the workers in the 1992 annual survey rated two program characteristics related
to crisis intervention as extremely important: 24-hour availability of the
worker (50%) and initial contact with family within 24 hours (78%).
Moreover, service summary data indicate that crisis intervention was
provided to nearly half of the families (48%). However, regional variations were significant ($p = 0.03$), ranging from 39 to 57% of the cases.
These data are difficult to interpret. It appears that crisis intervention
was not applied universally or even in the majority of cases, perhaps
with good reason—it may not have been needed. As we noted earlier,
however, workers did report using the approach more than any other
identified.

Use of Time Limits

The use of brief treatment in family preservation programs grew out of
the assumption that families experience a crisis at the point of referral
and that the crisis is time limited (usually from 4 to 6 weeks duration).
The appeal of brief treatment is twofold. First, it forces workers to limit
the range of problems to be addressed through services. In our study,
several workers described the 90-day time limit as helping them to orga-

nize and focus their efforts, thereby making overwhelming situations more manageable. Second, the pressure of a short deadline motivates action to solve problems. Some workers noted that the short-term nature of the family preservation program placed an identifiable endpoint on their relationship with clients, which they found motivating in another way. Since program families experience severe economic, social, and personal stresses (some of which are likely to be intractable), time-limited relationships with clients were often viewed with relief.

The success of time-limited approaches depends on the willingness of the worker to accept the basic philosophy and have the necessary resources available for problem resolution. Many workers remained unconvinced that brief services could benefit families who experienced numerous environmental and personal difficulties. Some had real difficulty understanding how meaningful change could be accomplished in 90 days or less. Only 19% of the Family First workers surveyed in 1992 expressed the belief that the 90-day time limit was a very important program characteristic. One worker said:

> A lot of times the 90 days just does not seem to be enough. I often feel the best thing would be to continue working with a client to prevent homelessness or whatever from happening again, but all we get is a chance to solve that immediate crisis.

And another worker:

> Because of the way things are handed to us, it's too short. We're given an incomplete investigation and an incomplete assessment. There's not enough time. In most cases, the information is not even given to you with any recommendations. Right when you get to a cooperation point with a client, it's too late because only two weeks remain.

Others suggested that the short time limits led them to terminate their relationships with clients before either party felt that the time was right. The discomfort challenged them to adapt, as one worker described:

> I try to talk to families about limits immediately. Sometimes when strong attachment develops I have to remind them of limits to avoid a sense of rejection . . . sometimes it's frustrating when I feel good stuff is occurring and it feels premature to let them go. Clients often plead for more contact: "Just drop in and see me." I'm learning to give a stronger message about the finality of 90 days to avoid disappointment later.

Of course, there were some workers who indicated that time limits were valuable even when significant problems remained at the 90-day point. It was not clear, however, that Family First staff were given much help in adapting their approach to families (or the systems approach advocated in the training they received) to the time limits of the program.

While the brevity of Family First services posed real constraints, there were several options workers could pursue for helping families over a longer period of time. These included linkage to other community resources, providing less intensive family maintenance services over a longer period of time, and turning families back to DCFS for continued services following Family First involvement. Many workers relied on these services to carry on the problem solving efforts they had begun. This amounted to using the Family First program to conduct a comprehensive assessment of family problems and to provide emergency services.

SUMMARY AND CONCLUSION

The Family First initiative posed a major challenge to the program's designers. Illinois is a large state with a diverse geography and population. Program services were carried out through contracts with over 60 private social service agencies. Although some uniformity was desired, program flexibility was believed to be an important component of the statewide program. To that end DCFS did not pursue a single program model, instead encouraging local programs to figure out ways to best meet the needs of their client families. Of particular interest to us was the extent to which the program contained elements considered to be the hallmarks of family preservation programs: time-limited services that are family focused and home-based; a mix of concrete and counseling services that are crisis oriented; community linkages for ongoing family support; small caseloads; and workers who are available around the clock.

Like most family preservation programs in other states, Family First was designed to be short term and time limited. Though the intent was a 90-day program, our data indicate that 60% of the families were served for a longer period of time. Many workers suggested that because of the number and severity of problems suffered by program families, it was unrealistic to think that meaningful improvements could be achieved within the prescribed time. In response, DCFS did not enforce strict time limits, but liberally permitted caseworkers to extend their work with families beyond the 90 days. Furthermore, many cases were not closed in DCFS at the conclusion of Family First services. Nearly one-half of the cases were expected to receive services and monitoring after leaving the Family First program.

Findings from analyses of data on service characteristics confirm that Family First cases received early and more intensive services, as well as a wider range of services, than control group cases. Greatly reduced caseloads in Family First permitted workers to spend more time with clients in their homes and to access a greater variety of services than would have been possible in the absence of the program.

Family First workers drew on their clients' capabilities, as measured by worker reports of parental involvement in services. Family First cases were distinguished from those receiving regular services by the increased level of participation of parents in developing their case plans and in carrying out problem-solving tasks. Parent interviews suggested that Family First clients had a positive relationship with their caseworkers, although differences between the experimental and control groups were significant only in the Chicago East region.

We expected that a family focus would be a central element of the work with clients. This was not generally the case. Problems addressed through services were usually tied to the initial allegations and were expected by workers to have an impact on family functioning. Caseworkers most often reported using individual counseling as their major approach. This may have been due, in part, to the large number of single parents and infants in the program and to the reluctance of some workers to involve extended family members in sessions.

Although staff attitudes about job conditions were fairly positive, more than one-half of the respondents reported average or low morale in their agency. Staff turnover was found to be higher for Family First caseworkers than for supervisors or homemakers.

Interviews with agency administrators and line staff were helpful in identifying sources of tension between the provider agencies and DCFS. We found that differing philosophies and lack of experience in working with protective service families were major factors in the close monitoring of some agencies by DCFS. For many providers, balancing an interest in family functioning with the need to protect the child was a difficult task. For others, it was striking a balance between client self-determination and child protection. Particularly in Chicago, the court played an important role in determining the problems to be addressed and the services to be provided to families.

The Family First program, like most social programs, has been imperfectly implemented and has been heavily criticized by the media, politicians, and national advocates of placement prevention programs. It has come under fire by some for giving "undeserving" families too much in the way of concrete supports, by others for not following a prescribed model of service, and by still others for not serving the families for whom the program was intended. We return to discuss the pressures on the program in Chapter 8.

NOTES

1. Analysis of data for this chapter was performed by Amy Chak and Lucinda Fox.

2. This mean was affected by the provision of extensive homemaking services to three families.

3. Of the 722 Family First cases for which data are available for this question, 18% of the cases were perceived by workers to have been unsuccessful. An open-ended question asked workers to state the reasons for their response. Categories were developed based on an examination of approximately 30 responses to the question. Two research assistants coded responses. Interrater reliability was 0.74, using Cohen's kappa.

4. Interrater reliability was 0.80 using Cohen's kappa.

5. Two of the most recent evaluations conducted in California (McDonald and Associates 1990) and New Jersey (Feldman 1991) reported smaller proportions of family preservation cases were provided with concrete services (10 and 68%, respectively).

6. For Family First cases, this percentage is 17% higher than reported for financial assistance when workers were asked to select from a list those services they provided to the family (Table 5.3). Workers may have interpreted the two items differently. The term *cash assistance* was used by DCFS and was widely understood to refer specifically to emergency funds available to families in the Family First program.

7. How cash assistance was used was an open-ended question. Analytic categories were developed based on an examination of approximately 100 responses to the question. Two research assistants coded responses for the analysis. Interrater reliability was established at 0.82, using Cohen's kappa.

8. Some cases in the regular services group were referred to private agencies for services (although they were not referred to private agency Family First programs). Workers indicated that private agencies had primary responsibility for only 9% of the regular service cases.

9. Data from the annual survey of Family First workers indicate that their median caseload was 5.

10. Level of significance for regional variation with respect to focus on families: $p < 0.001$.

11. In Lake Villa/Waukegan, 41% of the primary caretakers, 34% of other adults, and 60% of the children were usually cooperative. Thirty percent of the primary caretakers fully participated in the development of their service plans, 40% agreed with their service plans, and 39% usually completed their tasks.

12. Regular services parents who reported not having a caseworker since referral were probably cases that were closed after random assignment with no further DCFS involvement. Family First parents in Lake Villa/Waukegan and Peoria who reported that they did not have a caseworker since referral may have

misunderstood the question or errors may have been made in asking the question.

13.   Statewide, 50% of the Family First staff were white, 40% were African-American, 8% were Latino, and 2% were unspecified others.

14.   Data collection on staffing patterns ended early during the final year of the study. Because data on hires and departures were not available for the entire year, they are not included in the analysis.

Chapter 6

The Outcomes of Family First[1]

What were the effects of the Family First program? In this chapter, we examine this central question by looking at what happened in families during and after their involvement with the program. We look at the effects of the program on out-of-home placements, child maltreatment, progress toward individualized case objectives, the closing of cases in the public child welfare system, and child and family functioning.[2] We begin by presenting data on selected outcomes for all cases referred to Family First during the first four years of the program. We then focus on the effects of Family First relative to those of regular services, using data from the randomized experiment. We examine regional variations and the effects of case and service characteristics on outcomes of interest. These analyses provide progressively refined tests of the effects of Family First. We also present results from interviews with parents regarding effects of the program on child and family functioning and clients' views of services.

TIER 1: ALL FAMILY FIRST CASES

We begin by looking at outcomes for all families referred to the program over a four-year period.

Out-of-Home Placement of Children

The prevention of out-of-home placements is a central goal of family preservation programs, one that was examined in our study and in most evaluations in this area.

Data on out-of-home placements of children were available for 6,456 families (99% of those who received Family First services in the first four years of the program)[3] and 10,608 children who were in their homes at the time of referral.[4] We examined the risk of placement at both the family and child level; that is, we calculated the probability that a family would experience placement of one or more children and the probability that an individual child would be placed at various points in time. The statistical technique we used was survival analysis.[5]

At one month after referral, the risk of placement for a family was .05; that is, 5% of all families were likely to experience placement of one or more children within 30 days of referral (see Figure 6.1). At the family level, the risk of placement increased slowly to .12 at three months, .18 at six months, .23 at one year, .30 at two years, and .33 at three years after referral. For individual children, the risk of placement was .03 at one month, .13 at six months, .19 at one year, .24 at two years, and .27 at three years.

Thus, we find that 77% of families served by the program were intact and 81% of the children remained with their families at one year after referral. Findings such as these have been used by some observers to suggest that family preservation programs "prevent" placements in a substantial number of cases. However, it is not appropriate to draw conclusions about the effects of a program without knowing what the risk of placement would have been in the absence of family preservation services—that is, without data from a control group. We will return to

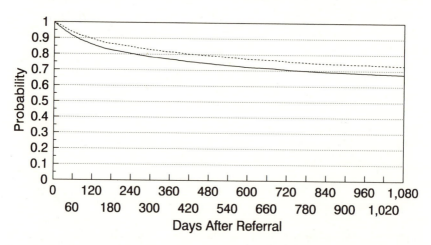

Figure 6.1.   Results of family-level (solid line) and child-level (dashed line) analyses of the probability of avoiding placement (all Family First cases).

this issue below when we present data from the randomized experiment.

As noted in the first chapter, the criteria for referral to Family First changed over time and some workers believed that easier cases were sent to Family First in later years. To determine whether the risk of placement changed over time, we examined placements that occurred among families who were referred to Family First during each of the calendar years from 1989 to 1992. There were no significant differences in the risk of placement among these entry cohorts. Hence, there is no evidence that cases became "easier," at least in terms of the likelihood of placement.

Overall, 45% of all placements were with relatives. The proportion of placements with kin ranged from a low of 26% in Marion to 59% in the Chicago South region. Family First workers said that they had initiated the decision to place a child in 63% of the placements that occurred during Family First services.[6] When placement was initiated by other parties (for example, the courts), workers usually agreed with the decision (workers agreed "greatly" in 68% of the cases, "somewhat" in 22%, and "not at all" in 10%).

Subsequent Maltreatment of Children

In addition to the prevention of out-of-home placement, family preservation programs are concerned with the safety of children who remain in their homes. Thus, we report on various types of child maltreatment following referral to Family First.

In Illinois, reports of child maltreatment are made to and recorded by the State Central Register (SCR). "Indicated" reports are those in which allegations of maltreatment are substantiated through a child protective services investigation. Here, subsequent maltreatment is defined as the presence of one or more indicated reports of maltreatment after the date of referral. Since we relied on official, substantiated reports of maltreatment, some incidents of child maltreatment are not captured in our data (either because they were not reported or because there was not enough evidence to substantiate a reported incident). Data on subsequent maltreatment were available for 6,255 (96%) of the families served during the first four years of the Family First program.

Within one month of referral, the probability that maltreatment would recur in a family was .06. The risk increased to .13 at three months, .19 at six months, .26 at one year, .35 at two years, and .40 at three years after referral (Figure 6.2). The risk of maltreatment for individual children was quite similar to that found in the family-level analysis.[7] There were no

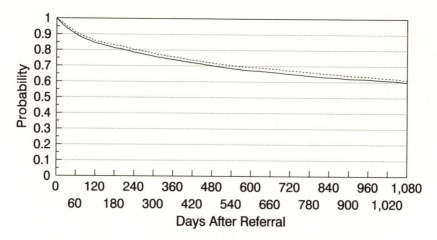

Figure 6.2. Results of family-level (solid line) and child-level (dashed line) analyses of the probability of avoiding maltreatment (all Family First cases).

significant differences among entry cohorts (those referred to Family First during 1989, 1990, 1991, or 1992) in the risk of subsequent maltreatment. As with placement, the rates of subsequent maltreatment were quite low.

Among families with at least one substantiated report of child maltreatment within the first year after referral to Family First,[8] 41% had indicated allegations of inadequate supervision and 32% were charged with substantial risk of physical injury to children. In Illinois, the allegation of substantial risk of physical injury to children means that there is a "real and significant danger" of physical injury or sexual abuse to the child. It is used when the specific nature or extent of harm cannot be defined or when violence or intimidation directed at a child has not resulted in physical injury although an injury could result from the continuation of these acts. "Inadequate supervision" (a neglect allegation) and "risk of physical injury" (usually an abuse allegation) are the most common allegations in Illinois. They are less precisely defined than other allegations and thus are broader categories. Investigators sometimes use them as catchall categories, incorporating situations in which workers believe there is considerable risk, although the risk may not be well defined. Less frequent types of maltreatment included physical injury to children (in 18% of families with indicated reports within one year of referral), medical neglect (14%), environmental neglect (10%), substance misuse (7%),[9] inadequate food (6%), sexual abuse (5%), and inadequate shelter (3%).[10]

Case Closing in DCFS

One of the goals of Family First was to address the problems that led to families' involvement in the child welfare system so that many families would no longer need to remain in the system. This goal has become more important in recent years, because of pressures to reduce caseloads throughout the child welfare system. For some families, case closure in DCFS represents a welcome end to the state's intrusion into their lives. For others, it may mean that needed services are more difficult to obtain.

Data on case closing in DCFS were available for 6,238 families (96%) served in the first four years of the program. Approximately 14% of all cases served in Family First were likely to be closed by DCFS within three months of referral (Figure 6.3). The probability that a case would be closed increased to .35 at six months, .52 at one year, .68 at two years, and .76 at three years. Once cases were closed by DCFS, the likelihood of reopening was fairly small. For example, within one year after case closing only 13% of closed cases were reopened.

The above analysis indicates that relatively few children in the Family First program as a whole were placed in substitute care or suffered from reported and confirmed maltreatment during and after involvement in the program. Further, about half of the cases were closed in DCFS within

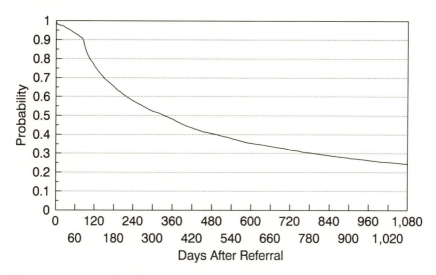

Figure 6.3. Probability that a family case will remain open in DCFS at various points in time (all Family First cases).

one year after referral. However, as we have suggested at several points, these data cannot be used to indicate the effects of the program. The randomized experiment described in Chapter 3 was implemented to provide evidence of program effects.

TIER 2: THE EXPERIMENT

As described in Chapter 3, the experiment was conducted in seven sites around the state. Between April 1990 and April 1992, cases in these sites were randomly assigned to Family First or to the regular services of the department. Cases in which the random assignment was violated were not included in the analysis of data. Since many regular service group assignments were violated in Rockford, this site was dropped from the analysis. A total of 995 Family First and 569 regular services cases were included in the analysis, although the number of cases for which various pieces of information was available varies (see Table 6.1).

We begin by examining overall differences between Family First and regular services groups (using survival analysis).[11] We then refine this analysis by examining site-level variations, the effects of case characteristics, and the influence of several aspects of service on case outcomes. This strategy may be outlined as follows:

1. Determine overall differences between Family First and regular services groups in outcomes
2. Determine site-level variations in outcomes
    a. Differences between Family First and regular services groups within sites
    b. Differences between Family First and regular services groups, controlling for site-level variations
3. Determine relationships between case characteristics and outcomes
    a. Effects of case characteristics on outcomes within the Family First and regular services groups
    b. Differences between Family First and regular services groups, controlling for variations in case characteristics and site
4. Determine effects of service characteristics on outcomes, controlling for variations in case characteristics and site.

Proportional-hazard models were used to examine the effects of case characteristics and sites on the probabilities of placement, maltreatment,

Table 6.1: Availability of Data on Cases in the Experiment, by Experimental Group and Site

	Family First cases						Regular services cases					
	Cases with data on maltreatment		Cases with data on placement		Cases with data on case closing		Cases with data on maltreatment		Cases with data on placement		Cases with data on case closing	
Site	N	%	N	%	N	%	N	%	N	%	N	%
Chicago East	389	100.0	386	99.2	360	92.5	231	100.0	225	97.4	221	95.7
Chicago South	274	100.0	271	98.9	262	95.6	141	100.0	133	94.3	130	92.2
East St. Louis	59	100.0	58	98.3	56	94.9	31	100.0	31	100.0	30	96.8
Lake Villa/Waukegan	85	100.0	85	100.0	84	98.8	61	100.0	60	98.4	58	95.1
Peoria	112	100.0	110	98.2	104	92.9	63	100.0	63	100.0	63	100.0
Springfield	76	100.0	74	97.4	72	94.7	42	100.0	40	95.2	37	88.1
Total	995	100.0	984	98.9	938	94.3	569	100.0	552	97.0	539	94.7

and case closing.[12] Simultaneous equations were developed to test the effects of service characteristics on outcomes.[13]

Placement

The risk of placement in both the Family First and regular services experimental groups was quite low. For families in the Family First group, this risk was .06 at one month after referral, .13 at three months, .20 at six months, and .27 at one year. Among families in the regular services group, the likelihood of placement was .07 at one month after referral, .13 at three months, .17 at six months, and .21 at one year (see Figure 6.4). The risk of placement for individual children was lower than the risk for families, but the trends over time were similar (see Figure 6.5).

Although the risk of placement was low overall, cases in the Family First program had a statistically significant higher risk of placement than families who received regular services (Figure 6.4). The same pattern was found in the child-level analysis of the risk of placement (Figure 6.5). These results are of obvious concern, since they suggest that the program had effects opposite those intended: Families in the program were more likely to have a child placed than those not receiving these services. It is possible that extensive contact with family members by program staff serves a "case finding" function, which increases the likelihood that families will lose one or more children.[14] However, between-

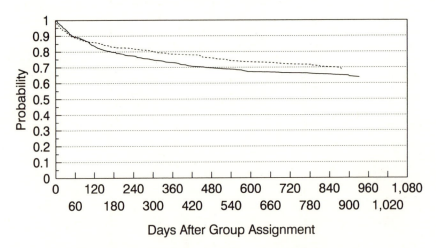

Figure 6.4. Probability that a family will remain intact (all cases in the experiment). Family First, solid line; regular services, dashed line.

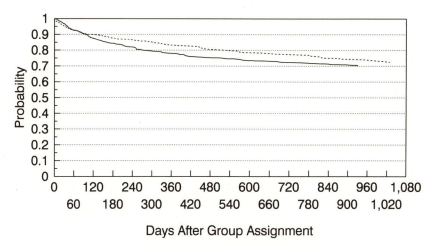

Figure 6.5. Probability that a child will not be placed (all cases in the experiment). Family First, solid line; regular services, dashed line.

group differences in placement rates did not appear until after families left the Family First program (at four months after referral in the family-level analysis) so it is unlikely that case finding explains the differences. Another possibility is that the events or behaviors that triggered placement among Family First and control cases were different. There is some anecdotal evidence that families who received family preservation services were thought to have been "given a chance" to change. That is, once "reasonable efforts" have been made to prevent placement, workers' tolerance for potentially harmful behaviors may be lower and they may be more likely to take custody of children. Finally, it should be noted that differences between groups in placements rates disappeared when case characteristics were taken into account, as we shall see in a later analysis.

Since the data on control cases represent the risk of placement among cases referred to Family First had they not received family preservation services, we can conclude that few cases in the program were at "imminent risk" of placement.[15] We believe that this is one of the most important findings of this study and we discuss it further in the final chapter.

We examined the duration of placements for the first child placed from each family and for all children that experienced placement. The program had no significant effect on the duration of placements in either analysis (Figure 6.6).

Slightly more than half (55%) of all placements among Family First cases were with relatives compared with 49% of those in regular services

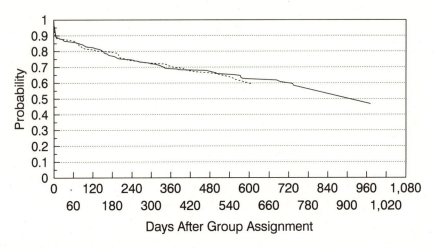

Figure 6.6. Probability that a child in placement will remain in placement (all placed cases in the experiment). Family First, solid line; regular services, dashed line.

cases (a nonsignificant difference). These proportions varied considerably among sites but within-site differences between experimental and control groups in types of placements were not significant.[16]

When workers reported that a child had been placed (on the service summary form), they were asked whether they initiated the decision to place, and if not, whether they agreed with this decision. Overall, Family First workers said that they initiated 69% of the placements that occurred while families were in the program. In contrast, regular services workers said that they initiated 27% of the placements that occurred in their cases within approximately 90 days of referral.[17] This pattern varied considerably across sites.[18] The overall difference between groups may reflect the fact that casework responsibility for regular services cases often changed hands within DCFS in the first 90 days after random assignment. Regarding the placement decisions that they didn't initiate, Family First and DCFS workers agreed "greatly" with the decision to place the child in about the same proportions (73% of the cases in Family First and 79% in regular services).

Subsequent Maltreatment

The possibility that children left in their homes might experience further harm is of paramount concern in the child welfare system. Insofar as workers choose between placement and family preservation, they must have some confidence that referral to family preservation will not often be accompanied by further harm. One might expect that children left in their own homes with family preservation services would experience more maltreatment than children placed in foster care, although, one hopes, only slightly more. However, as indicated by the above data on placement in the control group, workers do not generally consider referral to family preservation and placement as alternatives. Hence, the data on subsequent maltreatment have a different meaning than would have been the case had most control group children been placed. The question now is whether two groups of children, both of whom were largely left at home, experienced different levels of maltreatment. The hope now is that children in families receiving family preservation would have experienced less maltreatment.

Survival analysis showed that the Family First program had no significant overall effect on the risk of subsequent maltreatment (Figure 6.7). Analysis at the child level showed that children in the Family First group were significantly more likely to experience maltreatment than those in regular services (Figure 6.8); but the large number of children in this analysis makes it relatively easy to detect statistically significant differences and the differences between groups were slight. As with placement, the rates of subsequent maltreatment in both groups were relatively low.

In response to the finding that the program did not affect the recurrence of child maltreatment, program administrators hypothesized that

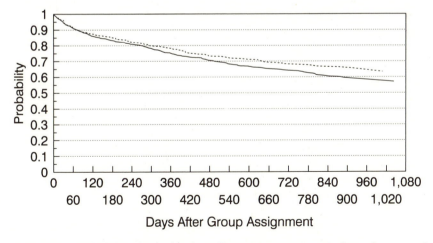

Figure 6.7. Probability that a family will not experience an indicated report of abuse or neglect following random assignment (all experimental cases). Family First, solid line; regular services, dashed line.

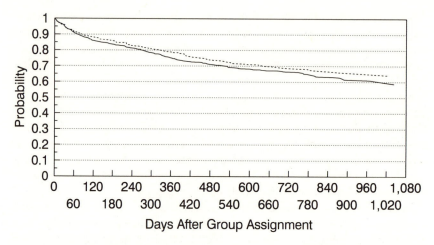

Figure 6.8. Probability that a child will not experience a subsequent indicated report of abuse or neglect (all cases in the experiment). Family First, solid line; regular services, dashed line.

Family First might reduce the severity of subsequent maltreatment. To determine whether there were systematic differences between Family First and regular services cases in the types of child maltreatment that occurred following random assignment, we compared percentages of cases with specific types of child maltreatment (indicated allegations). The categories of maltreatment that we examined included severe physical injury (abuse or neglect that resulted in death, brain damage, subdural hematoma, internal injuries, wounds, or torture), other physical injury, risk of physical harm, sexual abuse, substance misuse, inadequate supervision, inadequate food, medical neglect, environmental neglect, inadequate shelter, and other. Family First cases were significantly less likely to have experienced indicated allegations of medical neglect.[19] There were no other significant differences between groups in types of maltreatment.

Few studies of family preservation programs have examined the incidence of serious injury or death to children who remain in their homes. At the beginning of the Family First program, DCFS administrators and private agency service providers paid considerable attention to the risks involved in providing in-home services to families who had abused or neglected their children in the past. The potential risks to children were clearly articulated and plans were developed to handle "disasters," which were thought to be inevitable. Throughout the Family First evaluation, we paid particular attention to the incidence and handling of cases in which children died.[20] Among the 1,564 cases in the experiment, ten child fatalities were recorded in the Child Abuse and Neglect Tracking System. Seven deaths occurred in the Family First group; of these, three children died during family preservation services and four died after services to their families had ended. Following child protective service investigations, two deaths (both of which occurred while Family First services were being provided) were attributed to child abuse or neglect. Of the three fatalities that occurred in the control group, none were attributed to maltreatment. Since the total number of cases in the program exceeded that in the control group, a larger number of child fatalities among Family First cases is expected. However, the number of deaths that occurred in this sample is quite small and cannot be used to draw conclusions about the effects of the Family First program on the likelihood of child fatalities.

Providing in-home services to families who have abused or neglected their children entails some risks. As we indicated above, we might expect somewhat higher levels of maltreatment to children in family preservation programs compared with those in foster care. Since foster care was often not an alternative to Family First, we might have expected that the program would have resulted in less maltreatment compared to a group in which most children were left at home without the services. The data suggest that the program did not result in materially higher levels of harm to children, nor did it reduce this risk.

Achievement of Case Objectives

While policymakers focus on such objectives as the reduction in placements and maltreatment and the control of costs, such things are not the immediate focus of day-to-day work in the field. Rather workers and families develop specific case objectives to guide their work. Family First and DCFS workers were asked to rate the extent to which case objectives were achieved within 90 days of referral, using a 4-point scale.[21] Workers could list up to 5 case objectives. Achievement ratings were made for each objective and mean ratings were computed for each case. Overall, Family First cases had significantly higher mean achievement ratings than regular services cases, suggesting that Family First clients made greater progress in reaching objectives.[22] However, interpretation of this result is complicated by a number of factors. There were some differences between groups in the types of case objectives identified by workers (see Chapter 5). There may have been between-group differences in the specificity of objectives. For example, if objectives for Family First cases were more specific and short term in nature, they may have been more easily attained. Second, there may have been differences between Family First and DCFS workers in their views of what constituted case progress. Since Family First workers had more contact with families and were part of an experimental program, they may have been more likely to identify changes or to believe that change was occurring. Of course, it is possible that significant progress was made in Family First cases, although these gains were small and apparently not directly related to the likelihood of placement, child maltreatment, or case closing.

Case Opening, Closing, and Reopening

One-fifth (20%) of all regular services cases were never opened for services by DCFS, while all of the Family First cases were opened. This result suggests that the program had a "net-widening" effect: some cases that would not otherwise have become involved in the child welfare system were involved because of the Family First program. We consider the implications of net-widening in the final chapter.

Although Family First cases were more likely to enter the child welfare system, the program had no long-term effects on whether families remained in this system (Figure 6.9). After five months, the chance that a case would be open in DCFS was remarkably similar in the two groups (.30 for Family First cases and .32 for regular services). Hence, for both groups, most of the cases appear to have been closed relatively quickly (about 70% within 5 months of referral). We analyzed cases that were closed by DCFS and found that there were no significant differences between Family First and control groups in the likelihood that a case would be reopened by the department: Six months after case closing, 8% of Family First cases and 7% of regular services cases were likely to be reopened (Figure 6.10), again fairly low proportions. Thus, there is no

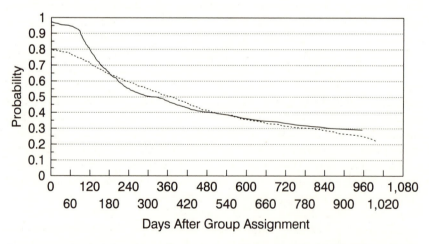

Figure 6.9. Probability that a family case will remain open in DCFS at various points in time (all cases in the experiment). Family First, solid line; regular services, dashed line.

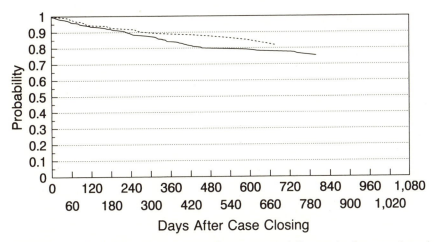

Figure 6.10. Probability that a case will not reopen (all cases in the experiment that closed). Family First, solid line; regular services, dashed line.

evidence that the program resulted in faster closing of cases or a reduced chance of subsequent reopening.

Variations in Outcomes across Sites

The experiment was conducted in six areas in different parts of the state. As indicated in Chapters 4 and 5, the clients served by Family First and the services provided to families varied across sites.[23] Thus it is possible that there were systematic differences in case outcomes across the sites. It is also possible that there were differences in outcomes between the experimental and control groups in some sites and not in others.

To test the latter hypothesis, we used survival analysis to compare the risks of placement, maltreatment, and case closing for families in the Family First and regular services groups within each site. We also conducted survival analyses for the risk of placement and maltreatment for individual children within each site. Results are summarized in Table 6.2. There were no significant differences between program and control groups (in either the family-level or child-level analyses) in the Springfield site. Children in the Family First group in Chicago East and Chicago South were more likely to be placed than those in the regular services group in those sites. Children in the Family First groups in East St. Louis, Lake Villa/Waukegan, and Peoria were more likely to be involved in subsequent indicated reports of maltreatment than children in the regular services groups in these sites.[24] In the Lake Villa/Waukegan and Peoria sites there were significant differences between groups in case opening and closing rates. In both areas, substantial proportions of cases

Table 6.2:   Results of Site-Level Analyses of Differences between Family First
and Regular Services Groups, by Site and Outcome

	Significance of difference between Family First and regular services (p-value)[a]				
	Placement		*Subsequent maltreatment*		*Case closing*
Site	*Family level*	*Child level*	*Family level*	*Child level*	*Family level*
Chicago East	.138 (+)	.035 (+)*	.778	.434	.092 (−)
Chicago South	.063 (+)	.002 (+)*	.395 (+)	.449	.340
East St. Louis	.366 (−)	.493	.211 (+)	.012 (+)*	.199 (+)
Lake Villa/Waukegan	.054 (+)	.179 (+)	.043 (+)*	.001 (+)*	.076 (−)[b]
Peoria	.576 (−)	.942	.250 (+)	.047 (+)*	<.001 (+)*
Springfield	.943	.733	.704	.321	.718
Overall	.031 (+)*	.002 (+)*	.072 (+)	.029 (+)*	.394

[a] The significance level reported here is from the log-rank chi-square test of difference
between groups. (+) indicates that Family First cases are more likely to experience the
event at the end of the observation period than regular services cases; (−) indicates
the opposite; blanks indicate virtually no difference between groups. Asterisks indicate that differences are significant at $p < .05$.

[b] The Wilcoxon chi-square test of differences between Family First and regular services
groups in Lake Villa/Waukegan was significant at $p = .005$.

in the regular services group (41% in Lake Villa/Waukegan and 32% in
Peoria) were never opened for services. In Lake Villa/Waukegan, Family
First cases remained open in DCFS longer than regular services cases,
although the opposite was true in Peoria, where Family First cases were
more likely to be closed after six months.[25] Thus it is evident that there
are some site-level differences in outcomes, sometimes favoring Family
First, sometimes regular services. These site-level differences are "averaged out" in the overall results.

What are the effects of Family First, taking into account these site
differences? Family First was still associated with an increase in the risk
of placement[26] while the program had no significant effect on subsequent maltreatment or case closing rates.

*Relationships between Case Characteristics
and Outcomes*

So far, we have found little evidence of the effects of Family First
services. However, it is possible that the program was more effective
for certain types of families than others. In many evaluations of this

type, various subgroups of cases receiving the experimental service are compared to determine those with the highest and lowest rates of success (see Chapter 2). However, such analyses do not indicate differential success of the program because of different "base rates" of success in the subgroups. For example, cases involving substance abuse might, in general, have higher rates of placement than those without substance abuse involvement, whether or not they received services. Hence, it is necessary to compare experimental and control cases within subgroups; for example, we must compare substance abuse cases receiving Family First services with substance abuse cases receiving regular services. We did these comparisons, using survival analysis, for each of the subgroups listed in Table 6.3.[27] Family First increased the risk of placement for single-adult households,[28] but had no effect on the risk of placement for other subgroups. The program had no effect on the risk of subsequent maltreatment for any of the subgroups. Family First appeared to speed the rates of case closing in DCFS for families with marital problems, those with housing problems, and those who had a child with health problems.[29] A substantial proportion (.31) of families with a teenage primary caregiver were not opened for services if they were assigned to the control group; although Family First increased the likelihood that teenage parent cases would be opened initially, the program had no long-term effect on whether such cases remained open in DCFS. We do not believe that these few subgroup effects should be used to guide decisions about the targeting of family preservation programs.

As noted above, analyses of the relationships between case characteristics and outcomes within treatment groups have been undertaken in other studies and we also conducted them. Within both Family First and regular service groups, placement rates were significantly higher among families with cocaine problems, those with other drug problems, and those in which protective custody had been taken within one year prior to referral (Table 6.4). Among Family First cases, the risk of placement was significantly lower for cases that were new to the child welfare system compared to families who had more than one report of maltreatment prior to referral. Among regular services cases, housing problems, alcohol problems, and problems related to children's health, development, or learning were associated with an increased likelihood of placement.

Within both groups, the risk of subsequent maltreatment was significantly lower than average for cases that were new to the system and higher for families with cocaine problems (Table 6.5). In addition, among Family First cases, the risk of subsequent maltreatment was lower for families in which a child had been injured prior to referral, lower

Table 6.3: Characteristics of Cases in the Experiment, by Group

Case characteristic	Family First cases			Regular service cases			p-value[b]
	Valid N[a]	N in subgroup	Percentage of total	Valid N[a]	N in subgroup	Percentage of total	
New to child welfare (A sequence)	976	629	64.4	553	374	67.6	
Prior physical injury	976	239	24.5	553	124	22.4	
Chronic neglect[c]	976	72	7.4	553	30	5.4	
Housing problems[d]	887	268	30.2	490	80	16.3	<.001
Poverty or resource deficit problems[e]	889	257	28.9	494	162	32.8	
Cocaine problems	872	291	33.4	477	167	35.0	
Other drug problems	872	37	4.2	477	16	3.4	
Alcohol problems	887	167	18.8	489	89	18.2	
Parents' chronic mental illness or emotional problems	887	272	30.7	489	100	20.4	<.001
Marital problems, domestic violence, or unresolved separation or divorce	887	243	27.4	489	108	22.1	.031

160

Characteristic	N	n	%	N	n	%	Sig.[b]
Child care skill deficits[f]	887	284	32.0	489	145	29.7	
Children's health, development, or learning problems	887	198	22.3	489	71	14.5	<.001
Teenage caregiver	895	72	8.0	506	47	9.3	
Single-adult household	895	500	55.9	506	235	46.4	<.001
Extended-family household	895	200	22.3	506	160	31.6	<.001
Protective custody within one year prior to referral	984	127	12.9	552	78	14.1	

[a] The valid N is the number of cases with available data from a specific source. It is the basis upon which percentages are calculated. The first three characteristics are derived from CANTS data, so the first valid N is the number of cases with valid CANTS records. The next nine categories (from housing to children's health, development, or learning problems. Teenage caregiver, single-adult household, and extended-family household are calculated from various items on the Service Summary household composition table. (For regular services cases, household composition data were obtained in the thirty- and ninety-day interviews described in Chapter 3. Thus, these data are available on some cases on which we do not have ninety-day service summary data.) The last category is derived from service summary data and from MARS/CYCIS data on children's living arrangements within a one-year period prior to random assignment.

[b] Indicates the significance level for differences between groups in the proportion of cases identified with the characteristic (based on chi-square tests).

[c] Three or more reports of neglect prior to referral.

[d] Includes dangerous housing, homelessness, and prior indicated allegations of inadequate shelter.

[e] Includes poverty and prior indicated allegations of inadequate clothing or inadequate food.

[f] Includes problems in physical care, discipline, or emotional care of children.

Table 6.4:   Results of Proportional Hazard Models of the Effects of Case Characteristics and Sites on the Risk of Placement for Family First, Regular Services, and Both Groups[a] (Percentage Change in Hazard Rate)

Characteristic	Family First cases	Regular service cases	Both groups
Family First services	—	—	9.3
New to child welfare (A sequence)	−38.5***	−15.9	−34.4***
Prior physical injury	−24.7	27.5	−13.5
Chronic neglect	10.1	61.7	13.1
Housing problems	1.8	87.3**	19.4
Poverty or resource deficit problems	9.6	−11.7	2.0
Cocaine problems	134.0***	185.0***	150.1***
Other drug problems	80.8*	225.7**	109.1**
Alcohol problems	15.0	56.3*	29.9*
Parents' chronic mental illness or emotional problems	23.0	41.0	34.7**
Marital problems, domestic violence, or unresolved separation or divorce	−15.3	37.6	−1.9
Child care skill deficits	16.8	41.0	28.1*
Children's health, development, or learning problems	11.6	68.3*	29.3*
Teenage caregiver	37.5	17.2	28.3
Single-adult household	15.9	−5.9	4.6
Extended-family household	32.0	13.2	20.7
Protective custody within one year prior to referral	96.9***	228.1***	141.2***
Chicago East	—	—	−16.3
Chicago South	—	—	−32.5
Lake Villa/Waukegan	—	—	−49.5*
Peoria	—	—	−40.0*
Springfield	—	—	16.5

[a] The significance of relationships between case characteristics and the outcome measure is
affected by the size of the estimated coefficient and the standard error of the coefficient (statistics that are not reported here). Thus, the absolute value of the percentage
change does not determine whether there is a significant relationship between the
characteristic and outcome variables.
*, $p < .05$; **, $p < .01$; ***, $p < .001$.

for families with marital problems, and higher for those in which protective custody had been taken in the year prior to referral.

Regarding case closing, in both groups, families with cocaine problems and those in which protective custody had been taken at some time
before referral were likely to remain in the public child welfare system
longer than cases without these characteristics (Table 6.6). Within the
Family First group, those who were new to the child welfare system
were likely to exit more quickly than others, while cases with substance
abuse problems other than cocaine were likely to remain open longer in
DCFS. In the regular services group, families with housing problems

and those with poverty or other resource deficits were likely to remain in the child welfare system longer than families without these problems.

By and large, the relationships we found between case characteristics and outcomes were not unexpected. They reflect the serious difficulties in dealing with cases involving substance abuse, housing problems, and other resource deficits, and cases with prior involvement in the child welfare system. When variations in case characteristics were taken into account, we found that the program had no significant effects on rates of placement, subsequent maltreatment, and case closing (Tables 6.4 through 6.6). Hence, the higher rate of placement for Family First cases

Table 6.5: Results of Proportional Hazard Models of the Effects of Case Characteristics and Sites on the Risk of Subsequent Maltreatment for Family First, Regular Services, and Both Groups[a] (Percentage Change in Hazard Rate)

Characteristic	Family First cases	Regular service cases	Both groups
Family First services	—	—	8.9
New to child welfare (A sequence)	−41.0***	−42.6 **	−42.9***
Prior physical injury	−36.1**	−12.0	−30.0**
Chronic neglect	11.0	27.1	9.1
Housing problems	13.9	6.8	13.3
Poverty or resource deficit problems	−4.8	4.7	−2.3
Cocaine problems	49.9**	79.6**	71.0***
Other drug problems	−34.7	63.4	−4.3
Alcohol problems	−11.3	10.0	−5.9
Parents' chronic mental illness or emotional problems	12.0	39.4	20.6
Marital problems, domestic violence, or unresolved separation or divorce	−26.0*	33.0	−9.3
Child care skill deficits	12.0	39.9	23.0*
Children's health, development, or learning problems	−.8	39.4	11.0
Teenage caregiver	18.5	40.8	31.5
Single-adult household	−.5	11.8	6.8
Extended-family household	−1.9	4.7	2.8
Protective custody within one year prior to referral	46.6*	7.6	35.7*
Chicago East	—	—	−27.9
Chicago South	—	—	−35.8*
Lake Villa/Waukegan	—	—	16.1
Peoria	—	—	−26.7
Springfield	—	—	−16.5

[a] The significance of relationships between case characteristics and the outcome measure is affected by the size of the estimated coefficient and the standard error of the coefficient (statistics that are not reported here). Thus, the absolute value of the percentage change does not determine whether there is a significant relationship between the characteristic and outcome variables.

*, $p < .05$; **, $p < .01$; ***, $p < .001$.

Table 6.6:   Results of Proportional Hazard Models of the Effects of Case Characteristics and Sites on the Risk of Case Closing for Family First, Regular
Services, and Both Groups[a] (Percentage Change in Hazard Rate)

Characteristic	Family First cases	Regular service cases	Both groups
Family First services	—	—	11.4
New to child welfare (A sequence)	29.1*	29.3	28.0**
Prior physical injury	11.0	26.0	19.1*
Chronic neglect	12.9	−9.6	9.6
Housing problems	−1.2	−42.6**	−10.9
Poverty or resource deficit problems	−6.7	−26.2*	−18.9**
Cocaine problems	−59.0***	−36.5**	−46.3***
Other drug problems	−47.5**	−42.4	−42.3**
Alcohol problems	−18.8	−18.1	−23.6**
Parents' chronic mental illness or emotional problems	−10.3	5.0	−12.0
Marital problems, domestic violence, or unresolved separation or divorce	11.5	−15.5	−4.5
Child care skill deficits	−12.5	−4.7	−14.5*
Children's health, development, or learning problems	−1.0	−23.0	−2.5
Teenage caregiver	−13.5	16.6	5.5
Single-adult household	−4.6	25.7	18.0*
Extended-family household	−8.3	−1.0	−1.0
Protective custody within one year prior to referral	−42.0***	−44.3**	−44.6***
Chicago East	—	—	28.4
Chicago South	—	—	40.4*
Lake Villa/Waukegan	—	—	156.8***
Peoria	—	—	127.3***
Springfield	—	—	100.7***

[a] The significance of relationships between case characteristics and the outcome measure is
affected by the size of the estimated coefficient and the standard error of the coefficient (statistics that are not reported here). Thus, the absolute value of the percentage
change does not determine whether there is a significant relationship between the
characteristic and outcome variables.
*, $p < .05$; **, $p < .01$; ***, $p < .001$.

disappears when variations in these case characteristics are taken into
account.

*Relationships between Service Characteristics
and Case Outcomes*

There is considerable debate in the field of child welfare about the
relative importance of various features of family preservation services.
Programs vary in the intensity, duration, and types of services provided

to families and there is little empirical evidence about the relative effects of variations in these aspects of services. The Family First program provided an opportunity to study such variations and their effects on families. The agencies in the program differed in the amount, type, and duration of services provided to families. In order to test the effects of variations in services, families would have had to be randomly assigned to different interventions. Although this was not the case in the Family First evaluation, our data do permit analyses of associations between service characteristics and outcomes.

In addition to differences across programs, service characteristics are likely to have been influenced by the characteristics of the individual case. Thus, in order to understand relationships between service characteristics and outcomes, we needed to control for variations in case and site characteristics. To do this, we developed systems of simultaneous equations in which the effects of service characteristics on outcomes were estimated using two-stage least squares. This approach allowed us to model the effects of case and site characteristics (exogenous variables) on both service characteristics and outcomes (endogenous variables), while examining relationships between services and outcomes (see Appendix C).

For all Family First cases in the experiment, we examined relationships between case outcomes and the following service characteristics:

(1) the number of days the case was open in Family First,
(2) hours of contact with caseworkers within the first 90 days after referral,
(3) hours of contact with homemakers within the first 90 days after referral, and
(4) number of concrete services provided.[30]

We thought these characteristics reflected some of the hallmarks of family preservation services, in particular, the length of service, the intensity of service, and the provision of concrete services. We might also have included the number of counseling services provided to a family but we believed that that variable was problematic because of ambiguity in the meaning of the categories of counseling services and their likely overlap.

Case outcomes were represented by three dummy variables indicating whether placement, subsequent maltreatment, or case closing occurred within one year after referral.[31] A similar analysis was conducted for all cases in the experiment, that is, Family First and regular service cases combined (the number of days open in Family First was dropped from this analysis). Since the provision of services varied greatly among sites, we tried each of the two-stage models with and without site as a predictor of outcomes.

Results of two-stage least squares estimation are summarized in Tables 6.7 through 6.9. None of the service characteristics were related to case

Table 6.7: Results of Two-Stage Least Squares Estimation of Effects of Service Characteristics on Placement within One Year after Referral[a]

	Model			
	Family First cases in the experiment		All cases in the experiment	
Variables in the model	With site variables	Without site variables	With site variables	Without site variables
Service characteristics				
Duration of Family First service (natural log)	−.151	.097	—	—
Number of hours of contact with caseworkers in the first 90 days of service (natural log)	.093	−.099	−.086	.009
Number of hours of contact with parent aides in the first 90 days of service (natural log)	.101	−.017	.228	−.026
Number of concrete services provided in the first 90 days	−.017	.022	−.017	.021
Case characteristics[b]				
Cocaine problems	.059	.133	.197	.145*
Alcohol problems	.059	.075	.084	.080**
Parental emotional problems or chronic mental illness	.053	.066	.091	.072*
Child care skill deficits	.004	.064	.011	.084*
Physical injury prior to referral	−.002	−.072	−.044	−.065
Number of prior reports of maltreatment	.011	.034	.049	.027
Placement prior to referral	.065	.124	.328	.212**
Sites				
Chicago East	.139	—	−.133	—
Chicago South	−.016	—	−.295	—
Lake Villa/Waukegan	−.116	—	−.324	—
Peoria	−.121	—	−.378	—
Springfield	.221	—	−.164	—
Other outcomes				
Indicated report of maltreatment within one year after referral	.651	.015	−.177	.059
Case closing within one year after referral	−.235	−.245	.027	−.121
Constant	.338	.128	.245	.096
Adjusted R^2	.098***	.109***	.063***	.130***

[a] The cells in this table contain parameter estimates (beta coefficients) for second-stage equations. *, $p < .05$; **, $p < .01$; ***, $p < .001$.

[b] Only those case characteristics that were significantly related to placement in a logistic regression analysis are included in these models.

Table 6.8: Results of Two-Stage Least Squares Estimation of Effects of Service Characteristics on the Reccurrence of Maltreatment within One Year after Referral[a]

Variables in the model	Family First cases in the experiment		All cases in the experiment	
	With site variables	Without site variables	With site variables	Without site variables
Service characteristics				
Duration of Family First service (natural log)	.244	−.309	—	—
Number of hours of contact with caseworkers in the first 90 days of service (natural log)	−.438	−.087	−.066	−.109
Number of hours of contact with parent aides in the first 90 days of service (natural log)	−.133	.027	−.097	.002
Number of concrete services provided in the first 90 days	.079	.050	.015	.064**
Case characteristics[b]				
Cocaine problems	.028	.065	.153	.130*
Marital problems	−.059	−.046	—	—
Poverty or resource deficits	−.041	−.055	—	—
Physical injury prior to referral	−.048	−.060	−.083	−.078
Number of prior reports of maltreatment	.020	.037*	.056**	.047***
Placement prior to referral	.021	.080	.175	.138
Child care skill deficits	—	—	.042	.069
Parents emotional problem or chronic mental illness	—	—	.060	.067
Sites				
Chicago East	−.186	—	−.159	—
Chicago South	.065	—	−.232	—
Lake Villa/Waukegan	−.004	—	−.138	—
Peoria	.152	—	−.228	—
Springfield	−.439	—	−.190	—
Other outcomes				
Placement within one year after referral	.580	.106	−.025	.029
Case closing within one year after referral	.080	−.075	.232	.148
Constant	.613	1.739	.143	.143
Adjusted R^2	.036***	.051***	.043***	.050***

[a] The cells in this table contain parameter estimates (beta coefficients) for second-stage equations.

*, $p < .05$; **, $p < .01$; ***, $p < .001$.

[b] Only those case characteristics that were significantly related to subseqent maltreatment in a logistic regression analysis are included in these models.

Table 6.9: Results of Two-Stage Least Squares Estimation of Effects of Service Characteristics on Case Closing within One Year after Referral[a]

	Model			
	Family First cases in the experiment		All cases in the experiment	
Variables in the model	With site variables	Without site variables	With site variables	Without site variables
Service characteristics				
Duration of Family First service (natural log)	−.616	−.132	—	—
Number of hours of contact with caseworkers in the first 90 days of service (natural log)	.366	−.110	−.038	−.104
Number of hours of contact with parent aides in the first 90 days of service (natural log)	−.005	.096**	.120	.144***
Number of concrete services provided in the first 90 days	−.008	−.011	−.041	−.038
Case characteristics[b]				
Cocaine problems	−.234	−.144*	−.167*	−.178***
Other drug problems	−.103	−.228*	−.204*	−.168*
Parental emotional problems or chronic mental illness	−.032	−.004	—	—
Chronic neglect	.081	.147	—	—
Teenage primary caregiver	−.233	−.095	—	—
Number of prior reports of maltreatment	−.051	−.007	.005	−.003
Placement prior to referral	−.309*	−.187**	−.246*	−.184**
Single-adult household	—	—	.071	.066*
Sites				
Chicago East	.535	—	.027	—
Chicago South	.499	—	−.012	—
Lake Villa/Waukegan	.425	—	.204	—
Peoria	.519	—	.100	—
Springfield	.809	—	.113	—
Other outcomes				
Placement within one year after referral	−.630	−.389	.154	−.124
Indicated report of maltreatment within one year after referral	.760	−.184	−.599	−.131
Constant	1.790	1.684*	.699**	.860***
Adjusted R^2	.077***	.138***	.081***	.092***

[a] The cells in this table contain parameter estimates (beta coefficients) for second-stage equations.

*, $p < .05$; **, $p < .01$; ***, $p < .001$.

[b] Only those case characteristics that were significantly related to case closing in a logistic regression analysis are included in these models.

outcomes either for Family First cases or for all cases in the experiment when regional variations in outcomes were taken into account. We then looked at relationships between service characteristics and outcomes without controlling for region (since region was related to both service characteristics and outcome, controlling for it might obscure service effects on outcome). Service characteristics still had no effects on placement. As for maltreatment, for all cases in the experiment, the more concrete services a family received, the more likely it was that they would experience an indicated report of maltreatment within one year after referral (this did not hold for Family First cases alone). One should not conclude from this that the provision of a range of concrete services increases the likelihood of maltreatment, since the direction of causality in the relationship between services and outcomes is not known. It is possible that the number of concrete services provided to families is a proxy for the severity of the case or the presence of multiple problems; maltreatment is probably more common in these families and they appear to receive more concrete services than others.

In the analysis of the relationship between service characteristics and case closing, without controlling for region, we found that the more contact families had with parent aides, the more likely it was that the case would be closed within a year after referral. It is possible that the type of help provided by parent aides speeded closing or that "easier cases" (defined here as those that were likely to close early anyway) received more services from paraprofessionals.

Thus, our findings suggest that the duration of family preservation services, intensity of contact with workers, and number of concrete services do not have significant overall effects on placement, maltreatment, or case closing. This is not surprising, since the problems and service needs of family preservation clients are diverse. It is possible that some approaches to family preservation are more beneficial than others for subgroups of families with specific needs. Brief treatment may be sufficient for some families, while others may benefit from longer programs. Similarly, the intensity of contact and amount of concrete services needed are likely to vary according to family circumstances. We will explore possible interactions between case characteristics, services, and outcomes in further research.

Summary of Tier 2 Results

Findings from the randomized experiment suggest that the risk of placement and the risk of subsequent maltreatment among families referred to the Family First program were quite low. Thus, it is not surprising that the program did not achieve substantial reductions in these risks, either overall or for any of the subgroups of cases we examined.

The program had no significant effect on the duration or type of out-of-home placements. To some extent, Family First had a net widening effect, resulting in the opening of additional cases in the child welfare system. However, the program had no long-term effect on whether families remained in this system. Substantial variations in case outcomes were noted across regions and between subgroups of families with different characteristics, but few effects of the program were found in the subgroups we examined. We found few significant relationships between duration of services, amount of contact with workers, or number of concrete services and case outcomes.

TIER 3: INTERVIEWS WITH PARENTS

The parent interview component of the Family First evaluation was designed to gather information about program effects on child and family well-being, clients' views of services, use of formal and informal social support, and significant life events. Parents in both the Family First and regular services groups of the experiment in Chicago East, Lake Villa/Waukegan, and Peoria took part in the interviews. The intent was to interview the parents at several points in time, providing a longitudinal view of their lives. Parents were first surveyed at least three months after referral to the experiment. The first round of interviews in Chicago East was conducted in the summer and fall of 1991. A second interview in Chicago East and initial interviews in the other two sites were completed in the spring of 1992. A third round of interviews in Chicago East and second interviews in Lake Villa/Waukegan and Peoria were conducted in the spring of 1993. A total of 154 Family First and 124 regular services parents were interviewed. (Details of the interview study and response rates are provided in Chapter 3.)

A number of comparisons are possible in these data. Of course, comparisons between the Family First and regular services groups are of interest, and we report those comparisons within experimental sites (since there are differences among sites and those differences might be obscured if they were combined). We also present comparisons across time. It is also possible to compare sites, but we do not dwell on those comparisons below.

Child and Family Functioning

Parents were asked about the presence or absence of a series of specific problems within each of the following eight domains of family functioning: housing conditions, economic conditions, physical child care, discipline and emotional care of children, children's academic adjustment, children's conduct, children's symptomatic behavior, and parental coping.[32] An overview of the problems reported by parents was provided in Chapter 4. Within each site, we examined differences between the Family First and regular services groups in the proportion of families who reported one or more problems in each of

Table 6.10: Percentage of Parents Who Cited at Least One Problem, by Time of Interview and Group in Chicago East[a]

Domains	First interview		Second interview		Third interview	
	Family First	Regular services	Family First	Regular services	Family First	Regular services
Housing	48	67	71	71	44	61
Economic conditions	31	44	49	45	37	51
Physical child care	21	22	42*	66*	22	40
Discipline and emotional care of children	27	20	51	50	39	47
Children's academic adjustment (≥ 5 years old)	16	18	40	54	19**	50**
Children's conduct (≥ 5 years old)	34	32	67	52	44	52
Children's symptomatic behavior (≥ 4 years old)	29	18	38	61	20	28
Parental coping	31	33	66	71	54	51

[a] Ninety-four families participated in the first interview. Because some questions were only relevant for families with children in certain age groups, the number of cases with valid data on each section varied. Children's academic adjustment was relevant for sixty-six families who had children age five or older and enrolled in school, children's conduct was relevant for sixty-nine families who had children age five or older, children's symptomatic behavior was relevant for seventy-four families who had children age four or older.

Seventy-nine families participated in the second interview. Of these, children's academic adjustment was relevant for fifty-four families, children's conduct was relevant for sixty families, children's symptomatic behavior was relevant for sixty-five families. One hundred and one families participated in the third wave. Of these, physical child care and discipline and emotional care of children were relevant for eighty-four families, children's academic adjustment for sixty-four, conduct problems for sixty-seven, and symptomatic behavior for seventy-one families.

Asterisks indicate significant differences between groups: *, $p < 0.05$; **, $p < .01$. The differences between Family First and regular services groups were not statistically significant, with two exceptions. Significantly fewer Family First parents reported problems with physical child care at the time of the second interview ($p = .03$). Significantly fewer Family First parents reported problems with children's academic adjustment at the time of the third interview ($p = .01$).

these areas. For each family we also determined the proportion of problems reported out of all those we asked about in each area. Mean proportions for the Family First and regular service groups were then computed at each point in time. Our analysis of between-group differences on these measures was aimed at testing the hypothesis that Family First resulted in improvements in the lives of children and families. However, it is possible that the program increased parents' awareness—and reporting—of the problems their children and families experienced.[33]

In Chicago East, at the time of the first interview (at least 90 days after case assignment), more parents reported problems in housing than in other domains (Table 6.10). Differences between Family First and regular services groups in the proportion of families with problems were not significant in any domain at the first interview. At the time of the second interview in Chicago East, significantly fewer Family First parents reported problems with physical child care than regular services parents.[34] At the time of the third interview, significantly fewer Family First parents reported that their children were having problems in school.[35] Differences between groups in other domains were not significant. Thus, at each point in time, Family First parents reported fewer problems than regular services parents in one of eight domains, but the domain was different at each point (Table 6.10). We discuss differences across time in Chicago in more detail below.

At the time of the first interview in Lake Villa/Waukegan, a higher percentage of parents in the Family First group reported problems in discipline and emotional care of children compared with the regular services group;[36] none of the other differences between groups were statistically significant (Table 6.11). At the time of the second interview in Lake Villa/Waukegan, there were no significant differences between groups in the proportion of parents who reported problems in various domains. In Peoria, there were no significant differences between the Family First and regular services groups in the percentage of parents who reported problems in various domains at the time of the first or second interviews (Table 6.11).

Thus, there were few differences between groups in the proportion of families who reported problems in various domains. Similarly there were few between-group differences in the proportion of problems families reported within each domain (see Tables 6.12 and 6.13). For the second and third waves,[37] we ran two-way analyses of variance to examine the effects of region and experimental group on the proportion of problems reported by parents in each domain; the results showed that the effects of the experimental group were not significant in any of the domains, at either point in time.[38]

Table 6.11: Percentage of Parents Who Cited at Least One Problem at the Time of the First Interview, by Group in Lake Villa/Waukegan and Peoria

Domain	Lake Villa/Waukegan[a]				Peoria[b]			
	First interview		Second interview		First interview		Second interview	
	Family First	Regular services	Family First	Regular services	Family First	Regular services	Family First	Regular services
Housing	51	35	54	55	55	42	61	44
Economic conditions	56	48	54	38	58	50	46	38
Physical child care	49	39	33	33	53	42	47	44
Discipline and emotional care of children	62*	30*	47	48	55	46	51	57
Children's academic adjustment (≥ 5 years old)	44	54	40	53	72	72	72	56
Children's conduct (≥ 5 years old)	68	62	59	82	77	67	80	77
Children's symptomatic behavior (≥ 4 years old)	44	64	45	39	50	65	64	68
Parental coping	69	65	63	72	76	75	80	77

[a] In Lake Villa/Waukegan, sixty-two families participated in the first interview. Of these, children's academic adjustment was relevant for thirty-eight families, children's conduct for forty-one families, and children's symptomatic behavior for forty-six families. In the second interview, sixty-eight parents participated; questions on physical care of children and discipline and emotional care of children were relevant for sixty-three families, children's academic adjustment for forty-two, children's conduct for forty-four, and children's symptomatic behavior for forty-nine families.

[b] In Peoria, sixty-two families participated in the first interview. Of these, children's academic adjustment was relevant for forty-three families, children's conduct for forty-four families, and children's symptomatic behavior for forty-six families. Seventy-six parents participated in the second interview; questions on physical care of children and discipline and emotional care of children were relevant for sixty-six families, academic adjustment for forty-seven families, children's conduct for fifty-seven families, and children's symptomatic behavior for fifty-five families.

Asterisks indicate significant differences between groups: *, $p < .05$.

Table 6.12: Mean Proportion of Problems Reported in Each Time Period, by Group in Chicago East[a]

Domains	At referral		First interview		Second interview		Third interview	
	Family First	Regular services	Family First	Regular services	Family First	Regular services	Family First	Regular services
Housing	0.26	0.28	0.13*	0.24*	0.24	0.25	0.15	0.23
Economic conditions	0.22	0.21	0.13	0.16	0.19	0.20	0.11	0.23
Physical child care	0.15	0.10	0.05	0.04	0.06*	0.14*	0.05	0.12
Discipline and emotional care of children	0.16	0.12	0.06	0.03	0.09	0.14	0.10	0.14
Children's academic adjustment (≥ 5 years old)	0.20	0.10	0.04	0.06	0.11	0.19	0.06*	0.18*
Children's conduct (≥ 5 years old)	0.15	0.21	0.07	0.15	0.15	0.17	0.10	0.20
Children's symptomatic behavior (≥ 4 years old)	0.18	0.09	0.08	0.06	0.11	0.17	0.05	0.09
Parental coping	0.34	0.24	0.11	0.10	0.24	0.32	0.19	0.27

[a] The proportion of problems is the number of problems reported by the parent in each domain divided by the total number of problem items applicable in that domain.

This table only includes the sixty-nine parents who participated in all three interviews. Of these, children's academic adjustment was relevant for forty-nine families, children's conduct for fifty families, and children's symptomatic behavior for fifty-four families.

Asterisks indicate significant differences between groups: *, $p < 0.05$. The difference between Family First and regular services groups were not statistically significant with three exceptions: The mean proportion of housing problems reported at the first interview was significantly lower for Family First parents ($p = .04$). Family First parents reported significantly fewer problems in physical child care at the second interview ($p = .01$) and fewer problems in children's academic adjustment at the time of the third interview ($p = .02$).

Table 6.13: Mean Proportion of Problems Reported in Each Time Period, by Group in Lake Villa/Waukegan and Peoria[a]

Domains	Lake Villa/Waukegan[b]				Peoria[c]			
	First interview		Second interview		First interview		Second interview	
	Family First	Regular services	Family First	Regular services	Family First	Regular services	Family First	Regular services
Housing	0.14	0.11	0.15	0.14	0.17*	0.08*	0.15	0.10
Economic conditions	0.23	0.16	0.20	0.17	0.20	0.16	0.15	0.19
Physical child care	0.12	0.07	0.05	0.05	0.14	0.10	0.12	0.15
Discipline and emotional care of children	0.21*	0.08*	0.14	0.11	0.15	0.12	0.15	0.15
Children's academic adjustment (≥ 5 years old)	0.11	0.17	0.13	0.11	0.22	0.26	0.29	0.26
Children's conduct (≥ 5 years old)	0.20	0.19	0.19	0.23	0.29	0.18	0.33	0.29
Children's symptomatic behavior (≥ 4 years old)	0.14	0.22	0.07	0.12	0.14	0.21	0.28	0.23
Parental coping	0.31	0.19	0.21	0.20	0.28	0.26	0.30	0.33

[a] The proportion of problems is the number of problems reported by the parent in each domain divided by the total number of problem items applicable in that domain.

[b] For Lake Villa/Waukegan this table only includes the fifty-two parents who participated in both interviews. Of these, children's academic adjustment was relevant for thirty families, children's conduct for thirty-two families, and children's symptomatic behavior for thirty-eight families.

[c] For Peoria, this table only includes the fifty-nine parents who participated in both interviews. Of these, children's academic adjustment was relevant for forty-one families, children's conduct for forty families, and children's symptomatic behavior for forty-three families.

Asterisks indicate significant differences between groups: *, $p < 0.05$.

Change over Time in Child and Family Functioning

For families who participated in multiple interviews, we computed the proportion of problems reported in each domain at each point in time.[39] We then compared the mean proportion of problems in the groups within each site. Results are shown in Tables 6.12 and 6.13.

In the initial interview in Chicago East, we asked respondents about the presence of problems at the time of referral as well as at the time of the interview. Hence, we have data for this group on problems at four points in time, although the data for the first point are retrospective. In all of the problem domains, Family First parents reported fewer problems at the time of the first interview than at the time of referral. The number of problems reported by these parents increased in the second interview and declined again in the third interview (with the exception of discipline and emotional care, which increased slightly between the second and third interviews). Similarly, regular services parents in Chicago East reported fewer problems at the time of the first interview than at referral. However, the proportion of problems reported by this group in the second interview increased and then remained relatively stable between the second and third interviews (Table 6.12 and Figures 6.11 through 6.18). Repeated-measures analysis of variance (ANOVA) showed that in all domains there were significant differences in the mean proportion of problems reported over time.[40] In general, the pro-

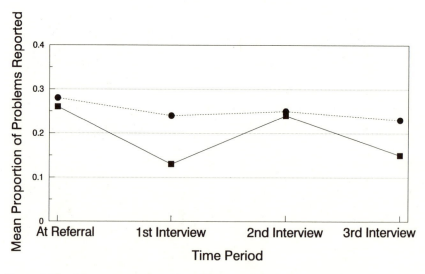

Figure 6.11. Mean proportion of problems reported in housing over time, Chicago East. Family First, solid line; regular services, dashed line.

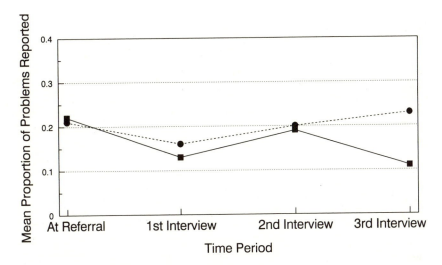

Figure 6.12. Mean proportion of problems reported in economic conditions over time, Chicago East. Family First, solid line; regular services, dashed line.

portion of problems reported decreased between referral and the first interview,[41] increased between the first and second interviews, and then decreased between the second and third interviews. In repeated-measures ANOVA, differences between groups over time are indicated by the interaction of group membership and time; in all but one do-

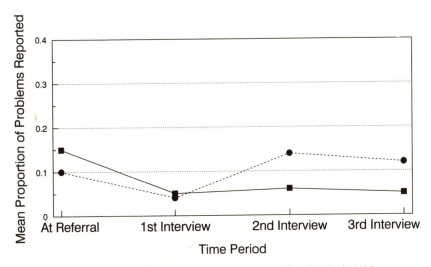

Figure 6.13. Mean proportion of problems reported in physical child care over time, Chicago East. Family First, solid line; regular services, dashed line.

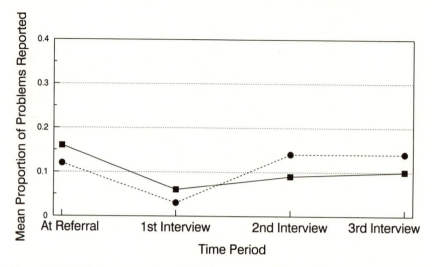

Figure 6.14. Mean proportion of problems reported in discipline and emotional care of children over time, Chicago East. Family First, solid line; regular services, dashed line.

main (children's academic adjustment), these interactions were not significant. The interaction effect in academic adjustment ($p = .017$) was linear; over time, the mean proportion of problems reported in this domain decreased for Family First cases while it increased for regular services cases.[42] Since eight domains were examined, the risk of overall

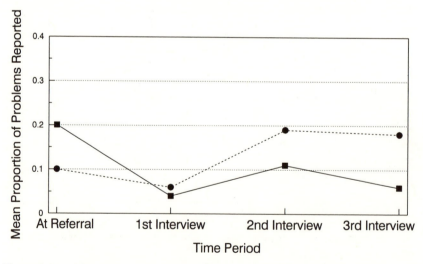

Figure 6.15. Mean proportion of problems reported in children's academic adjustment over time, Chicago East. Family First, solid line; regular services, dashed line.

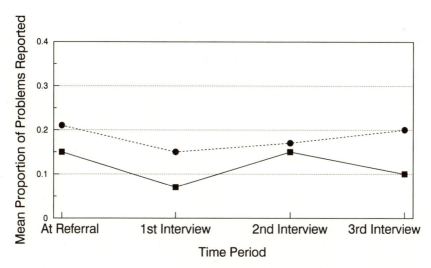

Figure 6.16. Mean proportion of problems reported in children's conduct over time, Chicago East. Family First, solid line; regular services, dashed line.

("experimentwise") Type I error is substantially higher than the risk for each of the eight tests. The significant result in the one area of academic adjustment should be viewed in this light. Experimentwise Type I error can be controlled through doubly multivariate analysis of repeated measures. We conducted such an analysis for cases in Chicago

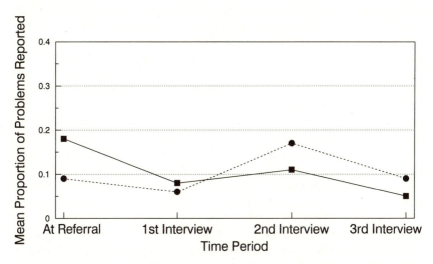

Figure 6.17. Mean proportion of problems reported in children's symptomatic behavior over time, Chicago East. Family First, solid line; regular services, dashed line.

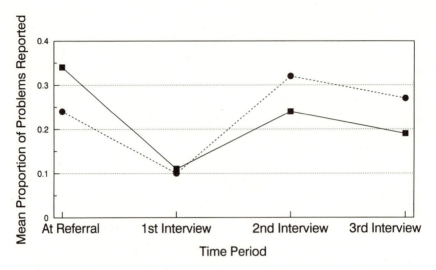

Figure 6.18. Mean proportion of problems reported in parental coping over time, Chicago East. Family First, solid line; regular services, dashed line.

East, looking at the effects of time and group membership on the mean proportion of problems in five domains at once (the domains were housing conditions, economic conditions, physical child care, discipline and emotional care, and parental coping; other domains did not have the same number of cases, for example, children's academic adjustment applied only to families with school age children). Again, changes over time were significant (but only the cubic effect), although the interaction between group and time was not significant ($p = .254$). Thus, Family First did not have a significant impact over time in the mean proportion of problems reported across these five domains.

In Lake Villa/Waukegan, Family First parents reported fewer problems in physical child care, discipline and emotional care of children, children's symptomatic behavior, and parental coping at the time of the second interview, compared with their reports in the first interview. Parents in the regular services group reported fewer problems in children's academic adjustment and symptomatic behavior in the second interview, compared with the first (Table 6.13). Repeated-measures AN-OVA showed a significant interaction between group membership and time in parental coping; this means that the decrease (from .31 to .21) in the mean proportion of problems reported in coping between the first and second interviews for Family First cases was significantly different from the more stable trend for regular services cases (.19 to .20). There were no significant differences between groups in trends over time in the other seven domains.

Peoria Family First parents reported fewer economic problems but more problems in children's academic adjustment and symptomatic behavior at the time of the second interview, compared with their reports in the first interview. Regular services clients reported more problems in physical child care, children's conduct, and parental coping in the second interview, compared with the first (Table 6.13). There were no significant interactions between group and time in any domain.

Parents' Views of Change over Time

In addition to asking about specific problems in each domain, we asked parents whether changes had occurred in the domains and in their lives as a whole.[43] In Chicago East, at the first interview, parents who reported problems in specific domains were asked to compare their situation at the time of the interview with their situation at the time of referral. In the first and second interviews in Lake Villa/Waukegan and Peoria and the second and third interviews in Chicago East, questions about perceptions of change over time were asked somewhat differently. All parents, not just those who reported problems in a particular area, were asked to compare their situation at the time of the interview with their situation three months earlier.

In the first interviews in Chicago East, significant differences were found between Family First and regular services parents (favoring the Family First group) in perceived changes in housing, economic conditions, and physical child care.[44] This is due, in part, to the fact that more regular services parents than Family First parents reported their situation worsened in these three domains. In the other domains, the differences between groups were not significant. There were no significant differences between groups in parents' perceptions of change in their lives as a whole between the time of referral and the first interview. At the time of the second interview, parents in the Family First group were significantly more likely than those in the regular services groups to report recent improvements in discipline and emotional care of children.[45] At the time of the third interview, Family First parents were more likely to report improvements in housing and economic conditions.[46] There were no other significant differences between groups, either in overall change in the families' situations or in perceived change in other domains in the second and third interviews.

In Lake Villa/Waukegan, significantly more Family First than regular services parents reported improvement in discipline and emotional care of children, children's academic adjustment, and their families' overall situation at the time of the first interview.[47] There were no differences between groups at the time of the second interviews.

In Peoria, significantly more Family First than regular services parents reported improvement in their children's conduct at the time of the first interview.[48] Differences between groups in perceptions of overall change or improvement within other domains were not significant in the first interviews. There were no significant differences in the second interviews.

Thus, there were few differences between Family First and regular services parents' in perceived improvements in family and child functioning. The differences we did find favored the Family First group; these appeared primarily in the first interviews and disappeared in later interviews.

Personal Efficacy

Family First workers told us that efforts to "empower" clients were an important part of the program. They hoped that their efforts would build clients' self-confidence and encourage them to advocate for themselves in future interactions with service providers. Thus, we attempted to test the hypothesis that Family First had an impact on clients' feelings of self-efficacy. In the second and third waves of interviews, parents were asked a series of questions about their personal strengths (data from the second wave are presented in Table 4.6). None of the differences between the Family First and regular services groups in any region were statistically significant. Thus, the program had no detectable effect on our measures of parents' sense of self-efficacy. Parents in both groups responded confidently about their ability to do things as well as others and make things better for their children (over 90% agreed with these statements). Less than a quarter of the parents said they did not have much to be proud of. Over three-quarters of the parents said that most of the things that happened to them were under their control, although about 40% felt that what happened in their lives was mostly determined by powerful people. About 40% of the parents said that they felt helpless in dealing with their problems. Half of Chicago East parents and about 30% of the parents in Lake Villa/Waukegan and Peoria felt that when they got what they wanted it was usually because they were lucky.

Use of Formal Support

One of the objectives of the Family First program was to link families to other resources in the community. Often this is interpreted by workers as the referral of families to formal services. In the first round of interviews in Chicago East, parents in the Family First group were significantly more likely than regular services cases to say that they had received clothing (27 vs. 4%), financial assistance (23 vs. 2%), food (31 vs.

4%), furniture (31 vs. 2%), toys or recreational equipment (15% vs. none), transportation services (32 vs. 9%), parent education services (19 vs. 4%), and family counseling (29 vs. 11%).[49] There were no significant differences between groups in the second and third interviews in Chicago East or in the first and second interviews in the Lake Villa/Waukegan and Peoria sites.

Since Family First cases in Chicago often remained in the program beyond 90 days (see Table 5.1), it is likely that the initial differences between groups reflected distinctions between services provided under Family First versus regular DCFS services in that site. However, the program had no lasting effects on service utilization in any of the three sites.

Use of Informal Support

In addition to linkages to formal services, workers suggested the program might help clients establish more positive connections to family and friends who could be relied upon for assistance in times of need. The engagement of informal support systems is viewed as particularly important in short-term services when clients' problems may not be fully resolved at the point of termination. Studies have shown that informal social support may have positive influences on parents and both direct and indirect effects on child development, although it is not clear how informal support can be harnessed in services for children and families (Tracy and Whittaker 1987).

In our interviews, parents were asked about availability and use of family and friends for support. In all three sites, there were no differences between the experimental groups in parents' reports of the availability of informal support at the time of the first interview (see Tables 6.14 and 6.15). In Chicago East, at the time of the first interview, a higher percentage of Family First parents reported that they had received physical assistance (e.g., help with chores) in the past month, compared with regular services parents in that site.[50] However, this difference disappeared by the time of the second interview (Table 6.14). In the other two sites, no differences in receipt of support were found in the initial or subsequent interviews. These results suggest that the effects of Family First on families' informal support networks were quite limited and short-lived.

Relationship with Caseworker

Parents were asked a number of questions regarding the quality of their contacts with their caseworkers. Parents rated various aspects of caseworker activity on a scale of "never" to "always" (scored 1 to 4). A score was created by averaging the numerical values of each parent's

Table 6.14: Availability and Receipt of Informal Support (%) at the Time of the First and Second Interviews, by Group in Chicago East[a]

| | First interview | | | | Second interview | | | |
| | Availability | | Receipt | | Availability | | Receipt | |
Type of support	Family First	Regular services	Family First	Regular services	Family First	Regular services	Family First	Regular services
Material aid	71	63	42	37	63	58	37	32
Physical assistance	71	57	63*	39*	66	58	54	40
Child care assistance	65	61	48	44	59	55	46	47
Advice: raising children	58	63	42	54	56	63	44	47
Advice: other	44	46	27	28	44	58	27	42
Listen to problems	83	72	73	54	76	68	51	61
Praise: general	73	70	46	44	66	71	61	50
Social activities	90	80	67	52	76	82	68	74
Total N of cases[b]	48	46	48	46	41	38	41	38

[a] Asterisks indicate significant differences between groups: *, $p < .05$. None of the differences between Family First and regular services groups were statistically significant with the exception of one item on the receipt of physical assistance at the time of the first interview.

[b] Since some cases were missing data on specific items, percentages are based on the number of cases with valid data on each item, not on the total number of cases.

Table 6.15: Availability and Receipt of Informal Support (%) at the Time of the First Interview, by Group in Lake Villa/Waukegan and Peoria[a]

| | Lake Villa/Waukegan | | | | Peoria | | | |
| | Availability | | Receipt | | Availability | | Receipt | |
Type of support	Family First	Regular services	Family First	Regular services	Family First	Regular services	Family First	Regular services
Material aid	64	78	31	30	76	71	47	38
Physical assistance	64	65	49	44	82	88	74	67
Child care assistance	69	87	49	52	76	83	60	63
Advice: raising children	51	65	44	44	71	63	51	33
Advice: other	49	57	26	30	68	63	53	38
Listen to problems	64	74	56	57	87	88	68	67
Praise: general	69	65	36	44	87	88	63	58
Social activities	74	96	69	78	87	96	84	88
Total N of cases[b]	39	23	39	23	38	24	38	24

[a] None of the differences between the Family First and regular services groups were statistically significant.
[b] Since some cases were missing data on specific items, percentages are based on the number of cases with valid data on each item, not on the total number of cases.

Table 6.16:   Satisfaction with Service at the First Interview (%), by Site and Group[a]

	Chicago East[a]		Lake Villa/ Waukegan[b]		Peoria	
	Family First	Regular services	Family First	Regular services	Family First	Regular services
Satisfied	90	44	69	69	76	54
No particular feeling	4	40	21	25	14	21
Not satisfied	6	16	10	6	11	25
Total N of cases	48	45	39	16	37	24

[a] In Chicago East, Family First parents were significantly more satisfied with service than those in the regular services group ($p < .001$). Differences between groups were not significant in Lake Villa/Waukegan or Peoria.

[b] Twenty-eight percent of regular services cases in Lake Villa/Waukegan refused to answer the question or said that the question was not applicable.

responses on 17 items.[51] Parents who reported they did not have a caseworker between the time of referral and the time of the first interview were excluded from this analysis.[52] Questions on parents' relationship with their caseworkers were asked only in the first interview.

In Chicago East, Family First parents rated their relationships with their caseworkers significantly more positively than parents in the regular services group (the mean rating across all items was 3.48 for Family First parents compared with 2.90 for regular services parents, $p < .001$). Family First parents rated their caseworkers significantly higher on 10 out of 17 items (Table 5.6), particularly on items related to skills and professionalism, worker's availability, and worker's expectations. In Lake Villa/Waukegan, Family First parents also rated their relationship with their caseworkers more positively than regular services parents, a difference that approached statistical significance at the .05 level (mean ratings of 3.23 vs. 2.80, $p = .055$). Family First parents rated their caseworkers significantly higher on 3 out of 17 items, particularly on items related to worker's availability. In Peoria, although the Family First parents' mean rating (3.47) was higher than regular services parents' (3.20), the difference was not significant. Only one of the between-group differences on specific items was statistically significant in the Peoria site. Overall, there is evidence that Family First parents were more positive in their assessments of their relationships with workers.

Satisfaction with Services

At the time of the first interview in Chicago East, parents in the Family First group were significantly more likely to express satisfaction with the services they had received than parents in the regular services group (90 vs. 44%, $p < .001$) (Table 6.16). In Lake Villa/Waukegan, 69% of parents in both groups reported that they were satisfied with the services they received. In Peoria, 76% of Family First parents and 54% of regular services parents reported that they were satisfied with services (the difference between the two groups was not significant). As with parents' views of the relationships with their caseworkers, the Family First program had a significant impact on overall satisfaction with services in the Chicago East region, but not in the other two sites.

SUMMARY AND CONCLUSIONS

We examined the effects of Family First in a number of areas including out-of-home placement of children, child maltreatment, achievement of case objectives, family and child functioning, and case opening and closing. The principal evidence for effects comes from our experimental study, in which cases were randomly assigned to Family First or regular child welfare services in six regions of the state.

Overall, Family First cases were more likely to experience placement than regular services cases, although this difference was rather small and disappeared once variations in case characteristics were taken into account. We suggest two possible explanations for the slight increase in the risk of placement among Family First cases. First, through extensive contact with families in their homes, the program may serve a "case finding" function. Second, workers' tolerance for conditions that are potentially harmful to children may be reduced once "reasonable efforts" to prevent placement have been made. Overall, the Family First program had no effect on the type or duration of placements.

Although Family First was aimed at preventing out-of-home placements of children, the risk of placement among families referred to the program was quite low. As a result, it is not surprising that the program did not result in a reduction in placements. This raises important questions about the targeting of family preservation programs, an issue to which we return in the final chapter. Targeting problems, particularly those related to "creaming," have been observed in a variety of social programs. We suggest that the targeting problem in family preservation is not just the result of attempts to steer "easier cases" into these programs (creaming). Difficulties in predicting future placements and conflicting messages about the purpose and uses of these programs contribute to the targeting problem.

The program had no substantial effect on subsequent maltreatment of children. Compared with regular child welfare services, intensive in-home services neither increased the risk of harm to children nor provided additional protection from such harm. Differences between groups at the family level were not significant; the results of child-level analyses suggest that the program may result in a slight increase in the likelihood that individual children will be involved in further substantiated reports of maltreatment. Again, it is possible that the program served case finding and net-widening functions; that is, Family First workers may have detected new evidence of risks to children and they may have identified other children who were harmed. In spite of the fact that there are only slight differences between groups in subsequent maltreatment, there is some evidence that medical neglect of children was less likely to occur after Family First services.

Family First workers' ratings of the achievement of objectives in Family First cases were significantly more positive than DCFS workers' ratings for regular services cases. This suggests that Family First clients may have made more progress during the initial 90-day service period. However, as noted in Chapter 5, there were differences between workers in the two groups in the types of objectives identified. There may also have been differences between groups in criteria used to gauge family progress.

Overall, Family First had a net-widening effect in that it resulted in an increase in the number of cases opened for services in the public child welfare system. However, the program had no lasting effect on the length of time that families remained in the child welfare system, nor did it affect the likelihood that families would return to this system after their cases had been closed.

Thus, we find little evidence that the Family First program affects the risk of placement, subsequent maltreatment, or case closing and some evidence that Family First may be related to short-term progress on case objectives. However, these results must be viewed in the context of considerable variation among sites and variations in outcomes that are due to characteristics of cases and the services provided to them. There are substantial differences between sites in the risks of placement, subsequent maltreatment, and case closing. For example, the risk of placement within one month of referral to Family First ranges from .02 in Lake Villa/Waukegan to .26 in East St. Louis (these figures are based on data from the control group that represent the risk of placement in the absence of family preservation services). We also noted wide variation across sites in the degree of net-widening. In addition, there was substantial variation across sites in the amounts, types, and duration of services provided to Family First and regular services cases.

We examined the effects of Family First for various subgroups of families. Results show that the program increased the risk of placement for single-parent families, although it had no effect on placement for other subgroups. The program had no effect on subsequent maltreatment for any of the subgroups we examined. Family First appeared to accelerate the rates of case closing in DCFS for families with marital problems, housing problems, and children with health problems.

The duration of services, amount of contact with workers, and number of concrete services provided to families were not substantially related to rates of placement, subsequent maltreatment, or case closing. It is possible that these and other characteristics of family preservation services are related to outcomes for certain subgroups of families with specific needs. Thus, although some families may require a longer treatment period than others, duration of services is not a predictor of case outcomes for family preservation clients overall. Similarly, the intensity of services provided and use of specific types of services may be important only for certain subgroups. In future work we will look at "what works best for whom in family preservation," by examining relationships between service characteristics and outcomes for specific subgroups in the Family First experiment.

In the area of child and family functioning, we found modest differences between program and control groups. In each of three waves of interviews in Chicago East, we found differences favoring the Family First group in one out of eight domains. However, these improvements were not stable over time: Family First clients reported fewer problems in housing at the first interview, fewer problems in physical child care at the second interview, and fewer problems in children's academic adjustment at the third interview. In repeated-measures analysis of variance, we found that the Family First program had significant effects in the mean proportion of problems reported in Chicago East in one domain only: The proportion of problems reported in children's academic adjustment tended to decrease over time in Family First cases, while it increased among regular services cases. In Lake Villa/Waukegan, Family First clients reported significantly more problems in discipline and emotional care of children at the first interview, compared with regular services cases, although there were no differences between groups at the time of the second interview. In Lake Villa/Waukegan, the proportion of problems reported in parental coping decreased between the first and second interviews for Family First cases, while this proportion remained steady in reports from regular services cases. In Peoria, Family First clients reported significantly more housing problems at the time of the first interview compared with regular services cases, a difference that disappeared by the second interview. Thus, the effects of the program in eight domains of family and child functioning were small and short-lived.

The program had no significant impact on parents' feelings of self-efficacy or on the availability of informal social support. Improvements in the receipt of informal support were quite limited and disappeared over time. The program had no lasting effects on the use of formal services.

In one of the three sites in which we interviewed parents (Chicago East), Family First clients rated their relationships with their caseworkers significantly more positively and expressed greater satisfaction with the services they received than families who received regular services in that site. Overall differences between groups in Lake Villa/Waukegan approached statistical significance; again Family First clients rated their caseworkers more positively. Differences between groups in Peoria were not significant. The difference in Chicago East may have to do with the nature of regular services in Chicago; families in this group had very little contact with caseworkers within 90 days after random assignment. Our interviews with DCFS workers indicate that this was often due to delays in the assignment of a caseworker. Hours of contact in the first 90 days for Family First cases in Chicago East were 16 times those for regular services cases (see Table 5.1). Regular services cases in Lake Villa/Waukegan and Peoria had more contact with workers than regular services cases in Chicago. It is interesting to note that the four- or five-fold increase in amount of contact provided by Family First in these two sites did not produce significant differences in client satisfaction.

It is quite possible that the Family First program had effects beyond those captured in our study. Certainly some families benefited from the casework and concrete services they received. Others may have found the program unnecessarily intrusive and even harmful. Based on the data reported here, we conclude that the benefits of the program were modest and short-lived.

Family First represented a dramatic improvement in the responsiveness of the child welfare system to the needs of families. In addition to responding more quickly to these needs, the program represented improvements in the quantity and quality of services provided to clients. The fact that these changes did not result in more substantial benefits for families is certainly disappointing. However, given the complex nature of the problems that bring families into contact with the child welfare system, the absence of substantial improvements in other social service systems upon which these families depend, and the limited availability of follow-up services for many child welfare clients, it seems unrealistic to expect lasting changes in families as a result of short-term family preservation efforts. We return to these themes in the final chapter.

Although we did not analyze data on the costs of services provided to families in the program and control groups, several assumptions can be made regarding costs. Since there were no substantial differences between groups in placement rates, the program clearly did not result in any savings in foster care costs. If anything, Family First may have resulted in a slight increase in the costs of foster care in Illinois. In addition, the net-widening function of the program in several regions and the increased intensity of services provided to families statewide suggest that Family First may have contributed to an overall increase in the costs of child welfare services in Illinois.

NOTES

1. Analysis of data for this chapter was performed by Amy Chak and Lucinda Fox.

2. Data on out-of-home placements, subsequent maltreatment, and case closing were derived from DCFS administrative data on case events that occurred through March 31, 1993. Data on subsequent maltreatment came from the DCFS Child Abuse and Neglect Tracking System (CANTS) file. Data on placement and case closings were derived from the DCFS Management and Reporting System (MARS) and Child and Youth Centered Information System (CYCIS) files. Information on case characteristics comes from the Chapin Hall Service Summary form and from CANTS. Data on workers' views of case outcomes are drawn from the service summary form. Information on clients' views of services and data on child and family functioning come from our interviews with parents. These data sources are described in greater detail in Chapter 3.

3. A total of 6,522 families were identified to us (by DCFS or the provider agencies) as having received Family First services between December 1, 1988, and December 31, 1992.

4. The child-level analyses only included children identified on the household composition table of the service summary form. As described in Chapter 3, the first version of the service summary form did not include a household composition table. These data were also not available for families that were referred to the program in nonexperimental sites after April 1, 1991. In all, we received household composition data for 3,833 families (59% of those referred during the first four years of the program). These families had a total of 10,608 children who were living in their homes at the time of referral. While administrative data can tell us how many children in a family were placed, household composition data are needed to identify the total number of children (and the number that were not placed). Thus, household composition data provide the denominator needed to calculate placement rates at the child level. All families with valid administrative data are included in the family-level analyses of placement, while the child-level analyses are limited to cases with both administrative and household composition data.

5. Survival analysis estimates the likelihood of events (such as out-of-home placement, subsequent maltreatment of children, and case closing) while taking into account the varying "observation periods" for different cases. Since cases were referred to Family First over a four-year period, the length of the observation period (the time period in which outcomes could be detected) varied across

cases. Our survival analyses determined the probability that families or children "survived" without experiencing an event at various points in time following referral to the program. The results of these analyses can also be used to determine the probability that a family or child will experience certain events (e.g., an indicated report of maltreatment, placement of one or more children) at various points in time after referral.

6.   On the service summary form, workers were asked to list each child placed out of the home and to note whether they had initiated the placement and, if not, whether they agreed with the decision to place the child. Data on workers' views of 1,199 individual (child) placements were available for this analysis.

7.   For individual children, the risk of maltreatment was .05 at one month, .12 at three months, .17 at six months, .25 at one year, .33 at two years, and .39 at three years after referral.

8.   Indicated allegations were recorded for 1,386 (25%) of the 5,485 families referred to Family First before April 1, 1992. The allegations involved 3,001 children. This analysis only includes cases with a minimum observation period of one year. We count here only the first indicated allegation for each family; of course, some families had more than one during this period.

9.   In Illinois, the allegation of substance misuse usually indicates that a baby tested positive for an illegal substance at birth.

10.   These categories are not mutually exclusive. Families could have indicated allegations in one or more categories.

11.   See note 5. Here, survival analysis was used to determine whether there were differences between Family First and regular services cases in the risk of placement, child maltreatment, and case closing. Thus, it provides a test of the hypothesis that Family First had an effect on the likelihood of these events.

12.   Proportional-hazard models are a group of statistical techniques designed to estimate the effects of several independent variables on the risk (hazard) of the occurrence of an event over time. Like multiple regression analysis, these models provide estimates of the effects of independent variables controlling for other variables in the model. The Cox Proportional Hazards Regression Model is employed in this analysis (Cox 1972). (For a description of the considerations that led to our choosing the Cox model, see Appendix B.) This model allows us to compare the relative importance of the effects of several variables (e.g., case characteristics) on the probability of the occurrence of an event such as subsequent maltreatment, placement, or case closing.

13.   For a description of this approach, see Appendix C.

14.   As indicated below, one-fifth of the regular services cases were not opened for services by DCFS following random assignment. Although these "never opened" cases may have been those least in need of service, they were also not subject to the kind of scrutiny that accompanies child welfare services. Placement rates in this group were quite low: there were none at three months after random assignment, 6% at six months, 7% at 12 months, and 10% at 18 months. These rates were significantly lower than the placement rates for other regular services cases.

15.   It might be claimed that these results are due to the implementation of the experiment; that is, the experiment might have had substantial effects on referral patterns, resulting in the referral of less severe cases to the program. This might happen because the experiment required more cases (to fill the control group) or because of other changes in decision-making practices. To assess

the plausibility of this hypothesis, we compared placement rates for Family First cases in the experiment and those referred to nonexperimental sites during the two-year period in which the experiment was conducted. The risk of placement was significantly higher for families in experimental sites compared with those in nonexperimental sites (for example, at six months after referral the risk was .20 in experimental sites and .17 in nonexperimental sites; at one year it was .27 vs. .23.; and at two years it was .34 compared with .28). The result was opposite that expected if the experiment had had the hypothesized effect. We found no significant differences in rates of subsequent maltreatment among Family First cases in the experiment compared with rates in nonexperimental sites. We also compared rates of placement and maltreatment among families referred to experimental sites before and after random assignment began. We found no significant differences in these comparisons. Although we cannot conclude definitively that the experiment had no effect on the character of cases referred, there is no evidence of such an effect.

16. In Peoria, 25% of placements in Family First were with relatives, compared to 6% in regular services cases. At the other extreme, in Chicago South, 65 and 67% of the Family First and regular services placements, respectively, were with relatives.

17. These results are based on workers' reports on 396 child placements in the Family First group and 141 in the regular services group. Differences between groups are significant (Chi-square = 75.21, d.f. = 1, $p < .001$).

18. In the Chicago East, Chicago South, and Springfield sites, Family First workers were significantly more likely to have initiated placement decisions than regular services workers. In the Lake Villa/Waukegan site, Family First workers were significantly less likely to initiate placements than regular services workers. Differences between groups were not significant in Peoria and East St. Louis.

19. It is possible that this difference is due to Type I error, since we examined a number of associations involving group assignment.

20. In addition to reports of child maltreatment and fatalities recorded in CANTS, our sources of data included interviews with Family First and DCFS workers. Many Family First workers were familiar with our interview protocols on these cases and often called our attention to cases in which children had died. As a result, we learned of several fatalities that were not recorded in CANTS. These included cases in which a medically fragile child died, deaths due to accidents, and some cases in which the cause of death was unclear or was attributed to Sudden Infant Death Syndrome. We had no similar informal source of information on fatalities that occurred in the control group; thus, for purposes of comparison we rely only on fatality cases reported in CANTS.

21. The steps on this scale were 1, no progress on objective; 2, minimally achieved; 3, partially or moderately achieved; and 4, substantially achieved.

22. The mean for Family First cases was 2.9 compared with a mean of 2.6 for regular services cases ($F = 21.528$, $p < .001$).

23. Table 5.1 shows that Family First cases in Chicago South received an average of 131 hours of contact with caseworkers and parent aides in the first 90 days of service, while Family First cases in Springfield received an average of 35 hours. For regular services cases, the mean hours of contact ranged from 67 in East St. Louis to about 4 hours in the two Chicago areas. In East St. Louis, Family First cases received an average of 6 different types of concrete services, compared with an average of 3 in the Springfield program. In Springfield, regular services cases received about the same number of concrete services as the Family

First cases in that site. In Lake Villa/Waukegan and Peoria, 70% of the Family First cases left the program within 108 days, while only 37% of the Chicago South cases completed the program in that time. Over 45% of regular services cases were closed in DCFS within 108 days in the Lake Villa/Waukegan and Peoria sites (most of these cases were never opened for services), compared with 10% in East St. Louis.

24. In the child-level analysis, the risks of placement among children in the experimental and control groups in Lake Villa/Waukegan were similar for the first two months, after which time differences between groups appeared: At three months the risk was .19 for Family First and .10 for regular services; at one year the risks were .37 and .16; at two years, .44 and .26. The risk of subsequent maltreatment for children in the Family First group in East St. Louis was .18 at one month after referral, compared with .06 for children in the control group; at one year the risks were .46 for Family First and .23 for regular services; at two years, .49 and .37. In Peoria, the risk of subsequent maltreatment was similar in both groups until six months after referral; at that point the risk was .15 for children in the Family First group and .12 for those in regular services; at one year the risk was .27 for Family First and .18 for regular services (an adequate number of observations was not available for children in this site at two years after referral).

25. In Lake Villa/Waukegan, the probability that a family case would be closed at four months after referral was .39 for Family First and .48 for regular services. At six months, the figures were .49 for Family First and .57 for regular services; at one year, .68 and .72; at two years, .80 and .87. In Peoria, the probability that a family case would be closed at four months after referral was .34 for Family First and .37 for regular services. After six months, Family First cases in Peoria were less likely to remain open in DCFS than regular services cases in that site (for Family First cases, the probability of case closure was .58 at six months, .75 at one year, and .91 at two years; for regular services the probability was .37 at six months, .49 at one year, and .69 at two years).

26. The result was obtained using proportional-hazard models. Within both groups, the risks of placement and maltreatment were highest in the East St. Louis site, while case closing rates were lowest in that site. Overall, Family First was associated with a 21.5% increase in the risk (hazard rate) of placement. The percentage change in the hazard rate that is associated with a certain case characteristic is interpreted as the proportional difference in the probability of an event, comparing cases with and without the characteristic. For example, a 50% increase in the hazard rate (risk) of placement for chronic neglect cases (those with three or more indicated reports of maltreatment prior to referral) indicates that the probability of placement among these cases is 1.5 times that of cases without chronic neglect. Thus, if the risk of placement for nonchronic neglect cases were .10 at a given point in time, the risk for chronic neglect cases would be .15 at that time point (see Blossfeld, Hamerle, and Mayer 1989).

27. Operational definitions of the case characteristics included in these models are provided in Appendix D. It is important to note that workers may define these characteristics in different ways. In particular, the amount of information bout family problems that was available to Family First and DCFS staff varied. Family First workers were more likely to identify housing problems, parents' mental illness or emotional problems, marital or other domestic problems, and children's health, development, or learning problems (Table 6.3). There were also differences between the Family First and regular services groups in reported family structure. Single-adult households were identified more often in the

Family First group, while households that included extended-family members were more commonly identified among regular services cases.

The absolute values of zero-order correlations among pairs of case characteristics were very low (most were less than .1 and all were less than .42). Correlations between sites and these case characteristics were all between −.2 and .2.

28. For this group, the risk of placement at one year after referral was .29 for Family First cases and .20 for regular services.

29. For families with marital problems, the probability that the case would be closed by one year after referral was .57 for Family First and .30 for regular services. For families with housing problems, the likelihood of case closing at one year was .51 for Family First and .30 for regular services. For families who had children with health problems, the probability of case closing at one year after referral was .58 for Family First and .32 for regular services.

30. The natural logs of the first three service characteristics were used in the two-stage least squares models, since the distributions of these variables are skewed, having long right tails.

31. Variables in the equations designed to predict case outcomes included service characteristics, case characteristics that were found to be related to outcomes (in logistic regression analysis), and the other outcome variables (e.g., the dummy variables for subsequent maltreatment and case closing were included in models designed to predict placement).

32. Information on victimization of children was also collected, but these data are not reported here because of low frequencies and questions about the validity of the data. Few parents reported that their children had been harmed. We suspect that actual harm to children is not accurately reflected in these data.

33. It is possible that the program raised parents' awareness of family problems while it reduced the severity of these problems. However, the notion that the program had a "consciousness raising" effect is a convenient post hoc explanation when parents receiving family preservation services report problem levels equivalent to or higher than those reported by control group parents. In contrast, differences in the opposite direction tend to be interpreted as evidence of program effects on outcomes.

34. Chi-square $= 3.761$, d.f. $= 1$, $p = .052$.

35. Chi-square $= 5.610$, d.f. $= 1$, $p = .019$.

36. Chi-square $= 4.424$, d.f. $= 1$, $p = .035$.

37. The second wave included second interviews in Chicago and first interviews in the other sites. The third wave involved third interviews in Chicago and second interviews elsewhere. We combined interviews in this way because the duration of time between referral and second-wave interviews (and between referral and third-wave interviews) was relatively similar across sites.

38. In the second wave, we found significant regional effects on the proportion of housing problems reported; families in the Chicago site reported more problems in this area than those in the other sites. Interactions between experimental group and region were significant in explaining variations in the mean proportion of problems reported in physical care and discipline and emotional care of children; Family First cases in Chicago reported a lower percentage of problems in these two domains compared with the control group in that site, while parents in the Family First groups in other sites reported more problems in these domains than regular services cases. In the third wave, there were significant regional differences in the proportion of problems reported in physical child care, children's academic adjustment, children's conduct, and children's symp-

tomatic behavior. Families in the Peoria site reported more problems in all of these domains.

39.   This analysis only includes families who participated in all three waves in Chicago East ($N = 69$) and in both interviews in the other two sites (52 families in Lake Villa/Waukegan and 59 in Peoria). The proportion of problems is the number of problems reported by the parent in each domain divided by the total number of problem items in that domain.

40.   Orthogonal polynomial transformations of the time variable were used, yielding linear, quadratic, and cubic estimates of trends. This time effect was cubic (rather than linear or quadratic).

41.   If the program increased clients awareness of family problems, we might expect to see this effect in parents' retrospective reports of the problems they were experiencing at the time of referral. Compared with regular services cases, parents in the Family First group reported a higher mean proportion of problems in five of the eight domains at the time of referral. However, none of these differences were statistically significant.

42.   The test of linear differences in the interaction between group and time was significant at $p = .002$. For the test of quadratic effects, $p = .588$; for cubic effects, $p = .561$.

43.   In each domain and regarding the family's situation overall, we asked whether things were a lot better, a little better, about the same, a little worse, or a lot worse.

44.   For housing, Tau-b $= .352$, $p < .001$; for economic conditions, Tau-b $= .302$, $p < .001$; for physical child care, Tau-b $= .374$, $p < .001$.

45.   Tau-b $= .188$, $p = .046$.

46.   For housing, Tau-b $= 0224$, $p = .009$; for economic conditions, Tau-b $= .180$, $p = .027$.

47.   For discipline and emotional care, Tau-b $= .218$, $p = .037$; for academic adjustment, Tau-b $= .256$, $p = .060$; for overall situation, Tau-b $= .213$, $p = .050$.

48.   Tau-b $= .273$, $p = .031$.

49.   For clothing, Chi-square $= 7.437$, $p = .006$; financial assistance, Chi-square $= 7.308$, $p = .007$; food, Chi-square $= 9.731$, $p = .002$; furniture, Chi-square $= 12.077$, $p < .001$; toys and recreational equipment, Chi-square $= 5.287$, $p = .021$; transportation, Chi-square $= 6.348$, $p = .012$; parent education, Chi-square $= 4.715$, $p = .030$; family counseling, Chi-square $= 4.876$, $p = .027$.

50.   In Chicago East at the time of the first interview, almost two-thirds (63%) of the Family First cases reported that they had received physical assistance within the past month compared with 39% of regular services cases (Chi-square $= 4.241$, d.f. $= 1$, $p = .039$).

51.   Prior to averaging, the values of negative items were reversed.

52.   Fifteen percent of regular services cases in Chicago East, 23% of Family First and 26% of regular services cases in Lake Villa/Waukegan, and 37% of Family First and 25% regular services cases in Peoria reported that they had no caseworker. Most of the regular services parents who reported not having a caseworker since referral were involved in cases that were closed after random assignment with no further DCFS involvement. Family First parents in Lake Villa/Waukegan and Peoria who reported that they did not have a caseworker since referral may have misunderstood the question or errors may have been made in asking the question. Our client tracking system indicates that all of these Family First cases had been served by a Family First provider; the duration of services for these cases was between 9 and 344 days (with a median of 97 days).

PART III

Chapter 7

Issues in the Evaluation of Family Preservation Programs

The developers of family preservation programs claimed that these services would prevent the placement of children in substitute care. The natural response to that claim is, Prove it. The demand for evaluation is increased when substantial resources are allocated from the public purse. Evaluators who venture into this arena are buffeted by many forces. Family preservation programs have become high-profile endeavors, often enmeshed in political tugs and pulls. There are many interest groups, all claiming to represent the best interests of children and families. Although lip service is paid to the ideal of "objectivity," defenders of programs often look to evaluators to provide ammunition for their arguments and when the evaluators fail to produce they are roundly attacked. Glowingly positive evaluations fare no better, being dismissed by detractors of the programs as uncritical. What is the proper stance for an evaluator? We believe that it must somehow combine hope and skepticism—hope that the programs will be found to provide important benefits for children, families, and society and skepticism born of long experience with social programs that fail to live up to their billings. Since evaluations are usually paid for by organizations that have an investment in positive results, researchers may feel a particular need to satisfy those interests. In this circumstance, it is particularly important that evaluators maintain a position of dispassionate skepticism.

In this chapter, we consider some of the issues that we and other evaluators of family preservation programs have faced. In the process, we take up three common criticisms directed at evaluators: You haven't measured the right outcomes (or the measurements were no good). You didn't describe the program operations well enough. Your design didn't allow you to answer your questions.

OUTCOMES

Although the term *evaluation* has been broadened to include virtually any study of programs, in its original meaning it was concerned with detecting the effects of programs (Suchman 1967:27). So it is a description of cause and effect, of specifying independent and dependent variables and their causal relationships. We begin with the dependent variable.

Among social programs, family preservation programs as originally conceived were remarkable (though perhaps not unique) for their singularity of purpose: the prevention of placement. However, as we have seen (Chapter 1) there are ambiguities that need to be resolved in the definition of placement. How does one treat placements in homes of relatives, informal placements, runaways, and placements for only a few days? In addition, as we have observed elsewhere (Schuerman, Rzepnicki, Littell, and Associates 1991), placement, as an outcome variable, is a curious thing. In the aggregate, placements are considered undesirable, because staying in the natural family whenever possible is considered to be good for children and because placement is very costly. But in individual cases, when a child is placed it is considered to be in the best interests of the child. Of course, errors of judgment are made, but in nearly all cases of placement, the decision-maker believes it is the best alternative. This is unlike outcome measures in other programs. For example, getting a job is almost always better than unemployment, so if a client in a job placement program fails to get a job, it cannot be considered to have been a good outcome.

A number of observers have suggested that the goals of family preservation programs be broadened to include other objectives, including improvements in family and child functioning, the delay of placement, or other desirable outcomes. There have even been suggestions that we determine success through "process" measures, indications of services offered and delivered (Suchman 1967:16). A cynic might suggest that this changing of goals is tantamount to "bait and switch." The matter of expanding goals has divided the advocates: Some purists insist on maintaining the preeminence of the placement prevention objective, others embrace broader goals (Littell, Schuerman, Rzepnicki, Howard, and Budde 1993; Haapala, Pecora, and Fraser 1991).

Sometimes measures of success are suggested because of their presumed relationship with more ultimate objectives. For example, one reason to measure improvements in family and child functioning is that they are assumed to be related to things like placement. If the family is functioning better, the risk of placement should be lower. The problem here is that while such relationships may exist, they are often not strong.

We then have a chain of causal connections in which the connections are relatively weak: Intervention is somewhat related to improved family functioning and family functioning is somewhat related to placement so the relationship between intervention and placement is quite small.[1] Thus, achievement of intermediate objectives should never be assumed to assure the achievement of ultimate objectives. One might measure child and family functioning as ultimate outcomes but not because they are assumed to be related to other things. Ultimately desired effects should be examined directly.

These considerations also apply to other presumed effects of family preservation and other social programs. Family preservation programs are sometimes assumed to reduce the need of families for other social services, perhaps for some time to come, with concomitant savings in costs to society. An extreme example is the claim that family support programs reduce the likelihood of future serious offenses by children, thereby reducing costs of incarceration. Claims such as these depend on long and quite shaky causal chains.

Even shakier is the determination of the success of a program on the basis of process measures. We refer here to measures of the intervention itself. In family preservation programs these might include hours of contact, the delivery of various services, the quality of the services, measures of the quality of the relationship between the worker and family, and the satisfaction of the client with the services. Such variables are obviously important in assessing the quality of implementation of the program but they cannot be taken as outcome measures. Any assumption that such things are related to ultimate outcomes begs the main question of evaluation: Did the services help? We again have the problem of assumed chains of causality.

A major problem in evaluation of social programs arises from the fact that services are often highly individualized. As we discuss in more detail below, this is a central feature of family preservation programs. Services are individualized because the goals for individual families (at least the proximate goals) vary. It is, therefore, often suggested that evaluations seek ways to measure the achievement of individualized goals, through approaches like goal attainment scaling (Kirusek and Sherman 1968). In our evaluation we did this in a modest way by examining workers' assessments of the achievement of individual objectives by families. There are considerable technical difficulties in using individualized measures like these, primarily those of comparability of objectives and of workers' ratings of achievement.[2] We think it is useful to attempt to deal with these problems and try to get at achievement of individualized objectives. However, such measures can never take the place of summary assessments of the effects of family preservation pro-

grams. After all, these programs are intended to have broad social benefit, so individual achievements should add up to measurable effects for
society.

Whenever a program has multiple goals the question arises, How are
these goals to be combined in an assessment of the program? This is
partially a political problem, but the evaluator must weigh in with his or
her interpretations of the data. How will it be determined that the program gets a "passing grade"? Must all of the objectives be met or only
one? Or is the grade to be assigned on the basis of a combination of
achievements on the objectives? Perhaps the "tests" should be weighted
in some way so that one objective predominates (the "final exam"?).
Multiple goals lead to much debate about these questions among the
constituents of the program. Since these questions are rarely answered
definitively, ambiguity remains about how the outcomes of programs are
to be judged. This is one of the sources of arguments about just how
much existing programs have accomplished.

A single, unambiguous goal is nirvana for the evaluator, a nirvana
that is destroyed when practitioners or policymakers discover multiple
goals. Evaluators must then deal not only with the problem of how data
on the achievement of multiple goals are to be combined but also with
developing or choosing measures for each of the goals. There is a whole
industry devoted to the proliferation of measures of family and child
functioning. Many pages of journals and many hours of conferences are
devoted to debates about the relative merits of various measures. The
evaluator must sort through these debates to settle on the measurement
procedures he or she will use. And completed evaluations will always be
criticized for not measuring the "right" things or for not having used the
"best" available measures.

Despite all of these problems we believe that it is appropriate for
programs like family preservation to have multiple goals and to examine
their achievement in evaluations. Programs do have multiple effects,
some of which are desirable, and it is reasonable to consider those effects as objectives of the programs. Furthermore, the effects of social
programs are limited. A program's accomplishments in regard to any
one objective may be unremarkable but the sum of its effects may justify
the social investment. And it must be noted that the political process
appears to require some ambiguity, with multiple goals being used to
appeal to diverse constituencies.

Side Effects

An additional reason to examine multiple effects is the problem of side
effects. Any intervention may have undesirable side effects that ought to

be taken into account in its assessment (Suchman 1967:40). In family preservation programs the most obvious such side effect is increased risk of harm to children because they are left in their own homes rather than being put into foster care. It is therefore important to determine the extent to which such harm occurs. We did this by examining data on subsequent indicated allegations of harm.

The problem of determining undesirable side effects in medical and social experimentation is figuring out what to look for. Some, like the death of program participants, hit you in the face (although one does need to determine whether the death could have been prevented had the individual not participated in the program), but others will not be detected unless you look for them. Many such effects cannot be anticipated. Nonetheless, it is important in the design of a study to think about possible negative side effects and to try to find ways to measure them.

System Effects

So far, we have considered only effects at the individual family level, although those effects are assumed to add up to benefits for society. Another approach is to look at effects on overall statistics, trends in the numbers of children placed or in the rates of children placed (say as a proportion of children involved in reports of harm or of indicated cases). Although these are the things that we hope the program will ultimately change, there are a number of problems in using them as outcome measures. The number of children placed is subject to myriad influences, many of them outside the child welfare system. These influences change over the course of time, so it is impossible to claim success for a program merely because improvements in gross statistics occur or to declare program failure when the statistics deteriorate. As to examining changes in rates, one must be alert to the possibility of changes in the character of denominators. For example, changes in the ratio of children placed to the number of children involved in indicated investigations may be due to changes in the way decisions about indicating a case are made.

It is often hoped that family preservation programs will have other system effects, influences on the way the system works, beyond the effects of the program on individual families. For example, the introduction of family preservation programs may well have had effects throughout the child welfare system on how decisions are made about cases. Anecdotal evidence suggests that the values embodied in family preservation programs, values such as the importance of maintaining the family whenever possible, have come to be widely accepted by child welfare workers. Protective service investigators may have become less aggressive in removing children from their homes and more willing to refer to in-home services, whether or not those services are "family preservation" programs.

The identification of system effects poses special problems for evaluators. It is usually not possible to detect them through randomized experiments. Like other effects, they must be anticipated if evaluators are to develop convincing evidence for them, although the possible existence of unanticipated effects may be uncovered through qualitative techniques. In the case of attitudes and values, it is desirable to take baseline measures before a new program is instituted so that systematic before-after analysis is possible. The difficulties involved are such that few evaluations undertake systematic examination of system effects. When such effects are claimed, the evidence is often anecdotal and post hoc.

Elusive Outcomes

A concern about evaluation often expressed by practitioners is that the desired outcomes are subtle and thus not detectable through the crude tools of social science. Alternatively, an advocate might admit that the effects are small and suggest that they are then unlikely to be detectable, but that they are nonetheless socially significant. In the case of evaluations of family preservation programs, these concerns appear unwarranted. As suggested above, the primary objective of such programs, placement prevention, is clear and not at all subtle. The effects are also supposed to be quite large.

We take the position that the effects of social programs must be detectable, even given the shortcomings of scientific method. Programs without observable effects simply cannot be defended, particularly in the present political climate. Very often, as in the case of family preservation programs, the efforts are intended to have quite large effects, effects that should be robust enough to be observable even with less than perfect methods. At the same time, problems in measurement of outcomes must be recognized. For example, in our study, as in others, the state administrative data system was used to determine whether a child has been subsequently placed. These systems are certainly not flawless (to our knowledge, systematic examination of their reliability has not been undertaken). In addition, placements that take place outside the state's purview are not recorded in these systems. Another example is the detection of subsequent harm to children. Here we again depended on the state data system. Clearly, there are many harms that are not reported to the state child abuse and neglect hotline, and some real harms that are reported are not "indicated" because of lack of evidence. We return to the problem of data quality below.

THE BLACK BOX AND THE MILLION MODELS

On the input side of the equation there are two related problems: the description of the black box that is treatment and inevitable variations in intervention. Researchers are often admonished to open up the black box by providing a thorough description of the services that were delivered, to describe the model that was used. An evaluation is of limited use if what was done in the program is not known. We must know the details of program operation so that we can replicate it, if it is proven effective, or avoid mistakes, if it is a bust. Furthermore, it is desirable to examine the effectiveness of various components of a program and it is impossible to do that if the components are not identified.

But the achievement of this ideal is far from straightforward. To begin, there are no generally accepted standards as to what constitutes an adequate description of an intervention. What level of detail is necessary? What degree of specificity? Some details are relatively easy to provide—the length of service, the frequency of contact, the caseloads of workers—but specifying these structural aspects of service leaves one quite unsatisfied. They do not get at the heart of the matter, the real character of the service.

One solution is to try to identify the general principles that lie behind practice activities. Ideally, the principles should identify those aspects of practice that make a difference. Writing in the field often appears to assume that these critical aspects are codified in models (we have discussed the matter of models in Chapter 1). The problem is that there are many important aspects of practice that are not incorporated in models. Nonmodel aspects of practice, including things like the commitment or ingenuity of the worker and the character of the relationship between worker and client, may be far more important than models in explaining variations in outcomes. Furthermore, models are never implemented exactly as they are designed, so actual practice must be observed and described in some way.[3]

A major difficulty lies in the fact that each case is unique, at least in some respects. Good workers individualize the services provided to clients. In a way, a new model is invented for each case. We then have what might be termed the "million model problem."[4] We might hope that common aspects of service are important in determining outcomes, but the individualized creativity of workers may be more important.

A related problem has to do with the "level" at which one examines practice. Models provide more or less general principles, they do not provide detailed instructions as to what to do in every practice situation. The management of the moment-by-moment interaction with the client is largely left to the practitioner operating within general guidelines. But these moment-to-moment events are likely to be quite critical to the success of a program. Examination of these interactions has not been undertaken in major evaluations of family preservation programs. Obtaining accurate data on interactions appears to require audio or video recording or direct observation, something that is quite expensive, particularly in a large-scale evaluation. Electronic recording can also be quite intrusive.

So the evaluator must search for the proper level of description of program activities. Mere structural features are not enough, nor is the identification of the prescribed model of practice. But practice activities will always be described in generalities—we cannot describe every interaction with every client. The resulting description is likely to be incomplete and unsatisfying and will probably provide only general guidance for those who wish to replicate the service. It will be left to future program planners and practitioners to fill in the blanks. In the end, evaluations may be seen as assessments not of models or particular services but of general approaches to the provision of service.

One additional note regarding the description of practice: Programs change over time and multisite programs vary in the way they are conducted in various locations. Contextual elements such as the availability of resources, public support, and media scrutiny play major roles. Not only do service characteristics vary, but also referral criteria and practices. It is important to try to describe such variations, the reasons for them, and how they relate to outcomes.

THE DESIGN OF STUDIES

Two major dimensions of research design have occupied commentators on family preservation evaluation: the experimental vs. nonexperimental and quantitative vs. qualitative dichotomies. We begin with the standard principle of research texts: The design of a study should be determined by the questions asked. The principal objective in family preservation evaluation is to determine effects, and we take the position that that objective requires the use of quantitative experimental designs. By *experimental* we mean the use of experimental and control groups constructed through random assignment in which the control group receives either no service or an alternative service, such as regular services.

Experience with the evaluation of family preservation programs provides a classic demonstration of the necessity for experimental studies, as we have shown in Chapter 2. Early studies that followed only cases that were served in such programs found high levels of "placement avoidance," that is, few of the families served experienced placement of a child. Subsequent experimental studies have demonstrated how misleading those early evaluations were. These evaluations assumed that virtually all of the families served had children that were "at imminent risk" of having a child placed, an assumption that has been found to be incorrect (Rossi 1991). The problem is that examination only of a group receiving service does not tell us what would have happened in the absence of service. It is necessary to look at a comparison group that does not receive the service or that receives an alternative treatment. The experimental studies of family preservation have found a low rate of placement in the family preservation groups but also a comparably low rate in the comparison groups. Hence, claims that family preservation caused reductions in placement are impossible to sustain.

It is now well accepted that we need comparison groups in evaluations of social programs (Rossi and Freeman 1993). The comparison group must be comparable to the experimental group at the outset of service. The best way to ensure that comparability is through random assignment of a pool of eligible clients to the two groups. Because it is not easy to implement random assignment, alternative methods of constructing comparison groups are often employed (resulting in "quasi-experimental" studies, see Rzepnicki, Schuerman, and Littell 1991). For example, other cases in the child welfare caseload that are thought to have characteristics similar to those of the service group are located. However, such cases are almost invariably different from those in the experimental group. After all, they were not selected for the service. Sometimes, comparison groups are chosen from other areas of the state, but this method is also inadequate because of differences in social conditions in various areas, including differences in available services. Hence, the comparability of groups constructed in nonrandom ways is rarely convincing. Only one type of nonrandom comparison group is potentially useful: The overflow or waiting list control group. Subjects in such groups are presumably similar to those receiving service because they have been referred and would have received the service had it been available. However, experience indicates that it is often impossible to construct overflow or waiting list groups that are large enough for statistical analysis. In many situations it is also possible that knowledge that services are or are not available affects the decisions of referral agents, with the result that overflow or waiting list clients are not similar to those receiving service. Finally, waiting list designs may often be manipulated by workers, for example, by re-referring cases when an opening becomes available.

In thinking about nonexperimental approaches to evaluation of family preservation programs, it is well to consider the well-known "threats to validity" identified by Cook and Campbell (1979). The operation of one of these threats is particularly ubiquitous in the evaluation of social programs: statistical regression. Programs such as family preservation serve persons who are identified as having serious problems; they are at the extreme end of the variable "problems." Persons who are at the extreme of a variable at a particular point in time are often there because of the combination of a number of random factors. At a later point, one or more of those random factors is likely not to be present (they "regress" to a less extreme level). The individual will have improved, but this is merely because of chance, not because of treatment. Thus, we expect that, on average, clients of social programs will improve, simply because the reason they were chosen to be in the program is that they were having problems. Experimental designs control for the effects of regression since the experimental and control groups will experience it to about the same degree.

Experiments are often not conducted because they are very difficult to mount and maintain. But they are clearly not impossible, as we and others have demonstrated. There is now a large body of social experimentation. A major difficulty in implementing experiments is the resistance of administrators, workers, and other interested parties. Considerable time is often required to negotiate and monitor the conduct of an experiment. In our study, random assignment was not begun until nearly a year and a half after the evaluation was begun, during which time we held innumerable meetings about the proposed experiment with personnel at all levels in DCFS and the private agencies, even though DCFS had proposed the experiment in the first place (see Chapter 3).

Objections to experiments often center around ethical issues, particularly the denial of services to members of control groups. We restate here the now familiar arguments around this issue (Rivlin and Timpane 1975). The purpose of experimentation is to determine whether a service is beneficial to clients; hence, it is presumably not known that the service is of benefit. Thus, in depriving a group of a service, it is not known that we are depriving them of a benefit. A problem with this argument arises when, as in the case of family preservation, the service includes what might be considered to be "inherent" benefits, services such as cash assistance, housing, or day care that are valued in and of themselves, not just because they might serve ultimate objectives. We believe that such services should be much more widely available, not just as components of programs like family preservation (we take up this matter again in the last chapter). If that were the case, objections on the grounds of inherent benefit would have less force.

Services like family preservation are usually limited in their availability. When that is the case, there is a further justification for denying services to a control group. Some families will not get the service in any case, so some rationing procedure is required. The most equitable rationing procedure is often random allocation, it ensures that everyone in an eligible pool has the same chance to receive the service. The argument rests on the assumption that everyone in the pool is equally deserving of service or that it is impossible to make reasonable distinctions among pool members as to their deservingness. In the case of family preservation programs, it is certainly possible that some families might make better use of service than others. However, although practitioners can always make arguments as to how important it is for particular families to receive services, we believe that it is quite difficult to make these distinctions prior to actually beginning work with a family.

In the end, ethical questions must be resolved through a weighing of benefits: the benefit to clients who would fall in the control group of receiving the service versus the benefit to future clients of the knowledge gained through an experiment. Both benefits are future presumed benefits—neither can be guaranteed. So judgments must be made about their likely achievement.

A further objection to randomized experiments in evaluations of social programs is that the imposition of an experiment changes the service. Sometimes the changes are thought to be harmful, but in any event it is argued that the experiment will not provide an accurate view of effects in the absence of an experiment. It is well known that study of something sometimes changes it, and the manipulations that are involved in experimentation can be particularly intrusive. While being studied no doubt has an effect on the conduct of an intervention, we believe that these effects are often over-estimated and do not necessarily invalidate the results. But the experimenter must be alert to evidence of such effects and try to assess their importance. In our study, the services were provided by private agencies that accepted referrals from DCFS. The agencies were not involved in the process of selecting clients, so it is unlikely that the experimental procedures (which governed who was referred) had an effect on the services received by families in the Family First experimental group. The experiment may have affected the services provided to the control group in at least one region, Springfield, where some families were provided with enhanced services beyond the "regular services" of DCFS. It is also possible that the experiment had an effect on referral practices, if only because it required a larger pool of clients to fill both the experimental and control groups. In Chapter 3 we provided some analyses to test this possibility.

Problems in Maintaining the Integrity of Experiments

Even when one is able to mount an experiment, it is not easy to keep it going. The conduct of a large-scale experiment requires the cooperation of a large number of people. New procedures must be followed and these are often resisted. Workers who are unconvinced of the value of the study or who have ethical objections may seek to undermine the work in various, often quite imaginative ways. Obviously, the support of high-level administrators is essential, particularly when the experiment is mounted in a highly bureaucratized and hierarchical organization. However, in a large and decentralized organization such as DCFS, high-level support is not enough. One needs local controls as well, procedures that maximize the likelihood that the experimental protocol will be followed. In Chapter 3 we detailed some of the processes we used to try to keep the experiment on track. But in a large experiment there will be violations: failures to submit cases to random assignment and efforts to switch the assignment of cases. It is important to track these violations and to estimate their effects on the data and their interpretation.

Another problem in our study is that the experiment may have affected the decision-making of DCFS investigators. An investigator who deemed a case appropriate for Family First could not be sure that the case would receive those services. This uncertainty might have affected the way decisions about the case were made.

Still another limitation of our study is that Family First cases in the experiment were not randomly assigned to specific providers. Once families were assigned to Family First, referrals to providers were handled at the discretion of DCFS staff. This limited our ability to test the effects of specific programs within sites that had more than one Family First service provider.

Qualitative and Quantitative Approaches

As we indicated above, we believe that the assessment of the effects of programs like family preservation requires the use of quantitative designs. The objectives of these programs are social benefits that are countable: reductions in numbers of children placed in substitute care, reductions in costs, improvements in average levels of family functioning.

Sometimes the resulting numbers do seem to speak for themselves: Placements were or were not reduced or costs did or did not increase. But the usefulness of the numbers is often much enhanced by additional understandings: How was the intervention implemented and how did it change over time? What was done with families? How did the workers think about their work? What did the families think about their workers? Such questions are often best approached with qualitative methods: conversations with program participants in which their "personal knowledge" is sought (Rossi and Freeman 1993:83, 437). As we have detailed, in our study we attempted to meld quantitative and qualitative approaches to provide a more complete picture of the Family First program than would have been possible with one or the other alone.

PROBLEMS OF DATA QUALITY

A significant and often overlooked problem in evaluation of family preservation programs is that of the quality of data. We believe that this is often the weakest part of these evaluations. Information is frequently obtained from administrative data systems whose reliability and validity is either unknown or known to be shaky. Often it is known that some items in an administrative data system are quite weak. Researchers must be familiar with the way data are collected and coded for administrative data systems and know the "practice wisdom" that accumulates around such systems. Sometimes case records are used, records that are incomplete, designed to serve purposes other than research, and again of uncertain reliability. The records can be expected to reflect the biases and self-interests of the workers who compile them. Sometimes, as in our study, dependence is placed on specially designed questionnaires completed by workers. Obviously, workers' responses may be affected by the knowledge that their work is being studied, even though strict assurances of confidentiality are provided. Furthermore, such questionnaires often ask for judgments of things like the problems in the family and the degree of progress. Clearly, workers vary in the criteria they use for such judgments. Family preservation evaluations rarely provide adequate estimates of the reliability of measures such as these.

In our study, an unusually high level of effort was expended to ensure the accuracy of data but we depended on other people for much of this information: our data came from the DCFS computer files, from private agency and DCFS staff, and from clients. There are omissions and inaccuracies in these data. On some cases workers failed to complete the necessary forms, or they completed forms hurriedly or so late that their memory of the details of the case had dimmed. We have multiple sources of information for some events, such as placements and amounts of service provided, and thus can estimate the accuracy of information for those items.[5] However, we have no way to estimate reliability for a number of variables, including those involving judgments of workers.

An additional problem of data is what has been termed "experimental group–measurement interaction." This occurs when sources of data or the procedures used to gather data are different for the experimental and control groups. This problem exists in our study. We depended on workers for important information, in the case of the experimental group, on the Family First worker in the private agency; in the control group, on the DCFS worker responsible for the case. Moreover, Family First workers completed questionnaires about cases while DCFS workers were interviewed. We used different procedures because of the difficulty we encountered early on in obtaining data from DCFS workers on forms. Such differences in data gathering procedures may have had effects on the character of the information obtained. But a more important influence may be systematic differences in the attitudes and approaches to cases of the workers in the two groups, differences that we have documented above. In addition, workers in the private agencies had much smaller caseloads and provided more intensive services and thus tended to know families much better. Providing such services is one of the reasons for the Family First program, but this may have led to differences in the kinds and quality of data obtained from the two groups of workers. In addition, there were differences in the training and orientations of the workers in the two sectors.

One area in which group-measurement interaction may have occurred has to do with the identification of abuse or neglect and the decision to take custody of a child during the period of service. Family First workers had more contact with families than DCFS workers and thus may have been more likely to observe evidence of abuse or neglect. Many observers have suggested that this may result in an apparent attenuation of the effects of Family First. This matter may be viewed as either a measurement problem or as an effect of the program. It is possible, however, that Family First services had a "suppressing" effect, that is, the extensive surveillance that is involved may reduce the likelihood of abuse or neglect during the period of service. The suppression effect might be evident in an increase in reported abuse or neglect shortly after the termination of services.

It is likely that evaluations of family preservation will continue to make use of measures of uncertain reliability, validity, and sensitivity. The interpretations of the data should be tempered by those uncertainties, and efforts should be made to determine the reliability of sources like administrative data systems. More important, efforts should be made to deal with the problems of reliability and validity. Involving agency staff in the development and revision of data collection procedures often results in better quality information. Multiple sources of information should be considered, particularly for the central variables of the study. In our evaluation of Family First, we attempted to do this in a limited way, for example, by obtaining data on placement from the administrative data system, workers, and clients. Of course, when various sources yield differing data, the evaluator is left with the sticky problem of how to reconcile the differences.

It is desirable that efforts also be made to get as close as possible to the phenomena of interest and to avoid, as much as possible, the operation of self-interest in the gathering of data. We believe that it is important to talk directly with clients about their lives and their experiences with services. Consideration should be given to independent observations of family life and perhaps of the interaction of helpers and clients. In large evaluations, such observations might be made in small subsamples of cases.

WHAT DO WE NEED TO LEARN?

Longitudinal Effects

We have argued that the principal objective of family preservation evaluations is to determine the effects of the service. A major issue in the detection of effects has to do with time: Over what period of time do we look for effects? How long do we watch clients to see if there are effects (Glaser 1988; Rzepnicki 1991)? One might hope that guidance in answering these questions would be provided by theories of treatment, but family preservation theory, like most theories of social service, is notably silent as to projections of the length of time the intervention is effective. If the service is effective in turning people's lives around, the effects should be evident for the rest of their lives. But that seems grandiose. Lives, particularly those of family preservation clients, are buffeted by many forces, and interventions simply cannot be expected to immunize families forever from serious setbacks. So family preservation work cannot be expected to provide a lifetime guarantee. At the same time, it is not worth the investment if its effects are only momentary.

Evaluations of family preservation services have often been faulted for not having taken a long view, for not following families for a sufficient period of time. We believe that it is important to follow families for a reasonable period of time because it is important to determine how long the effects of treatment last. But extended follow-ups are not justifiable if no effects or marginal effects are found at the end or shortly after the end of treatment. If significant effects are not found early, they are highly unlikely to be found later. To our knowledge, delayed effects have never been found in social program experimentation and we doubt that they will be.

Benefit-Cost

Similar considerations apply to benefit-cost studies. As we noted in Chapter 2, there have been few careful studies of benefit-cost in family preservation, although there have been many claims of substantial savings from these programs (Edna McConnell Clark Foundation 1985, 1990; Pecora 1991). It is clearly important to be able to judge whether a program is worth the investment, but the first step is to show that it is effective. If it is not effective in reaching its service goals, it cannot be cost effective. So far, the field has not been able to show that family preservation programs are effective in reducing placement, so sophisticated analyses of benefit-cost are quite beside the point.

What Works for Whom?

Clearly a major task of family preservation research is to determine those components of service that make a difference overall and those components and combinations of components that are effective with various types of families. We think that the principal difficulty here is the development of categories of service activities and categories of cases that are meaningful in relation to each other. This is largely a conceptual task, although empirical work can contribute to it. But we need to develop more refined categories than "drug cases," "single-headed families," and "short-term intensive treatment." Then, of course, we need large enough samples to explore the relationships among our categories of activities and families.

The Need for Clinical Trials

It has been suggested that we need more small "clinical trials" of service approaches, in the style of experiments conducted by medical researchers. One reason to conduct such studies is the problems posed for evaluation by variations in the ways services are implemented, as identified earlier. In a clinical trial, the researcher controls the service given to clients in the hope that it will be delivered in the best possible manner, according to theory, and thereby give the program the best chance of success. We believe that small-scale clinical trials should be employed much more frequently in the development of child welfare services. Far too often, service ideas are developed, tested in uncontrolled circumstances, and then prematurely deployed in large-scale programs. But success in controlled circumstances does not guarantee success when the program is mounted on a large scale, when the researcher can no longer control the intervention. Hence successful clinical trials must be followed by studies of programs "at scale."

Basic Research

In this chapter, we have focused on the description of programs and the detection of effects. But the successful development of programs in child welfare requires other kinds of knowledge as well. Of particular importance is the development of greater understanding of how decisions on cases are made. We have talked throughout this book about the "targeting problem," the fact that most of the families served in family preservation programs are not at imminent risk of having a child placed. At the core of the targeting problem is the decision on the part of a worker to refer a case to a family preservation program. We need much greater understanding of the ways that workers make decisions to place a child in foster care, to refer to family preservation, to reunite a child with his or her family, and of all the other decisions that are made in the course of a child welfare case. Such knowledge would help us to improve those decisions and to better frame criteria for referral to programs like family preservation. There is a great deal of "basic" knowledge of this sort that is needed for the further development of programs for children and families.

NOTES

1. This idea is captured in path analysis, where the effect of a cause at one end of a causal chain on an effect at the other end is the product of the intermediate effects (assuming that there is no direct effect). Since the effect coefficients are usually less than one, the product is usually considerably less than any one of the intermediate effects.

2. For example, in our study, workers were quite inconsistent in the "level"

of objectives specified for clients. Some identified improvements in functioning (e.g., reduction in drug use) while others identified activities like attendance in a drug program. In addition, it appears that there was considerable variation in the standards workers used to assess achievement.

3.   No manual is ever totally complete. For example, recipes for cooking are often quite vague ("a dash of salt," "low heat"), the order of steps is sometimes not clear, and things are left out (you are rarely told to take the cake out of the oven after the instruction "Bake for 35 minutes"). Experienced cooks have no trouble with such instructions because they are readily able to fill in the blanks. In addition, recipes rarely tell you what to do when things go wrong. Again, that is a matter that is left to one's experience and ingenuity.

4.   The first author first heard this term in a "focus group" called together by officials of the Department of Health and Human Services to discuss evaluation of the provisions for family preservation services in the 1994 federal budget. The originator of the term is unknown.

5.   On these items we have information from both the DCFS computer files and the service summaries. This information was also obtained in our interviews with parents, so we have three sources of data on some cases.

Chapter 8

The Recent Evolution of the Family First Program

Over time, changes occur in programs and in the organizations in which they are housed. Such changes can constitute either opportunities or threats. In the five years the Family First program has existed, many events have shaped its development. During this time there have been two governors of the state and four directors of the Department of Children and Family Services. Other significant personnel changes have taken place and the influence of various actors has waxed and waned. The environment of the program has hardly been stable. These are not unusual circumstances for social programs.

In Chapter 1 we described the beginnings of the Family First program. We take up here where we left off there, in the middle of 1990. Our discussion is organized in terms of the state's fiscal years.

JULY 1990 TO JUNE 1991

In August 1990 Gordon Johnson stepped down as director of DCFS and Governor James Thompson named Jess MacDonald acting director. MacDonald had served in Governor James Thompson's administration as the governor's assistant for human services. He came to DCFS a few months before the gubernatorial election in November 1990. Since Thompson was not seeking another term, there was a great deal of uncertainty about the future leadership of DCFS. McDonald was to serve only until January 1991.

During the MacDonald administration, there was a major effort to settle several large class action lawsuits. After the election, it appeared that settlement of the lawsuits was of great interest to the incoming governor, Jim Edgar. The DCFS administration's interest in reaching settlements spilled over into discussions about the directions of the Family First program. (A discussion of the issues involved in the major lawsuits is provided below.)

It soon became clear that the MacDonald administration was deeply concerned about the Family First program. MacDonald was unhappy with the directions the program had taken. For example, he thought the program should be targeted toward families with older rather than younger children. He was eager to take action and was frustrated by what he perceived to be inaction on the part of DCFS staff and a lack of useful information coming from the evaluation. Serious consideration was given to reshaping the program in order to deal with pressures from legal advocates and to meet other needs that the administration saw.

The MacDonald administration considered broadening the target population and expanding the types of services provided under Family First. It was thought that the money spent on intensive services for relatively few families could go further by providing less intensive services to more families. The development of a continuum of family preservation services was suggested; this would include the provision of low-intensity services (e.g., DCFS casework), moderate-intensity services (a "diluted" version of Family First), and high-intensity services (something akin to Family First).

DCFS administrators also considered extending the service period from 90 days to 6 months. Difficulties in Chicago in the transfer of cases from Family First programs back to DCFS provided one impetus for this change. DCFS decided that providers would keep cases until DCFS had assigned a caseworker to the case and was ready to accept the transfer. This resulted in the extension of a large number of cases in Chicago, but this was seen as a temporary measure and there was no formal decision to extend program time limits.

There was a series of discussions between DCFS administrators and private providers about possible changes in the program. Providers were almost unanimously opposed to alterations in the major features of the program, but for different reasons. Some thought that the original intent of the program—to provide brief, intensive services aimed at placement prevention—was lost in proposals to expand the program's time limits. Others advocated that the intensity of services should be maintained but that the services should be provided for a longer period of time. Still others thought that the focus of the program should be shifted from placement prevention to other goals, such as strengthening family functioning.

The debate over new directions for Family First seemed to hit a crescendo at the time that Governor Edgar appointed a new DCFS director, Sue Suter, in January 1991. There was a brief lull in the dialogue about plans for the Family First program as Suter made significant changes in the organizational structure of DCFS, but the department soon renewed discussions about alternative visions of the program. Some of these alternatives were implemented. For example, in the Aurora region, the program was used to provide 30-day assessments for families who might or might not require intensive family preservation services.

The private child welfare agencies, especially the sectarian agencies, had long wielded substantial influence over policy and practice in the Illinois child welfare system in both the executive and legislative branches of state government. During the administration of Gordon Johnson, the private sector and DCFS had achieved a relatively comfortable relationship. During the first few months of the Suter administration, the department and the private agencies struggled to redefine that relationship. Some members of the new administration seemed unfamiliar with a system in which the private agencies had so much influence.

Upon taking office in January 1991, Governor Edgar decried what he claimed was the profligate spending of the previous state government and announced that it would be necessary to cut well over $1 billion from the state budget, a figure that increased to $1.8 billion by the end of the fiscal year. In this austere climate, DCFS was spared reductions and in fact was budgeted for a 12% increase. This was done in part because of pending lawsuits against the department. After substantial increases in FY 1990 and FY 1991, Family First was budgeted at about a level amount (the budget for FY 1992 was $21.284 million, a 6% increase over the previous year).

Influence of Lawsuits and the Media

As in many states, in recent years DCFS has been the defendant in a number of lawsuits challenging the department's handling of cases. During fiscal 1991 three suits in particular gained a great deal of attention. The suits created difficult cross-currents for family preservation: The *Norman v. Johnson* and *B.H. v. Suter* lawsuits reinforced the family preservation ethic, while *In the Interest of Ashley K.*, the "Sarah" case, called attention to its limitations.

Norman v. Johnson was a federal class action suit filed against DCFS by the Legal Assistance Foundation in Illinois on behalf of parents who had lost or were at risk of losing custody of their children because they were "unable to provide what (DCFS) accepts as adequate living circumstances for their children." The suit was settled by a consent decree in which DCFS agreed not to remove children from their homes "because of the living circumstances of the family, or lack of provision for the child's subsistence needs" unless the child's life or health was in imminent danger and "reasonable efforts" had been made to prevent removal of the child, or unless "such reasonable efforts, if provided, would not prevent or eliminate the need for removal." "Reasonable efforts" included provision of "hard" services such as assistance in locating and securing housing, temporary shelter, cash assistance, in-kind services including food or clothing, child care, emergency caretakers, and advocacy with public and community agencies providing such services. The consent order made provision for $800 or more in cash assistance to families in need. In addition, DCFS was to establish an advocacy program to assist families in locating secure shelter. Initially, DCFS elected to send some "Norman cases" to the DCFS family reunification program in Cook County and to Family First placement prevention programs in other regions.

B. H. v. Suter was filed by the ACLU in June 1988. This federal class action suit concerned all children placed in substitute case by DCFS. The suit was quite broad in scope, alleging that DCFS failed to provide these children with safe and stable placements and with other services, including those which might prevent placement or facilitate reunification. The suit involved an extensive process of discovery that included the appointment of a panel of experts to investigate the operation of DCFS. That panel reported in October 1990, making a series of recommendations for changes. This lawsuit is discussed in greater detail below.

The case *In the Interest of Ashley K.* generated far more media attention than any of the other cases, even though it concerned only one child (Norman and B. H. were both class action suits). The case became famous through the efforts of Bob Greene, a columnist for the *Chicago Tribune*, who called the young girl in the case "Sarah." The case concerned a child born to parents who were alleged to have abused drugs. The child was placed until the age of six with foster parents. The birth parents then successfully petitioned for return of the child. The foster parents contested the return of the child to the birth parents without avail. They also sought rights to visits with the child. Such rights were not provided for in the court order for reunification and were opposed by the birth parents. Following media attention and the intervention of then Governor Thompson, DCFS filed an appeal with the Illinois Appellate Court for foster parent visitation. The appeal was joined by Cook County Public Guardian Patrick Murphy. Governor Edgar filed an *amicus curiae* brief in support of the foster parents. In April 1991, the appellate court issued a stinging rebuke to the juvenile court judge in the case and ordered visitations between the child and the foster parents. The appellate court ordered further review of the decision to return the child to the birth parents and severely criticized the juvenile court and DCFS for the delays that had occurred in the case and the failure to make timely permanency plans.

The appellate court and media commentators also criticized DCFS and the juvenile court for attempting to reunify Ashley with parents who appeared to be inadequate. Other media critics, most notably Mike Royko in the *Chicago Tribune,* leveled the same accusation in other cases. These cases may or may not have been examples of the misapplication of family preservation values on the part of the juvenile court or DCFS, but in any event they gave pause to workers and judges who contemplated leaving a child in or returning a child to a birth family in which risks existed.

JULY 1991 TO JUNE 1992

During fiscal 1992, *B. H. v. Suter* came to dominate planning in DCFS. The suit was settled by a consent decree in November 1991. The consent decree called for a range of actions including reductions in caseloads of all workers dealing with children and families in which abuse or neglect has occurred, the provision of improved placement prevention and re-unification services, enhanced assessment services (to determine the medical, educational, and social service needs of placed children and their families), and more frequent and more effective case review mecha-nisms. The consent decree was hailed as a vehicle for a broad reform of the child welfare system in Illinois. However, except for caseload reduc-tions, it contained few provisions for change in services to the majority of families that DCFS serves: those in which placement of a child has not occurred and is not likely to occur. It also provided for little in the way of prevention. Thus, the consent decree represented somewhat less than a complete overhaul of the system.

The consent decree contained detailed timetables for performance of various activities and provided for the appointment of an independent monitor to ensure compliance. Joseph Schneider, formerly presiding judge in the Circuit Court of Cook County, was appointed as monitor. Monitoring of the decree is to continue at least through this decade. Partly as a response to the lawsuit, an elaborate planning process was established. Governor Edgar appointed a Child Welfare Advisory Group made up of representatives from the private sector, other state code departments, and DCFS. A number of internal DCFS implementation committees were established. These groups were asked to make still more recommendations for change in the child welfare system. A major early step required by the decree was the preparation by DCFS of an implementation plan, a draft of which was submitted in early June 1992. The implementation plan was revised twice as a result of complaints from a number of quarters, including the attorneys for the plaintiffs and the monitor.

Other lawsuits also influenced planning. In *Suter v. Artist M.*, the department challenged the right of individual children to sue in federal court under PL 96-272, the federal Adoption and Child Welfare Act of 1980. In the spring of 1992 the U.S. Supreme Court ruled in favor of DCFS. The failure of the Court to uphold the right of individual suit was greeted with relief by administrators in DCFS since it made it less likely that they would be harassed by a series of suits on behalf of individuals. Advocates for children viewed the decision as a setback.

The state continued to experience severe budget problems exacerbated by a continuing recession. Shortfalls in expected revenues caused midyear gubernatorial reductions in resources available to many state departments. The governor's budget for fiscal year 1993 continued the budget cutting. DCFS was largely immune to these reductions, and in fact was given a substantial increase in the proposed budget for FY 1993, to cover the costs of implementing the B. H. consent decree. Furthermore, it was necessary for the department to obtain a supplemental appropriation from the legislature to cover shortfalls in costs of substitute care in fiscal 1992. The budget that was finally adopted by the legislature and approved by the governor called for an allocation to DCFS about $20 million less than the governor's original budget. The amount for Family First was slightly less than the approximately $21 million allocated the previous year, a little more than $1 million less than an annualization of the previous budget.

Planning for the future of Family First was affected by concerns about the implementation of the B. H. settlement. The resources devoted to Family First were seen as potentially contributing to that implementation. Some DCFS administrators were concerned about the performance and results of the Family First program, particularly the placement prevention effort, a concern that was fueled in part by preliminary results of the evaluation. A number of changes in the program were proposed. Early in the year, some DCFS administrators considered efforts to "tighten up" the program by prescribing a particular model (e.g., Homebuilders) for the use of the private agencies. Consideration was also given to ways of ensuring that more families who were truly at risk of placement of a child would be referred to the program. These changes were not made. During the last half of the year steps were taken to convert one-third of the slots in the placement prevention program to "moderate intensity reunification." This new program, a version of the Family Reunification Program of Family First, involved families with children in placement from 4 to 12 months (the "intensive" Family Reunification Program was targeted at families of children in placement for

4 months or less). It was to offer a somewhat less intensive service than the original Family Reunification program. The shift caused consternation among some agencies that were asked to participate (not all were) because they felt ill prepared to offer the new services. Some of these agencies had no prior experience with foster care.

Toward the end of the year, a proposal to convert some of the remaining placement prevention services to less intense services for intact families was circulated by DCFS. Again, this proposal was met with resistance on the part of some advocates and agencies, in part because it represented a further "watering down" of the idea of intensive efforts to prevent placement. The proposal was not adopted.

The proposed shifts of resources to less intensive programs could be seen as efforts to enhance the range of service options available to families. These changes were also consistent with an argument in the department's B. H. implementation plan that the heavy investment in the relatively few families served by Family First was inequitable and should be spread around to more families. The changes in the Family First program were characterized as "midcourse corrections" by DCFS administrators and could be thought of as part of the natural evolution of a new program. However, private agencies and their workers experienced the changes (both real and rumored) as disruptive and destabilizing. Staff who had been hired for one purpose were now being asked to shift to other responsibilities or were being asked to work in more than one program. Some agencies experienced considerable financial stress as they attempted to meet shifting expectations while often coping with fewer referrals than were called for in their contracts. A few agencies found it necessary to lower their personnel requirements, accepting staff with B.A.s where previously they would have insisted on M.A.s. Other agencies reported that the development of several different programs within Family First strained their capacity to manage.

The department continued its plans to utilize Medicaid funds to support departmental activities, particularly Family First. The department wanted to use the Medicaid Rehabilitation Option, which requires that agencies be certified as Medicaid providers and that they adhere to certain procedures and billing practices. These requirements were new to the agencies and again, some resisted, in some instances claiming that the process would distort service provision. Furthermore, field tests indicated that medicaid billing might decrease payments to the agencies. Implementation of Medicaid funding for Family First was put on hold.

Toward the end of the year, the department decided to attempt to change the broad mandate of the Illinois Family Preservation Act, the legislation under which Family First operates. The Illinois Family Preservation Act of 1988 required that by January 1, 1993, these services be available to virtually all families in which an allegation of abuse or neglect has been indicated. The proposed change was in keeping with an effort by Governor Edgar to eliminate a number of other legal mandates for state services. The private sector vehemently objected to the proposed demandating of family preservation services, fearing that the department would then have carte blanche to eliminate or drastically alter these services. Further, they felt that demandating would reduce the pressure on the department to expand the availability of these services. As the legislative session drew to a close, a compromise was reached under which the date for full implementation of the mandate was delayed until July 1, 1995, with the understanding that the intervening time would be used to reshape the Family First program.

JULY 1992 TO THE PRESENT

The legislature was quite specific in its cutting of the 1993 DCFS budget: The reductions were to be concentrated in personnel costs. A total of 365 positions had to be eliminated primarily from the management ranks (including 50 management positions that had been eliminated in the governor's original budget). In August 1992, Director Sue Suter resigned, saying that she could not in conscience proceed with layoffs of that magnitude. Sterling Ryder was named acting director. The governor considered several possible appointees before Ryder was appointed as permanent director in the spring of 1993. Planning for the layoffs proceeded. The plan involved a reorganization of the eleven DCFS regions into four. Implementation of the personnel cuts was delayed because approval of the reorganization by the state's Central Management Service was required and because of the need for consultations with the staff union. Because of provisions for "bumping" (the provision in union contracts allowing persons in eliminated positions to take another job in the department) many people other than those in positions targeted for elimination were affected. The result was a considerable sense of turmoil in the organization and decision-making in a number of areas was disrupted.

In the spring of 1993, a substantial backlash against family preservation developed in Illinois. Participants in the attack included newspapers, state legislators, a congressman, and the Cook County public guardian, whose office is responsible for providing guardians ad litem for children in the Cook County Juvenile Court. The attack was precipitated by the deaths of several children in families who had been involved with the state. Some of these families had participated in the family preservation program. Critics pointed to what they believed were mistakes made by DCFS and the courts, mistakes such as leaving children with parents who were clearly abusive or returning children to homes that were unsafe. The results of our evaluation of the family preservation program (evidence that the program had failed to prevent substantial numbers of placements) were used to bolster the attack. The attack reached a crescendo following the death of Joseph Wallace, a 3-year-old whose mother allegedly hung him. Joseph had been placed in foster care and returned home three times, despite his mother's history of mental health problems. Blame for the situation was spread widely: to the state child welfare agency, the judge who returned the child home, the Public Guardian's Office, and others who had been involved in the case. It should be noted that the Wallace family was not involved in the Family First program.

Critics have alleged that the causes of such tragedies include the "policy of family preservation" (columnists often display their dismay at the idea by putting it in quotes) and federal legislation requiring that policy has been ridiculed. These critics claim that the idea of family preservation has been allowed to supersede the best interests of the child. Furthermore, it is claimed that family preservation programs "reward" families for their abuse of children. The response has been that common reaction to things gone wrong in our society: The laws must be changed. Late in 1993 the governor of Illinois signed a bill that sprinkles the phrase "best interests of the minor" throughout the Juvenile Court Act and efforts were made to require court approval of the provision of family preservation services to parents who have seriously abused their children.

The rush to legislative remedies recalls the old truism that extreme cases make bad law. We are witnessing another example of policy being driven by sensational cases. These legislative actions clearly ignore certain realities. Responsible child welfare professionals have always considered the best interests of the child to be preeminent (all of the RFPs issued by DCFS for Family First services have emphasized this idea). The preservation of families whenever possible is thought to be best for children. Further, no matter what laws are passed, some children will be killed at the hands of their parents. No society can monitor the workings of all its families and no legislation can completely eliminate bureaucratic or judicial errors in the cases of families who come to the attention of the child welfare system. Court review of services will further clog already overtaxed courts. And although mistakes are clearly made in the referral of cases to family preservation programs, there is no evidence that judicial review will improve such decisions. It is noteworthy that the Wallace case was reviewed several times by the courts.

Nonetheless, it must be noted that the experience in Illinois points up one fact about family preservation services that is often ignored by their advocates. These services are not perfect and insofar as children in families provided these services are at risk, leaving them in their homes will result in an increased likelihood of harms, including death (Gelles 1993). This is an inescapable result of the attempt to find a new balance between protecting the child from harm and maintaining the integrity of the family. This may seem to be in conflict with our suggestion that many families that are not at imminent risk of having a child placed (because there is not risk of serious harm) are referred to these programs. Of course, it is possible that both are true—most families are not at imminent risk but a few errors are made in referring cases in which serious harm ensues. Furthermore, there is the problem of the uncertainty of prediction. Things do change. Cases that appear to be quite "nonserious" can deteriorate quickly. And sometimes children can be protected in families in which serious harm has occurred in the past.

As for the future of Family First, it is clear that changes will be made, but it is not clear at this writing what they will be. The governor has appointed still another task force on family preservation in response to the legislative demands for change. In Chicago, DCFS is experimenting with a major change in the program. It has awarded a small number of contracts for Homebuilders-type programs and a larger number of contracts for longer term, less intensive, family preservation efforts with caseloads of 20. The reunification program is also due for change. The moderate-intensity reunification program has been largely abandoned, except in a few areas in which it seems to have been successfully implemented. Consideration is being given to reunifying some children without much preparation but with extensive monitoring of the family following reunification. Meanwhile, the impatience of many private sector providers is growing in the face of indecision on the part of DCFS. At least two have withdrawn from the Family First program.

Rather remarkably, given the atmosphere in Illinois, state appropriations for family preservation services have been maintained. Part of the reason for this is the B. H. consent decree, which requires a substantially increased investment in services. However, the program is bound to be affected by the intense publicity around child injuries and deaths and by legislative actions. Already there is evidence that judges, guardians ad litem, and social workers are more likely to take custody of children and more reluctant to return children home from foster care. Workers are being asked by lawyers and judges to "guarantee" the safety of children before they are returned home, a guarantee that is obviously impossible. In the last few months the foster care rolls have mushroomed. No doubt the system will find ways to live with the increasingly restrictive legislation. The system has a remarkable capacity to make use of ambiguities in law and regulation to adjust to pressures. Nonetheless, it is evident that the idea of family preservation has suffered a substantial setback in Illinois. It remains to be seen whether other states will have similar experiences.

Chapter 9

What We Have Learned—Directions
for Reform in Child Welfare

The message of this chapter is one of caution but not despair. Family First was an ambitious effort to combat the rising numbers of children in foster care, a problem that plagues child welfare systems nationwide. The state must be applauded for making this significant effort. It must also be applauded for insisting on a rigorous evaluation of the program. Family First made the lives of many families better through the provision of many needed services although those services do not appear to have had a significant effect on the likelihood of further harm to children or placement in substitute care.

THE OUTCOMES OF FAMILY FIRST

Data on the outcomes of Family First come from an experiment in which cases were randomly assigned to Family First or to the regular services of the DCFS. The experiment was conducted over a two-year period in six regions of the state: two in Cook County and four downstate.[1] The experiment is the largest randomized experiment on family preservation services conducted to date, involving almost 1,600 families (995 in Family First and 569 in regular services). Data are available on most of these cases on harm to children following referral to the experiment, placement in substitute care, and case closing. A substudy involving interviews with both Family First and regular services families was conducted with a sample of cases in three experimental areas. This substudy provides data on family functioning and levels of family problems at various points in time.

The central objective of family preservation programs and therefore the first concern in evaluations of these programs has been the prevention of placement in out-of-home care. Overall, we find little evidence that the Family First program has resulted in lower placement rates. In fact, families in Family First experienced placement of children at a slightly higher rate than those in the regular services group, a difference that disappears when case characteristics are taken into account. We also find no evidence that Family First resulted in lower risk of subsequent harm to children or in faster case closing in the public child welfare agency. When placement of children did occur, there was no difference between Family First and regular services in the length of placement or in the type of placement (that is, whether the placement was in the home of a relative).

There is evidence that some cases served in Family First would not have been opened in DCFS had Family First not been available. All of the Family First cases were opened, while 20% of the cases assigned to regular services were not. Since the cases were randomly assigned, it is likely that roughly the same proportion of Family First cases would not have been opened if the program were not available. The extent to which this occurred varied considerably among the sites. These results suggest the presence of a case finding or net widening effect of the program, an effect also found in some other social programs, for example, diversion programs in juvenile justice (Ezell 1989; Blomberg 1977, 1983).

While we found little difference between the Family First and regular services groups in rates of placement, in our view the more important finding is the low rates of placement in both groups. The risk of placement in the regular services group in the first month was about 7%, in three months, 13%, and after one year, about 21%. Since families were randomly assigned to both groups, it is evident that many, if not most, of the families receiving Family First services did not have a child at "imminent risk of placement." The results are consistent with findings from informal interviews with investigative staff responsible for referral decisions and interviews with staff of provider agencies. In these interviews we were frequently told that many of the families in the program were not at immediate risk of having a child placed. This "targeting problem" is a problem that has beset family preservation efforts in other states as well. The problem of targeting is not a new issue in social programs. We return to it below.

In our interviews with parents, we found evidence of some differences between Family First and regular services groups. In each of three waves of interviews in Chicago East, we found differences favoring the Family First group in one of the eight domains of functioning we examined; however, these improvements were not stable over time. Family First clients reported fewer problems in housing at the first interview, fewer problems in physical child care at the second interview, and fewer problems in children's academic adjustment in the third interview. An analysis of change over time indicated that the proportion of problems reported in children's academic adjustment in Chicago East tended to decrease over time in Family First cases, while it increased among regular services cases. In Lake Villa/Waukegan and Peoria, differences over time favoring the Family First group were found in one or two of the domains, but these effects were modest and short-lived. Overall, the program had no significant impact on parents' feelings of self-efficacy or on the availability of informal social support. Improvements in the receipt of informal support were quite limited and disappeared over time. The program had no lasting effects on the use of formal services.

We have found little effect of the Family First program on placement, subsequent maltreatment, and rate of case closing, and we have found that effects on family functioning are probably relatively limited. Nonetheless, we do not believe that these results need be taken as indicating that the efforts of the program were wasted. Many families received needed assistance with concrete needs and many parents were helped to learn better ways of relating to their children. In our interviews with families, those who had received Family First services expressed considerable appreciation for the services they were offered. In addition, there may have been effects of the service that we did not measure.

Our findings are similar in many respects to those of the controlled studies reviewed in Chapter 2. While results have varied across studies, most have shown that the risk of placement among family preservation clients was low to begin with, indicating problems in targeting, and that intensive, in-home services programs have not produced overall reductions in placement. The few studies that have examined program effects on the recurrence of child maltreatment have not found significant effects (Jones 1985; McDonald and Associates 1990). The finding that family preservation programs have modest, short-term effects on child and family functioning is supported by Feldman (1991) and Meezan and McCroskey (1993).

What Do the Findings Mean?

It is clear that the Family First program did not achieve the objectives set out for it. The question now is: What broader lessons can be learned from this experience? To what extent can these findings be generalized?

Findings of no or minimal effects of a program may have many possible explanations (Suchman 1967:144). Such a result many indicate that the program theory is defective, that it is not possible to achieve the desired objectives with the activities prescribed in the theory. Alternatively, the result may be due to the poor implementation of a good idea. Still another possible explanation of null results is that the research was flawed; for example, it was badly designed, the design had low statistical power, or there was too much error in the measurement of critical variables.

The hypothesis of poor implementation has been invoked with particular vigor by some observers of the results of the Illinois program. In Illinois the family preservation program was implemented through some sixty private agencies throughout the state. Although broad guidelines were established by the state (services of not more than 90 days, small caseloads, etc.) the agencies had considerable latitude in developing their programs. Question has been raised as to how good most of these programs were, given the lack of state guidance and oversight. Concern has been expressed about the adequacy of training of workers in the program.[2] Finally, criticism has been leveled at the state for failing to adopt a consistent and well-formulated model of practice, a model such as Homebuilders.

It is clear that our results must be taken as an assessment of a general approach to the prevention of foster care placement rather than an evaluation of a specific technology. The general approach was an implementation strategy that permitted (in fact, encouraged) variability. The wisdom of that strategy can be debated. On the one hand, it seems reasonable to argue that the state should have control over the services for which it contracts and should do everything possible to assure the highest possible quality in those services. On the other hand, no one "model" of family preservation has been proven to be superior to all others, so it seems reasonable to experiment with several and try to learn from that variation.

It is evident that the state could have done better in at least some respects. Program monitoring could have been more uniform (it varied throughout the state), even though a single model of service was not being employed. Programs like this can always use more training. There could have been more sustained attention to certain conundrums of service identified by workers, for example, the problems of dealing with substance abuse. And the state might have made greater attempts to deal with the problem of targeting.

Thus the focus of conclusions to be drawn could be on the failure of the state to properly implement a promising intervention, on the importance of adopting well-defined models of service, and on the need to maintain control over the implementation of those models. These are familiar lessons in the history of experimentation with social programs. But we believe the lessons of the Illinois experience go further than that.

At a minimum, the experience demonstrates the considerable difficulty in implementing programs of this kind: They take enormous resources, sustained effort, and great imagination to solve the myriad problems that arise in implementation. But beyond that, it is evident that in the assessment of social program implementation certain realities must be taken into account. Programs never implement models perfectly—the real world intervenes. They adjust to local conditions and change over time. "Model slippage" occurs, despite the best training and retraining efforts. Workers may not be as talented as the model requires. These problems increase when programs are "taken to scale," when they are implemented on a large scale, for example, statewide (Rossi and Freeman 1993:190). The available technology may simply be inadequate in the face of the problems it is expected to solve. Other states may well be able to do better but even heroic efforts are likely to fall short. Hence, the experience in Illinois may well be representative of what can be expected when we try to implement large-scale family preservation programs. At the risk of appearing overly idealistic, we suggest that truly useful program ideas should be those that are "robust" for variations in implementation. That is, a program model should work even if it is not implemented exactly as prescribed. Obviously there are limits to the violations that can be tolerated, but a program model that demands exact adherence is unlikely to succeed. It should not take an ideally implemented program to produce positive results.

It should be noted that in the Illinois program, although there was variation in the character of the work from agency to agency, the basic elements of the original plan for the program were by and large implemented. Services were much more intensive than those usually available to child welfare clients. Families were usually seen relatively quickly after referral, contact during the service period was frequent (though it varied among agencies), and, although they varied somewhat, caseloads were kept small. Families received many services that would not have been available in the absence of the program.

Targeting

As noted above, there is substantial evidence that the Family First program was delivered to many families for which it was not intended, families in which there was not an "imminent risk of placement."[3] What are the sources of the targeting problem? It is tempting to blame it on poor implementation of the program, inadequate training or supervision, incompetence of referring workers, or a desire by workers to frustrate the policymakers. However, we believe that the reasons for the problem are more complex.

The Meaning of "Imminent Risk of Placement."   To begin, there are problems with the phrase used to define the target group for family preservation programs: cases in which there is an "imminent risk of placement" (Berry 1991). While it is not unusual for criteria for social programs to be somewhat vague, this one is particularly ambiguous. All three of the operative words in this phrase are subject to multiple interpretations. *Imminent* is a term that conveys a sense of immediacy, but how imminent is left to judgment. *Risk* implies a prediction of the future, presumably a prediction of some behavior, but the prediction of human behavior is a notoriously uncertain matter. While *placement* may seem relatively unambiguous, it too may be interpreted in various ways. Is care by a relative a placement? Does placement imply involvement of a court or payment by the state? What about informal arrangements that do not involve the courts or foster care payment by the state?

The phrase *risk of placement* is problematic for other reasons as well. Why is the term *risk* used at all? After all, the person making the determination of "imminent risk of placement" usually must also make the decision on whether placement is needed now. Why not simply make that decision, then follow it with a decision as to whether the child is likely to be safe if the family is referred to family preservation?

All of the confusions around the phrase "imminent risk of placement" could be avoided by replacing it with a somewhat simpler and less ambiguous criterion such as "immediate placement is necessary unless family preservation services are begun immediately." Such a criterion would likely arouse considerable resistance since important interests are served in maintaining the ambiguity of the criterion. Ambiguity allows for more discretion in decision-making and gives workers greater latitude in referring cases they believe will benefit from the service. But the cost of the vagueness is increased referrals of cases in which placement would not occur and increased likelihood of disappointing evaluation results.

The "Placement Bias."   There are other sources of the targeting problem. No one claims that all cases in which placement occurs are suitable for family preservation services. Some cases involve continuing and immediate risks of severe harm to children such that chances cannot be taken. This is recognized by adding to the criterion "imminent risk of placement" the phrase "and can be protected if family preservation services are provided." The development of large-scale family preservation programs is based on the assumption that there are a large number of cases in that category. Part of the reason for believing the group is large is an assumption that there is a bias in the system in favor of placing children. Unfortunately there are no adequate estimates of the size of the group in which placement could be prevented with the provision of services. We believe that this group may be smaller than is often supposed. Proponents of social programs often overestimate the applicability of programs and thus the size of the target group (Rossi and Freeman 1993:63).[4]

Of course, mistakes are made in the decision to take placement. Mistakes are also made in the other direction: Children are sometimes left at home when they should be taken into custody, and serious harm ensues. It is these cases that are often sensationalized by the media. But the assumption that there is a bias in favor of placement may be incorrect.[5] It is possible that in most cases of placement, no services would adequately control the risk to children, at least no services short of virtually constant monitoring. Many investigative workers believe that even before family preservation programs were instituted they were preserving families whenever possible. Alternatively, it may be that the problem of "overplacement" is limited to certain jurisdictions, those with investigators, state's attorneys, or judges with a bias toward placement.

It has been suggested that the large number of cases in which children are returned home shortly after placement "proves" that there are many cases in which placement could have been prevented, presumably because this indicates that either a mistake was made or the family quickly changed for the better. We think otherwise. Short-term placements are sometimes beneficial, despite the wrenching experience they often entail for children and families. Sometimes a short-term placement enables a family, perhaps with help from the child welfare system, to change in ways that would otherwise have been unlikely. In other cases, a very severe risk may dissipate quickly, as when an abusive caretaker is no longer in the home. It has also been suggested that the variation among states in placement rates demonstrates that in some states there must be a bias in favor of placement. Unfortunately, as the discussion in Chapter 1 suggests, the data on placement rates in various states are not adequate to reach that conclusion. In particular, the definition of placement varies from state to state.

Finally, it has been suggested that results such as ours indicate an inability on the part of workers to adequately assess risk of placement. We think this notion misses the mark. Our interviews with referring workers indicate that when they refer cases to family preservation they often know that there is little risk of placement, at least in the short term. Rather, referrals are made because of the belief that the programs will benefit the clients.

Other Referral Criteria.   There are usually other, at least implicit criteria for referral to family preservation programs. A common criterion is that the family be willing to participate in services. Again, this criterion is a bit vague and subject to many interpretations, which are more or less restrictive. But again the question of how many families fit the criterion is relevant. Motivation for making use of help is a major part of the decision as to whether to place the child. So it has been suggested that any family that meets the requirements for referral to family preservation would not have a child placed anyway.

Creaming. The fact that relatively few cases in which there is an imminent risk of placement are referred to family preservation programs is taken by some as evidence of creaming. "Creaming," the acceptance into a program of persons who are relatively well off or most likely to benefit from the program, has been observed in a number of social programs (Rossi and Freeman 1993:177). We believe that it is an oversimplification to attribute creaming to most family preservation programs. There is evidence that the families served, while not at risk of having a child immediately placed, are generally quite troubled and in great need of help. Many have received considerable benefit, though the benefit does not show up in reduced likelihood of placement because that likelihood was low at the outset.

Limitations in Targeting Effectiveness. Of course, one of the ways to solve the targeting problem is to specify those groups of cases that programs are likely to benefit. Unfortunately, in our study we did not find evidence of substantial benefits for particular groups of families. Instead of specifying particular groups on whom to focus the program, we suggest here some different approaches to targeting.

The targeting of a program may be based on perceived need for services or on presumed benefit. The target groups that are defined by these two principles are by no means the same. Persons with great need may or may not benefit from the provision of service and those who benefit most from a service may not be those in greatest need. Those who determine social policy have a great urge to target those people who have the greatest problems, who are worse off, or who are costing the state the most money. Such targeting may also be justified on equity grounds. But these people may be those least likely to benefit from our efforts to help. The idea of triaging in the response to medical emergencies is relevant here: Cases that are very serious are considered hopeless so that services provided to them would be wasted (although minimal services may be provided to reduce suffering). Very mild cases are also treated in a minimal way since they are not likely to experience lasting disability in the absence of treatment. Cases in the middle are presumed to be able to make the most of service. The identification of this middle group is then the task of targeting.

In programs that are aimed at the alleviation of social problems, effective targeting depends on the provision of service to a group of people who are likely to benefit from the service. But programs are usually provided to at least some people who do not receive the intended benefit (though they may benefit in other ways). Such people fall in three groups: those who do not have the problem for which the program was designed, those who have the problem but who will get better even if they do not receive the service, and those who have the problem, receive the service, and do not get better. The major task for targeting technology is to find ways to identify cases that have the problem and will get better if they are given the service but would not get better without the service. The problem in family preservation targeting has been the inclusion of a large number of cases that do not have the problem (of imminent risk of placement).

There are a number of possible targeting strategies. We have mentioned two above: worst-case targeting and triaging. Targeting can be either inclusive or selective, broad or focused. Two concepts may be used in considering the problem of targeting: problem impact and targeting efficiency (Schuerman 1993). Problem impact is the number of cases that benefit from a program (as a proportion of the number of cases that have the problem) and targeting efficiency is the proportion of cases receiving the service who benefit.[6] It is of interest that these two ratios are somewhat independent: One can have a relatively large problem impact with low targeting efficiency by targeting very broadly. Vaccination programs are an example. Alternatively, one could target narrowly, achieving high target efficiency, and have little overall impact on the problem. Obviously, one could also have both low target efficiency and low problem impact.[7]

In programs like family preservation, it would be desirable to maximize both targeting efficiency and problem impact. However, there are likely to be limitations on the extent to which this ideal can be achieved. There are always pressures to expand or shift the target group of a program. Some of these pressures are political, arising out of the need to gain the support of diverse constituencies, but others are experienced in the field. Workers often encounter cases that they believe would benefit from a program even though the cases do not fit the criteria for referral. The criteria can always be stretched to accommodate those cases (social programs nearly always have at least one vague criterion that invites the use of judgment). To the extent that the target group is broadened, targeting efficiency is likely to suffer, since those in the broadened group are less likely to have the problem for which the program was designed. Sometimes the target group is subtly shifted away from that originally specified, as opposed to just being broadened (we have suggested that may have happened in the case of family preservation programs; see Littell et al. 1993). To the extent that the target group is shifted, problem impact will suffer.

Another part of the targeting problem lies in the process of reaching decisions to refer cases. Referral agents are usually found in public child welfare agencies and face significant problems in doing their jobs. These workers are often inadequately trained, have caseloads that are too large, and must make decisions based on little contact with families. These are at least theoretically solvable problems, but beyond them is a deeper difficulty: Information needed to make good referral decisions is often not available at the time the decisions must be made. This is due not just to the fact that there is insufficient time to get to know the family. The problem is that it is often not possible to determine how well a family will respond to service efforts until such efforts are begun. Significant factors in service outcome, for example, the motivation of the family to change, may not be determinable, even in the best circumstances, at the time a referral decision is made. Information on these factors emerges in the course of service, rather than being evident at referral. Insofar as this is the case, it constitutes an inherent limitation on targeting technology. These problems limit the extent to which we can identify cases that will not get better without the service but will get better with it. It is likely that these difficulties will have greater relative impact in large programs compared to small programs because of the greater difficulty in maintaining control of an ambiguous referral process in large programs.

We believe that the targeting of programs like Family First can be improved. Lower caseloads and better training would enable referring workers to better understand the problems their clients face and thus lead to better referral decisions. It is hoped that further research will lead to greater understanding of the characteristics of those who are likely to benefit from these programs. But as we have suggested, there are likely to continue to be limitations on targeting effectiveness.

The Limited Orbit of Most Family Preservation Programs

One limitation on the effectiveness of family preservation programs in reducing the numbers of children in foster care is the fact that many receive referrals from only one of the "stages" of child welfare cases: the investigative stage. That is, many, if not most programs seek to prevent the placement of children from families that are being investigated for a recent incident of abuse or neglect. However, a significant number of children are taken into care in the course of service to open cases, cases in which abuse or neglect may have occurred some time ago. In these cases, placement occurs because of a subsequent incident of harm or because conditions of risk have not improved sufficiently or have gotten worse. Still other placements occur for reasons other than abuse or neglect, including "dependency" (the unavailability or inability of parents to provide for their children) or adolescent incorrigibility. It is quite reasonable to limit the scope of referrals to family preservation programs, since to broaden it would weaken program focus and risk trying to be all things to all families. But it must be recognized that this limits the effect of the programs on placement caseloads.

Problems Arising from the Context of Family Preservation Programs

The success of family preservation programs appears to be very much conditioned on aspects of the environment in which they are implemented. Unfortunately, such contextual factors are often not taken into account in planning for implementation. Most programs depend on referrals to other services, services that are sometimes nonexistent or inadequate. We have often heard from workers about the unavailability of drug treatment, housing services, day care, etc.

We believe that a significant problem in the implementation of the Family First program was lack of adequate follow-up. The short-term, intensive services of the program must often be followed by continued attention to the needs of these families, an issue that has often been ignored in previous evaluations of similar programs. While DCFS made provision for ongoing services in those cases in which it was needed, we found that such provision was often haphazard and inadequate. Often, plans were made to transfer cases back to DCFS at the end of Family First for ongoing services or monitoring but the transfer was delayed because of caseload or other problems in DCFS. We believe the matter of aftercare is an area needing particular attention; there is relatively little theory to guide practice in this area.

The Overselling of Family Preservation

During the buildup of family preservation programs extensive claims have been made by advocates: Substantial numbers of placements will be prevented at little risk to children with benefits to the children in maintenance of familial bonds and substantial, if not enormous savings in foster care costs (Edna McConnell Clark Foundation 1990).[8] In part, the claims seem to have been motivated by political considerations, to obtain the support of legislatures. Some original supporters of the Illinois family preservation program have admitted to us that they did not really think that the program would have major placement prevention effects but that the claims had to be made in order to get the program passed by the Illinois legislature. For others, the claims of benefits appear to have been simply an excess of zeal. In any event, as has too often been the case in the selling of social programs, expectations were too high (Howard 1992). These expectations must now be tempered in light of this and other evaluations.

THE PRESENT AND FUTURE OF CHILD WELFARE

Many observers have declared that the child welfare system in the United States is in disarray. It is a system with impossibly high expectations: to solve major social problems by responding to individual cases. The technology for that response is underdeveloped and unable to meet the demands placed on it. The expectations are not only high, they are conflicting: We must protect children and preserve families and do it all with less money. And the major new development in the last twenty years, family preservation, appears to have come up short.

So what is to be done? Solutions to the problem of abuse and neglect will not come easily. It could be claimed that nothing less than massive reform of societal structures will do: alterations of basic relationships in society, together with major shifts in cultural values regarding responsibilities that we have for each other. But however desirable, that is unlikely to be achievable, at least in the near future, so we are left to devise more incremental approaches—meliorations (some would say mere palliatives).

Our incremental approaches must be based on a set of principles and on a thoroughgoing understanding of limitations. They must also deal with a set of core issues in the field. We begin with a discussion of these issues.

Core Issues

Social Conditions. Probably the most significant limitation on reform is that created by social conditions. Poverty, racism, inadequate housing, drug abuse, poor education, community violence, and poor prospects for achieving personal goals form a constellation of interrelated social conditions that severely limit the impact of any reforms in the child welfare system itself. Not all poor families abuse their children but abuse and neglect are found disproportionately in poor families. In families with fragile relationships, poverty is an extreme and chronic stress that increases the likelihood of child maltreatment. Family preservation is often expected to solve major social problems one case at a time. Significant improvements in such things as placement rates will depend on improvements in broader social conditions, conditions that are outside the purview of the child welfare system, at least as that system is currently constituted.

Time Horizons. A central issue in the consideration of reforms has to do with time horizons: whether we take a short- or long-term view. This may be considered at both the family and the system level. As for families, do we seek long-term solutions for individual families or will we be satisfied with temporary improvement in their situations? The impulse is to find long-term solutions, to fix families so that they will not trouble the state in the future. The problem is that we lack technology to reliably effect long-term solutions. Hence, we would put the emphasis on relatively short-term approaches, recognizing that this is less than totally satisfying since it means that the child welfare system or other systems of social support are likely to encounter these families repeatedly. In those cases in which substantial long-term change is possible, help to achieve it should be available.

Either a short- or long-term view can be taken with regard to system changes as well. The usual approach is short term, finding ways to deal with immediate fiscal pressures or with the latest child death splashed across the headlines. Here we hope for a longer-term view, a significant reform of the system having long-range implications. In most states, such a reform will require a substantial increase in resources devoted to child welfare.

The Protective vs. Treatment Functions. The tension between the values of protecting children from harm and respecting the integrity of the family results in a tension between protective and treatment functions of service. This tension is seen most clearly during the investigation of an allegation of harm to a child. To what extent should the activities of the investigative worker be directed at determining guilt and level of risk as opposed to determining what should be done to help the family? Some may hope that these are not opposing objectives, but in practice they are. The tension is often expressed in terms of the difference between a "social work" and a "police" approach to investigation of harm, and often both social workers and individuals with backgrounds in law enforcement are involved in the work. In most jurisdictions today the emphasis is on investigation, although workers may be urged to provide services (usually through referrals). Service delivery is clearly secondary.

While the tension between investigation and helping is clearest in the investigation of possible harm, it may occur throughout services to a case. Workers who provide services must monitor conditions in the home while trying to help. To the extent that workers are expected to detect harm or risk of harm, their effectiveness as helpers may be hampered.

Treatment vs. Prevention.   The extent to which reliance is put on prevention of harm as opposed to treatment of families in which harm has already occurred is a central issue for the child welfare reformer. The sentiment in most fields leans to prevention. It is clearly better to keep something bad from happening than to deal with it once it has happened. There are a number of possible confusions here. The term *prevention* is used in various ways, including activities that are designed to prevent harm in the first place as well as efforts to prevent recurrence of harm that has already occurred. Here we refer to prevention of harm in the first place.

Prevention may occur on a number of levels. As we have suggested above, broad social conditions contribute to the incidence of abuse and neglect so a major step toward prevention would be to change those social conditions. But prevention is often thought of in a narrower sense: the provision of services to families that are at risk of harming their children. These services are found in many "family support" programs. Such services include visiting new mothers, parent education, support groups, drop-in centers for parents, and efforts to identify parents who are "at risk."[9] So far, evidence of the effects of such preventive efforts is not encouraging: These services may be quite beneficial for parents but there is little evidence that they significantly reduce the incidence of child maltreatment (see Chapter 2). Part of the reason for this may be a targeting problem. By their nature, services to prevent a problem are usually delivered to a range of individuals, many of whom would not have developed the problem in the absence of the service. Family support programs are largely delivered to voluntary clients, those least likely to mistreat their children.

As is evident from the discussion so far, we favor preventive efforts on the grand scale (the elimination of poverty and drugs, the provision of adequate housing for all, the opportunity for education and employment) but we are skeptical about individually oriented prevention programs, at least insofar as they are directed at the prevention of child maltreatment. Family support programs and other child abuse prevention programs are laudable efforts because of the benefits they provide to families. But many of these services should be available to all families who might benefit rather than seeing them as preventing maltreatment.

Fragmentation of Services.   Much has been written about the problem of fragmentation in social services and vast sums have been expended in efforts to combat it. It is the perennial unsolved problem in the field. Child welfare program initiatives usually depend on external service resources, in the community and in other branches of state or local government. These initiatives often founder when resources are not available or when access to them is restricted. The problem is often attributed to lack of coordination, so various coordinating mechanisms are devised. Even when such mechanisms are present, difficulties continue to be encountered in the form of multiple assessments of cases by various providers of service and divergent views of case needs by providers.

In child welfare there are other sources of service fragmentation within the public system. The distinction between in-home and out-of-home services is sharply drawn, giving rise to unnecessary discontinuities in services. Within family preservation programs, the division into placement prevention and reunification programs leads to similar discontinuities. We believe these old distinctions should be rethought. We return to this issue below.

The Limitations of Service Technology. No doubt there are ways to improve the services delivered through programs like Family First but we think that there are likely to be significant limitations in the extent to which they can have effects on outcomes such as placement rates. While these services help some families, their effects are likely to be marginal and short-lived. The dominant influence of broad social conditions has been noted above. The services provided by Family First often came too late. By the time families come to the attention of the child welfare system, dysfunctional patterns of relationship have often become ingrained. Hence, our expectations for these programs must be quite modest. In particular, the effectiveness of counseling services is often limited with involuntary clients. These services depend to at least some extent on involvement of clients in efforts to help them. While a degree of involvement may sometimes be coerced and motivation for improvement may be developed in some clients, there are limits. The technology does not exist to bring about high levels of motivation in all clients. Given the prevalence of substance abuse among clients of child welfare agencies, it is important to note that most available drug treatment programs have limited success (Hubbard et al. 1989).

Housekeeping and Staffing

The reports of commissions, task forces, and investigative committees that are set up when disasters such as the death of a child occur often focus on what might be called "housekeeping" issues. Problems are often attributed to lack of responsiveness (or lack of responsible responsiveness) on the part of the various entities that become involved in cases of abuse or neglect. Often these problems are blamed on lack of coordination and communication. Mechanisms for improved communication and bureaucratic reorganizations are proposed to deal with these difficulties. Large caseloads, lack of adequate personnel to get the job done, and inadequate training and supervision are also often identified as central problems.

As our discussion implies, we believe that the solution to problems in the child welfare system must go beyond these kinds of issues. Nonetheless, solving problems of inadequate communication, coordination, and staffing would substantially improve the responsiveness of child welfare systems. Most systems would benefit from improved computerized databases that are more widely available to those who are involved. As an example, in Illinois, investigations of the death of Joseph Wallace (discussed in Chapter 8) have suggested that the courts should have access to the databases maintained by DCFS and that the computer systems of the courts and the state department be linked. To do this will require solving difficult technical problems, but we suspect that the greater difficulty will be overcoming the desire to protect turf. As to personnel matters, most state child welfare systems operate with too few staff and with staff who have too little training and inadequate supervision. Turnover is often rampant. We can deal better with these problems. What is missing is the will to make the necessary investments.

THE BASIS OF A NEW VISION

Efforts at reform must take into account the issues and limitations identified above. They must also be based on a set of principles. Reform must seek a reasonable balance between safety of the child and maintenance of family ties, recognizing that maintenance of those ties is usually in the best interests of the child if harm can be prevented. But reform must recognize that there can be no guarantees—total avoidance of maltreatment cannot be achieved and risks must be taken as part of any balance.

The Responsibility of the State

The most important requirement in reform is to be clear on the responsibilities of the government. We expect both too little and too much of the state. Too little because government could facilitate resolution of the social problems that contribute to child maltreatment. Too much because the state cannot prevent or even respond to all harms to children. Expectations of the state must reflect the limitations of technology and resources. The expansion of the purview of the child welfare system that has occurred in the last few decades should be stopped and reversed. This requires that lines be carefully drawn between our aspirations and what can be reasonably expected.

It may be useful to distinguish between responsibility for outcomes and responsibility for opportunities (this is similar to the distinction in civil rights law between equal outcomes and equal opportunities). The state cannot accept responsibility for the optimal development of all children. Nor should it even endeavor to assure the "well-being" of all children, given the impossibility of achieving that goal, even if well-being could be adequately defined and measured. On the other hand, the state can be seen as having a responsibility for encouraging the development of opportunities for advancing child development and for reducing as much as possible outright harms to children.

The determination of the responsibilities of the state in dealing with abuse and neglect must begin with a specification of the harms to which it will respond. We suggest that these harms be limited to those involving physical injury to the child, including injuries caused by either abuse or neglect. We would eliminate harms such as educational neglect and all but the most serious emotional neglect. Emotional harms can, of course, have serious effects on the child, on his or her development, and the state should encourage the development of services to help parents better relate to their children. But these services should be voluntary, outside the abuse and neglect response system. The scope of state investigative and coercive action must be limited and it is quite difficult to provide a definition of emotional harm that is both unambiguous and not overly inclusive (nearly all parents have at some time caused mental anguish in their children; for a discussion of efforts to define emotional abuse, see Giovannoni and Becerra 1979).

We suggest that physical injury to the child should be reason for state involvement but of course we do not mean to include all injuries. While we might like parents to abandon all corporal punishment, it is unreasonable to expect that it could be outlawed. And every parent is guilty of minor neglects that may cause minor harm to his or her child. So we must exclude "minor" physical injuries and injuries due to accidents in which neglect is not an issue, recognizing that this requires distinctions that may be fallible.

Another issue here is whether to condition state intervention on actual physical harm to a child or allow for involvement in cases in which there is risk of such harm. Including situations of risk as well as actual harm invites intrusion of the state into many more families, often on the basis of rather flimsy evidence. Again, it courts the operation of unfettered judgment. Nonetheless, we believe that the possibility of state involvement in situations of risk should not be precluded. We suggest that this be done only when there is "high" risk of "serious" harm, recognizing that those qualifiers may be criticized as ineffective hedges rather than substantive restrictions.

The Line Between In-Home and Out-of-Home Services

We believe that the sharp division between the realms of in-home and out-of-home services is not helpful to families and children. The bright line that is drawn when a child is placed in substitute care should be blurred (Fein and Maluccio 1992). Placement of a child is unavoidably disturbing to the child and family but it is made more traumatic by the way the system handles it. We suggest that efforts be made to lessen the sense of trauma that accompanies placement. Where it is appropriate, it would be made clear to all involved that efforts will begin immediately to return the child home. Under this conception, in-home and out-of-home services would constitute a continuum and movement between placement and home would be made easier. Placement should be viewed as a step in the process of helping that need not always indicate failure. Placements are often quite brief, and this should be recognized by emphasizing the anticipation that the child will return home shortly. Placements can often be thought of as respite from caretaking responsibilities and more use should be made of voluntary placements.

Such changes should be accompanied by a broadened view of the idea of permanency planning. At present, permanency planning is interpreted in most instances as placement prevention or reunification, rather than the broader meaning it originally had: the seeking of a permanent living arrangement for a child (Fein and Maluccio 1992).[10] Further, there is often more emphasis on planning than achieving permanency.

Services

We turn now to the matter of services in a reformed child welfare system. Our approach here must recognize that there is little evidence that many of the programs currently being tried have more than minimal effects. In particular, family preservation efforts have not produced the major results that were expected. In our view, this means that we must continue to experiment with service approaches. We believe that family preservation programs should be a part of the service mix in child welfare, but perhaps a smaller part than has sometimes been advocated.

In our view, any reasonable reform of the child welfare system will involve a substantial increase in the volume of services available to families, with perhaps some shifts of resources currently in the system. There should be many more alternatives for families and for workers who are trying to help them. We would begin with an expansion of voluntary, community-based services. In low-income communities, help with housing problems, day care, caretaking respite services, and other supports for parenting is more readily available to families who abuse their children than to those who do not. Often help of this kind is provided too late, after family relationships have deteriorated to the point of child maltreatment. This help should be much more universally available through community-based organizations that are responsive to the needs of their neighborhoods.

Part of the integration of the continuum of in-home and out-of-home services should involve a merging of placement prevention and re-unification efforts. There is much overlap in the kinds of activities and approaches in these programs (there are some differences too, notably the important role of visitation in reunification programs). Merging these programs would permit continuity of care, workers would not necessarily transfer cases to other workers when children are placed. At the very least, such cases would stay in the same program.

Another direction that we believe would be fruitful is the development of smaller, specialized programs for particular client groups. Family preservation programs are usually "generalist" programs requiring agencies to deal with a wide range of issues. As a result, the acquisition of expertise in dealing with particular problems is inhibited. An example of a specialized effort is a program for young, isolated, single parents, focused on parent training but also dealing with other problems this group encounters. Continuity of care ought to be a central feature of these smaller, targeted programs. There are other reasons to resist the urge to mount large-scale undifferentiated programs. Large programs have a high profile and therefore are more vulnerable to attack from detractors in the media and elsewhere. Further, smaller programs are better able to maintain control of the quality of services.

We believe that programs for family preservation should place heavy emphasis on provision of concrete resources for families, the teaching of skills of child rearing, and on resolving issues in the proper care of children. Programs differ a great deal in the extent to which they make use of "counseling" and "therapy." Counseling in which the efforts of parents are supported and in which they are helped to find better ways to relate to their children clearly has a place in the work. But in early efforts with a family we are skeptical of more elaborate forms of therapy in which more extensive changes in personality or familial relationships are sought in an atmosphere of coercion. Such services may be useful for families later when they can be offered on a voluntary basis.

The emphasis in family preservation programs is on short-term intensive work. We believe that short-term intervention is appropriate in many, but not all cases. Some families are able to benefit from this kind of service but others require more extended work. Many cases involve problems that will not be resolved in a short-term service, no matter how intense. Long-term problems tend to take a long time to resolve. Many workers think that drug abuse problems cannot be addressed in short-term programs. The chronic mental illness suffered by some parents often requires long-term treatment. Perhaps in such cases short-term service can be used for assessment purposes, but it ought not be considered to provide solutions. We need a range of service lengths and service intensities available for families. Of perhaps more importance, much more attention needs to be paid to what happens at the end of the program, however long a family has been in it. Whatever the length of service, some families will need continued attention.

CONCLUSION

There have now been a number of well-controlled studies of family preservation. While the results of these studies vary somewhat, they suggest that the effects of these programs in preserving families are likely to be quite limited. A major problem in attaining the placement prevention objective is that of targeting, a problem that we need to understand much better. It is possible that there are inherent limitations in the extent to which programs such as family preservation can be effectively targeted. For some families, the programs do provide important resources and may result in modest benefits in the form of improved family and child functioning but these benefits are likely to be time limited.

We have suggested that reform of the child welfare system will require attention to nearly all aspects of the system. First, expectations of the child welfare system ought to be scaled back—it cannot be expected to prevent all harm to children or to respond to every harm when it occurs. Beyond that, we need attention to the range of services provided in these systems. It is particularly important that we attend again to the foster care system. As family preservation programs have expanded, foster care has become demonized. Many children will continue to depend on foster care and in most states it needs to be improved, through better training and supervision of foster parents and through providing them the resources they need to do their jobs. And we need much more emphasis on permanency, in whatever setting that may be found for a child. More often than we are now prepared to admit, that will mean permanent foster care, and steps must be taken to reduce the inordinate amount of "bouncing" from one home to another.

As we have indicated, we believe that a wide range of service options should be available for families and children. As programs are developed, it will be useful to blur the distinctions between in-home and out-of-home care, to make movement between them somewhat easier. For some families, placement should be viewed as a useful tool to facilitate resolution of family problems that will help the family stay together.

Finally, we return to a theme we have discussed at a number of points: The effectiveness of reforms in the child welfare system will be limited by broad social conditions and the severely depleted communities in which many child welfare clients live. While expectations of the child welfare system should be scaled back, we should renew our expectations that society take responsibility for alleviating those conditions that increase the chance that a child will be harmed.

NOTES

1.   A seventh region was included in the experiment but deleted from the analysis for reasons specified above.

2.   DCFS did invest heavily in training of the private agency workers in the program. Our efforts to assess the quality of this training revealed a mixed bag. Some workers expressed appreciation for the training they received while others were disappointed. A frequent complaint was the lack of training on substance abuse issues.

3.   The problem of targeting has occurred in many other social programs, including family support programs, job placement efforts, and community mental health centers. Many community mental health centers were set up to deal with chronically mentally ill patients released from state mental hospitals but have focused on serving less disabled clients. There are remarkable similarities between the family preservation movement and the movement to substitute home care for nursing home care for the elderly. Early hopes that home care could substantially reduce the need for (and expense of) nursing home care have not been realized. In the large-scale National Channeling Demonstration and other studies it was found that large proportions of individuals referred to home care (on average, about three-fourths) would not have gone into nursing homes in the absence of home care. Weissert's comment on home care might well apply to family preservation: "Few interventions can save money if they give treatment three out of four times to people who do not suffer from the expensive problem that the treatment was supposed to avoid" (1991:69).

4.   This observation is similar to one made by Robert Boruch about the conduct of experiments. Boruch has pointed out that when experiments are

implemented the number of cases that appear to need the service often drops precipitously.

5.   Chapin Hall has undertaken some research to test the assumption that there are large numbers of cases in which placement could be prevented, including a study of the extent to which investigative workers in fact think about placement and family preservation services as alternatives and a study of the accuracy of decisions to place.

6.   Other ratios may also be important, for example, the success rate, which may be defined as the proportion of cases who benefit in the group that receives the service and would not recover spontaneously.

7.   For a discussion of the idea of "coverage efficiency" see Rossi and Freeman (1993:179). Suchman (1967:63) discusses the notion of problem impact.

8.   Claims of cost savings are often based on comparisons of the cost of an episode of family preservation with the cost of a year in foster care or with the cost of an average stay in foster care. Such cost comparisons are likely to be misleading for a number of reasons. First, as we have seen, many families referred to these programs do not have children at risk of placement, so for those cases no cost of placement has been forgone. But even if all families in the programs would have had children placed, the distribution of lengths of time that those children would have spent in placement is likely to be different than the distribution for placed children as a whole. In particular, it is likely that they would have, on average, spent less time in care than the overall average. This is because the population of cases served by family preservation programs does not include the most "serious," those likely to have very long periods of foster care. The cost comparisons also do not include an adjustment for the eventual placement of some children in families served in these programs.

9.   A program in Hawaii, called Healthy Start, is often cited as a model for such efforts.

10.   Adoption is also a permanent plan, an element of the child welfare system that we have not considered in this book. Efforts to improve adoption services are clearly needed, including enhanced recruitment of adoptive parents and greater supports for adoptions. But we think it unreasonable to expect adoption to play a much greater role in the system than at present. This is because of a mismatch between the number of children who might be adopted and the number of adoptive parents we can expect to recruit, and a mismatch between the characteristics of children available for adoption and the expectations of prospective adoptive parents. There are far more children available for adoption than there are adoptive parents willing to adopt them.

This raises the issue of termination of parental rights. Some observers have suggested that we should move more aggressively toward the termination of parental rights in those cases in which natural parents are clearly unable or unwilling to provide adequate caretaking, in order to free the child for adoption. We believe that it may often be useful to terminate parental rights to indicate that a decision has been made that the child will not return to his or her natural parents. However, to do this as a step in the direction of adoption is often illusory and holds out false hopes to the child who is unlikely to be adopted.

Appendix A

Summary of Controlled Studies of
Family Preservation Programs

STUDY	Jones, Neuman, and Shyne (1976); Jones (1985)
DESIGN AND SAMPLE SIZE	Families of 525 children were randomly assigned to the program or a control group.
TARGET POPULATION	Cases in which placement was thought to be imminent, families with children in placement, and those in which children had recently been returned home (here we focus only on the first group).
PROGRAM SERVICES	Demonstration services were provided by seven voluntary agencies in New York City (through subcontracts with Special Services for Children), the Monroe County Department of Social Services, and the Westchester County Department of Social Services. Both the program and control groups received traditional child welfare services (including counseling, financial assistance, medical care, family-life education, and day care). Intensive services were provided to cases in the experimental group over approximately 14 months. Caseloads in the experimental group were usually 10 families per worker and the families in this group received significantly more in-person contacts with workers.
OUTCOMES	
Placement	At the end of treatment, placement rates were significantly lower in the experimental group than in the control group (7% vs. 18%). Six months after the termination of services 8% of children in the

program group and 23% of those in the control group had been placed. A follow-up study of a subsample of 243 children in the experiment was conducted five years after the project ended. At that time, 34% of the children in the experimental group and 46% of those in the control group had been placed in foster care, a statistically significant difference. Note that sample loss at the time of the five-year follow-up (less than 50% were followed) limits the usefulness of these data.

Child maltreatment

At the five-year follow-up, 21% of 98 families in the experimental group had experienced one or more indicated reports of child maltreatment, compared with 25% of 44 control group families. The difference between groups was not statistically significant.

Child and family functioning

N/A

Other

N/A

* * * * *

STUDY

Hennepin County Community Services Department (1980)

DESIGN AND SAMPLE SIZE

Random assignment of 138 cases to experimental and control units of the county agency.

TARGET POPULATION

The families served had children under age 15 who "were at risk of placement, but who were judged by intake workers not to be at imminent risk of abuse or neglect" (Stein 1985:116).

PROGRAM SERVICES

Staff in the experimental group carried a maximum caseload of fifteen families, compared to caseloads of 22 to 40 families among workers in the control group. Experimental cases received an average of 40 hours of service, compared with 32 hours for control cases. All agency services were available to families in both groups; specific services provided to families were not described (Stein 1985).

OUTCOMES

Placement

The experimental group had a higher number of children placed in foster care (123 vs. 84 children in the control group); however, the total number of children in each group was not reported (Stein 1985). Of those placed, children in the experimental group spent slightly fewer days in placement (mean of 199 days) than those in the control group (mean of 208 days).

Child maltreatment	N/A
Child and family functioning	N/A
Other	N/A

* * * * *

STUDY	Halper and Jones (1981)
DESIGN AND SAMPLE SIZE	Randomized experiment involving 120 families with 282 children.
TARGET POPULATION	Families with children "at risk of placement."
PROGRAM SERVICES	Services were provided by Special Services for Children, the public child welfare agency in New York City. Families in both the experimental and control groups received counseling, homemakers, day care, and recreational, medical, legal, financial, and family planning services. The primary difference between groups was the intensity of services provided: over a one-year period, families in the experimental group had three times the number of in-person contacts with workers (an average of 39 vs. 13) and almost twelve times the number of telephone contacts (39 vs. 3.4). Project staff also had significantly more contact with collaterals and provided emergency financial assistance, vocational counseling, and housing assistance to families. They carried caseloads of eleven to twelve families, while the average caseload size for workers in the control group was eighteen families.
OUTCOMES	
Placement	During the project, 4% (6) of the 156 children in the experimental group and 17% (22) of 126 in the control group were placed in substitute care (a statistically significant difference).

Child maltreatment	N/A
Child and family functioning	N/A
Other	N/A

*   *   *   *   *

STUDY	Nebraska Department of Public Welfare (1981)
DESIGN AND SAMPLE SIZE	One hundred fifty-three families were randomly assigned to experimental or control groups.
TARGET POPULATION	Families at risk of placement because of actual or suspected child maltreatment.
PROGRAM SERVICES	Services were provided by the public child welfare agency in Nebraska. Workers in the experimental unit spent about 30% of their time in direct contact with clients, while those in the control unit spent about 20% of their time in either in-person or telephone contact with clients. The main difference between these units is that staff in the experimental group were under less time pressure and had more support and direction in decision-making. Information on caseload sizes and specific services provided to experimental and control families was not available (Stein 1985).
OUTCOMES	
Placement	Control cases required more public foster care, compared with experimental cases, which were more likely to be placed with relatives and friends. Although the exact number of children placed is not known, available data show that 4% (3) of 80 families in the experimental group and 11% (8) of 73 families in the control group had one or more children placed in out-of-home care, a nonsignificant difference. Data on informal placements with relatives and friends and on placements outside the project county were not available.
Child maltreatment	N/A
Child and family functioning	N/A

Other   N/A

* * * * *

STUDY   William and DeRubeis (1981)

DESIGN AND   Ninety families were randomly assigned to pro-
SAMPLE SIZE   gram and control groups.

TARGET   Families whose children were thought to be at
POPULATION   "risk of placement within the next two years."

PROGRAM   Services were provided by the Hudson County
SERVICES   (New Jersey) Special Services Project. All families
               received referrals to community mental health, day
               care, family planning, health care, and homemaker
               services. Those in the experimental group had access
               to legal advocacy, group therapy, and emergency fi-
               nancial services and were more likely to be referred
               for employment services, homemaker or teaching
               services, housing services, legal aid, and welfare as-
               sistance. Workers in the experimental group carried
               caseloads of 11 families each; caseload size for the
               control group was not reported (Stein 1985). Families
               in the experimental group received more home visits
               and had more contact with workers in their offices.

OUTCOMES

Placement   At the end of the three-year demonstration pro-
               ject, 24% (11) of families in the program and 18%
               (8) of those in the control group experienced place-
               ment (a nonsignificant difference). Children in the
               control group were more likely to be placed in re-
               strictive settings (such as residential treatment)
               and less likely to be placed with relatives than
               those who received more intensive services. While
               more control group children were returned to their
               families (7 vs. 3), reunification in the control cases
               was described as "unplanned and unsuccessful."

Child   N/A
maltreatment

Child and   N/A
family
functioning

Other   N/A

* * * * *

STUDY   Lyle and Nelson (1983)

DESIGN AND   Random assignment of 74 families to one of three
SAMPLE SIZE   traditional child protection units or an experimen-
                    tal, family-centered, home-based unit.

TARGET   N/A
POPULATION

PROGRAM   Services were provided by the Ramsey County (St.
SERVICES   Paul, Minnesota) child protective services depart-
                    ment. Families served in the home-based services
                    unit received a combination of counseling and
                    concrete services. Families in the control group
                    received traditional case management services.
                    Caseloads in the experimental unit were half the
                    size of those in the traditional units. Cases in all
                    units remained open for approximately 10 to 12
                    months.

OUTCOMES

Placement   Three months after services ended, 33% of families
                    in the experimental group had experienced place-
                    ment of one or more children, compared with 55%
                    of families in the control group. Of the children
                    who were placed, those in the experimental group
                    spent significantly less time in substitute care
                    (Frankel 1988).

Child   N/A
maltreatment

Child and   N/A
family
functioning

Other   N/A

                              *   *   *   *   *

STUDY   Szykula and Fleischman (1985)

DESIGN AND   Randomized experiment with families of 48 chil-
SAMPLE SIZE   dren. Cases were identified as more or less difficult
                    by workers, based on numbers of prior abuse re-
                    ports and types of family problems. Cases within
                    each difficulty group were randomly assigned to
                    program or control services.

TARGET   Clients were parents with children between the
POPULATION   ages of 3 and 12 who were considered at risk of
                    placement due to child abuse and neglect.

PROGRAM
SERVICES

A social learning treatment program was compared with regular child protective services. The program was conducted in the child protective service unit of Cascade County Social Services in Oregon. No data were provided on the type, duration, or intensity of services received by families.

OUTCOMES
Placement

The experimental program appeared to reduce the risk of placement among less difficult cases: 8% (1 of 13) of the children in the less difficult experimental group and 38% (5 of 13) of those in the comparable control group were placed. However, there was no significant difference between program and control groups in placement rates for more difficult cases: 64% (7 of 11) of children in the more difficult experiment group vs. 45% (5 of 11) in the control group. The overall effect of the program (for both groups) was not significant.

Child
maltreatment

N/A

Child and
family
functioning

N/A

Other

N/A

* * * * *

STUDY
DESIGN AND
SAMPLE SIZE

Wood, Barton, and Schroeder (1988)

An overflow comparison study conducted in conjunction with researchers at the University of California at Davis. Of the 50 families referred to the project, 26 received FamiliesFirst services as well as other county services. The remaining 24 families did not receive home-based services because of insufficient space in the program; these families received regular county child protective services.

TARGET
POPULATION

Families were referred to the project by child protective services staff. Eligible families had children who had been abused or neglected and were thought to be at risk of having at least one child placed out of the home. Target children in the in-home services group were somewhat older than those in the comparison group (average of 8.9 years vs. 5.4 years).

PROGRAM
SERVICES

In FamiliesFirst, masters-level therapists provided in-home services over a 4 to 6 week period to a maximum of two families at a time. They provided family therapy, help in practical matters of living, and liaison work with schools and other community services.

OUTCOMES

Placement

One year after intake, 25% (15) of the 59 children in the in-home services group were placed compared with 53% (26) of 49 children in the comparison group (a statistically significant difference). Children who were the focus of intervention were placed more often than their siblings.

Child
maltreatment

N/A

Child and
family
functioning

N/A

Other

N/A

*   *   *   *   *

STUDY

Mitchell, Tovar, and Knitzer (1989)

DESIGN AND
SAMPLE SIZE

Twenty-one cases were referred from the city Child Welfare Administration (CWA) and 22 from the Pius XII Court Designated Assessment Service. An overflow comparison group of 12 families was available for the Pius group; one of these 12 families was lost to follow-up.

TARGET
POPULATION

The average age of CWA children was 8.3, of Pius children, 13.3.

PROGRAM
SERVICES

This Bronx program was modeled after Homebuilders. The average length of service was 35 days.

OUTCOMES

Placement

Families in the overflow group had relatively fewer placements than those in the service group. At 3 months, 19% (4 of 21) CWA, 23% (5 of 22) Pius treatment, and 9% (1 of 11) Pius comparison families had experienced a placement. At 12 months, 24% (5) of the CWA, 27% (6) of the Pius treatment, and 18% (2) of the Pius comparison families had experienced placement. Apparently, all children who were placed were still in placement at the end of the one-year follow-up period.

Child
maltreatment   N/A

Child and   N/A
family
functioning

Other   N/A

*   *   *   *   *

STUDY   Schwartz and AuClaire (1989); Schwartz, Au-
                     Claire, and Harris (1991)

DESIGN AND   Nonrandom comparison group. Cases that were
SAMPLE SIZE   approved for placement were recorded on a log.
                     When an opening in the home-based service pro-
                     gram occurred, the log was consulted and the most
                     recent case was referred. If there were no cases
                     available, the next eligible case was referred. Cases
                     not referred to the home-based service were re-
                     ferred for placement services. A random sample of
                     cases, equal in number to those in the home-based
                     service group, was selected from the placement
                     services group as the comparison group. (It is not
                     clear why comparisons were not done with the
                     entire placement services group.) There were 58
                     cases in each group, selected during the period Au-
                     gust through December 1985.

TARGET   The children were at risk of placement for juvenile
POPULATION   offenses, were between 12 and 17 years of age, and
                     had "significant behavioral, family, school, health,
                     and substance abuse problems" (Schwartz, Au-
                     Claire, and Harris 1991:39).

PROGRAM   The program, conducted by the Hennepin County
SERVICES   Child Welfare Division, consisted of intensive
                     home-based services delivered by eight "specially
                     trained social workers." The service was intended
                     to last for four weeks. Workers carried caseloads of
                     two families.

OUTCOMES

Placement   Three of the experimental group cases were in
                     placement during the entire follow-up period and
                     were excluded from outcome analyses. Follow-up

extended until December 31, 1986. The authors believed that since the comparison group was almost
certain to have a placement at the beginning of the
study period (actually, 5 were never placed during
the study period), it would be appropriate to compare their placement experience after that placement with that of the home-based service group.
These "adjusted" comparisons are reported here.
There were 76 placement episodes involving 31
(56%) of the 55 experimental cases and 81 (adjusted) placements involving 34 (59%) of the 58
comparison cases.

Child   N/A
maltreatment

Child and   N/A
family
functioning

Other   N/A

* * * * *

STUDY   Feldman (1990, 1991)

DESIGN AND   One hundred seventeen experimental and 97 con-
SAMPLE SIZE   trol cases were randomly assigned in 4 of New
                   Jersey's 21 counties. Another 33 families were
                   "turned back" after random assignment to the ex-
                   perimental services (because they did not meet se-
                   lection criteria, the caretaker refused to participate
                   in the program, or the children were deemed at
                   imminent risk of harm and were removed from the
                   home); these cases were not included in the analy-
                   sis.

TARGET   Referrals came from local child welfare offices,
POPULATION   county family court or crisis intervention units,
                   and regional community mental health centers.
                   Referrals were reviewed by a local screening body;
                   screening criteria included "risk of placement."
                   Forty-six percent of the cases involved single-
                   parent households. The family preservation group
                   had a higher proportion of white families (51%)
                   than the control group (33%). About 20% of the
                   families in both groups had experienced placement
                   prior to referral. The mean age of "target" children

was 13 years. Reasons for referral were out-of-control behavior among target children (in 60% of the cases); abuse, neglect, or risk of abuse or neglect (25%); emotional disturbance or substance abuse among target children (13%); and emotional or substance abuse problems among parents (2%).

PROGRAM
SERVICES

The Family Preservation Services (FPS) program was modeled after Homebuilders. Services provided by private agencies involved a median of 31 hours of face-to-face contact between families and workers over a median of 6 weeks of service. In the first week of services, families received a mean of 13 hours of direct contact with workers. The median number of total hours of contact (including telephone and collateral contacts) per family was 48 (mean of 58). There were significant differences across sites in duration of services. Concrete services were received by 68% of the families in the experimental group. No information was provided on caseload size. Referring agencies were responsible for determining the kinds of services that were provided to families in the control group. Families in the control group typically received "traditional community services," including less intensive counseling services, referrals to other community resources, youth advocacy services, monitoring by the state child welfare agency, family court interventions, and out-of-home placement. Services received by control group families were thought to be much less intensive than those in family preservation programs, but, unfortunately, there was no systematic data collection on the nature and amounts of services provided to families in the control group. It was suggested that the services provided to control cases were similar to the kinds of follow-up services received by families in the experimental group (after FPS termination).

OUTCOMES

Placement

During the intervention period 17% of the families in the control group experienced placement of at least one target child, compared to 6% of families in the experimental group. At 6 months posttermination, 50% of control group families and 27% of families in the experimental group had experienced at least one placement. At one year posttermination 57% of families in the control group and 43% of those in the experimental group had experienced placement. (Differences between groups were statistically significant at each point in time.) For the first target child to enter placement in each family, there were no significant differences between the experimental and control groups in types of placements, numbers of placements, or duration of time in placement. Family preservation services appeared to result in reduced risk of placement for single-parent families (at one year after termination, 68% of the single-parent families in the control group experienced placement, compared with 49% in the experimental group).

Child maltreatment
N/A

Child and family functioning
Both the treatment and control groups made gains on the Family Environment Scale, Interpersonal Support Evaluation List, and Child Well-Being Scales, but there were few statistically significant differences between groups in the amount of change.

Other
Outcomes examined included changes in perceived social support, goal attainment, and client satisfaction. There were some differences between experimental and control groups in the amount of change in these measures (favoring the experimental group) but these were quite limited.

*   *   *   *   *

STUDY
McDonald and Associates (1990)

DESIGN AND SAMPLE SIZE
Three hundred four families were randomly assigned to family preservation or control groups (each group had 152 cases).

TARGET POPULATION
Families thought to be at imminent risk of placement due to abuse or neglect were referred by county child welfare agencies. The families had an average of 2.4 children whose average age was 6.7 years. Forty-seven percent of the primary caretakers were under 30 years of age; 49% of the families were headed by single parents; 59% were receiving pub-

lic assistance; 34% of the adults had not completed high school; 56% were unemployed. Reasons for referral included physical abuse (43% of the cases), child neglect (33%), sexual abuse (12%), emotional abuse (6%). Sixty-four percent of the families had experienced at least one placement prior to referral.

PROGRAM
SERVICES

Services were provided by private agencies and one public mental health agency in 8 counties in California. On average, the duration between referral and the initiation of services was 7 days. Services lasted an average of 7 weeks. Families received an average of 32 hours of direct contact with workers. (In addition, workers spent an average of 17 hours per case on "collateral services" and 10 hours per case on travel.) Services consisted of assessment, case planning, individual and family counseling, crisis intervention, parenting skills training, and service coordination. Concrete services (e.g., food, clothing, assistance with housing and utilities, and chore services) were provided in less than 10% of the cases. In most cases, services were provided by licensed therapists, although some projects used cotherapists or case aides. Follow-up services were provided by the family preservation projects to 42% of the families. (No data are available on services provided to the control group.)

OUTCOMES

Placement

Twenty percent of control group families and 25% of cases in the experimental group experienced placement within 8 months after random assignment (the difference between groups was not statistically significant). There were no substantial differences in lengths of time in placement or costs of placement. Children in the control group were more likely to be placed with relatives.

Child
maltreatment

Approximately 25% of families in both the program and control groups experienced an investigation of child abuse or neglect within 8 months after referral.

Child and
family
functioning

(Pre- and posttests were conducted with the experimental group only.)

Other

Placement costs for in-home services and control cases were comparable ($141,375 vs. $145,388) for the 152 families in each group. Average cost of providing intensive, home-based services was $4,767 per family served.

* * * * *

STUDY

Pecora, Fraser, and Haapala (1991, 1992)

DESIGN AND SAMPLE SIZE

Four hundred fifty-three Utah and Washington families in intensive home-based services based on the Homebuilders model and 26 families in an overflow comparison group in Utah. A 12 month follow-up was conducted with 263 families.

TARGET POPULATION

The criteria for referral were risk of imminent placement, safety of the child with service, and willingness of at least one parent to cooperate with service. The average age of the oldest child at risk of placement was 12.5.

PROGRAM SERVICES

In Utah a 60-day service model was provided in two sites by the state child welfare department, while in Washington a 30-day model was provided by the Homebuilders program (under contract with the state agency) in four sites. Families in the Utah program received an average of 23 hours of in-person contact with workers; those in the Washington program received 21 hours of in-person contact. Caseloads ranged from 4 to 6 families in Utah, while therapists in Washington carried caseloads of two to three families each (Pecora, Fraser, and Haapala 1992).

OUTCOMES

Placement

Service failure was defined as placement of a child outside the home for two weeks or more in a nonrelative setting during the provision of family preservation services or within 12 months following intake. Runaways were also counted as failures (Pecora,Fraser, and Haapala 1991). At termination, 9% of the 172 Utah children and 6% of the 409 Washington children in the treatment groups had been placed. The figures for the 12-month follow-up were 41% of 97 Utah children and 30% of 245 Washington children. In the Utah comparison group of 27 children, 23 (85%) were placed during the 12-month period.

Child maltreatment	N/A
Child and family functioning	N/A
Other	N/A

* * * * *

STUDY	Meezan and McCroskey (1993)
DESIGN AND SAMPLE SIZE	Two hundred forty families were randomly assigned to in-home services or regular child protective services.
TARGET POPULATION	Referrals were based on "caseworker judgment about need for the services" and were not limited to cases in which children were thought to be at imminent risk of placement.
PROGRAM SERVICES	In-home services were provided by two private child welfare agencies (the Children's Bureau of Southern California and Hathaway Children's Services); the control group received services from the County Department of Children's Services. Over a 3-month service period, families in the in-home services group received significantly more contact with workers than comparison cases (average of 9.6 vs. 4.2 contacts); in-person contacts for the program group were not only more frequent but also longer in duration (William Meezan, personal communication, November 1993).
OUTCOMES	
Placement	Data on placements were available for 231 families. At the beginning of the project 37 (34%) of the 108 families in the program group and 30 (24%) of 123 families in the control group had one or more children in placement. During the project, 19 (6%) of the 335 children in the experimental group were placed, compared with 34 (8%) of 424 children in the comparison group. At the end of the project (12 months after services ended), families in the experimental group had more children in out-of-home

placements than those in the comparison group (38 vs. 24%) (McCroskey and Meezan 1993).

Child maltreatment   N/A

Child and family functioning   Family functioning was measured on six scales: parent-child interactions, living conditions of the family, interactions between caregivers, supports available to parents, financial conditions of the family, and developmental stimulation of children. Families in both groups reported that they did not have significant problems in family functioning at case opening and did not see significant change in these areas at case closing. However, families in the in-home services group reported more improvements in living conditions and financial conditions at one year after termination, compared to controls. Parents in the program group also reported more improvements in their children's behavior between referral and the case closing, although there were no differences between groups one year after services had ended. Workers who provided home-based services reported that the families had significant problems in all areas of family functioning at case opening and made significant improvements in 4 of 6 domains at case closing. (The 4 areas in which improvements were noted were parent-child interactions, living conditions, supports available to families, and developmental stimulation given to children.)

Other   N/A

Appendix B

Selection of Proportional Hazard Models

Hazard models are a group of statistical techniques that are used to examine the effects of several independent variables on the risk (hazard) of the occurrence of an event over time. The hazard rate is the risk (or probability) that an event will occur at a given point in time, given that the event has not already occurred. As an example, in analyses of the risk of placement, the hazard rate is the probability that a family will experience placement at a certain point in time, given that a placement has not already been made in that family. The effects of each of the independent variables in a hazard model are estimated while controlling for the effects of other variables in the model.

The choices of hazard models can be divided into parametric (e.g., exponential, Weibull, Gompertz, and log-logistic) and semiparametric (Cox) models. Parametric hazard models require that one specify the relationship between the hazard and time. Exponential models assume that there is no dependence on time (the hazard is constant over time). In "monotonic" models (e.g., Weibull and Gompertz models) the hazard always increases or decreases over time (the dependent variable is the log of the hazard rate). There are also "nonmonotonic" models (e.g., the log-logistic model), in which the hazard may sometimes increase and sometimes decrease (i.e., the relationship between time and the probability of an event may be curvilinear), but these are difficult to estimate correctly (Allison 1984).

Theory may suggest that the hazard will decrease over time (the longer a case is open the more likely it is that it will stay open). However, it is difficult to distinguish this (time dependence) from the fact that cases most "at risk" (of, say, case closing) "fail" early on, so that the results are affected by selection bias or changes in the composition of the group that is "at risk" at different points in time. Another way to say this is that it is difficult to distinguish time dependence from differences in hazard rates across individuals. (This is not a problem in models that suggest that the hazard increases over time.)

Unlike parametric hazard models, the Kaplan-Meier (or product-limit) estimate of the survivor function (a nonparametric estimate) is not constrained to any particular form and can be compared to the results of hazard models to determine the best-fitting distribution. The goodness-of-fit of a model can be determined by comparing survival curves produced via several parametric hazard models with the Kaplan-Meier estimate of the survival function. The relative "fit" of different models can also be determined by comparing their log-likelihoods,[1] and by examining plots of residuals (i.e., deviations from the model), which should follow a straight line.

The procedure recommended by Allison (1984) for selecting a hazard model is to start with the exponential model; if the exponential model does not fit, monotonic models are tried; then if these do not fit, Allison recommends use of the Cox model, rather than nonmonotonic models. Analysis showed (via residual plots and log-likelihoods) that the parametric models (specifically, the exponential, Weibull, Gompertz, and log-logistic models) did not fit our data on the hazards for subsequent maltreatment, placement, or case closing (e.g., plots of residuals did not form a straight line). Yamaguchi advised us to use the Cox model, because it makes fewer assumptions about the path of the hazard function (Yamaguchi 1991, 1992).

The advantage of the Cox model is that it makes no assumptions about the relationship between time and the hazard rate (a relationship that is often difficult to specify). It does assume that, for any explanatory variable, the ratio between hazard rates for subjects with different values of the variable will be a constant (proportional) over time (thus, the percentage change in the hazard that is associated with a given change in a variable is supposed to be a constant over time).

It appears that we may be violating the proportionality assumption with respect to the experimental group variable in the hazard models on case closing, since the differences between Family First and regular services cases change over time (this is not a problem in the models of subsequent maltreatment or placement). The solution for this (according to Allison) is to develop different models for each subgroup, which we have done. However, this is not very helpful, since we still want to look at the effects of Family First on case closing.

There are several ways (graphical and statistical tests) to check whether the proportionality assumption is violated. The easiest way to test this is to plot the log-minus-log survival function for the two subgroups; these plots should be "roughly parallel" (Allison 1984). Our graphs of the placement and subsequent maltreatment log-minus-log survival functions for Family First and regular services cases show that the plots are not parallel.

Even when the proportionality assumption is violated, the Cox model is often a "satisfactory approximation" (Allison 1984). More problems arise through omission of important explanatory variables, measurement error, and dependence of censoring on other events than from violation of this assumption. Also, the proportionality assumption is always violated whenever time-dependent explanatory variables (e.g., age, duration in care, other variables with values that change over time) are used in the Cox model—and this is acceptable (Allison 1984).

The Cox model is most useful when one is interested primarily in the effects of explanatory variables and not in modeling the relationship between the hazard and time. This is another reason that Yamaguchi gave for using the Cox model in our work.

In the Cox model, the dependent variable is the log of the hazard rate. Thus, interpretation of the coefficients (which are asymptotically normally distributed) is not straightforward. As in logit models, it is useful to transform the coefficients in order to interpret them. We compute the percent change associated with explanatory variables in hazard models as $(\exp (b) - 1) * 100$ (see Blossfeld, Hamerle, and Mayer 1989) and this is the statistic that is reported in our tables (not the coefficient b).

NOTE

1. The log-likelihood is a by-product of maximum likelihood estimation. The procedure for comparing the fit of two models involves computation of twice the positive difference between the log-likelihood statistics associated with each model. The statistic derived from this computation has a Chi-square distribution (the degrees of freedom is the difference between the number of variables included in the two models) and can be used to test the null hypothesis that there are no differences between the two models (Allison 1984).

Appendix C

Estimation of Simultaneous Equations
Using Two-Stage Least Squares

In Chapter 6 we report the results of analyses using simultaneous equations to assess the effects of service characteristics on outcomes. Here, we discuss the rationale for this approach and the application of two-stage least squares techniques in our study.

In Family First, as in most social programs, the nature of services provided to clients depends in part on characteristics of the case. For example, some families are thought to require more intensive services or longer-term intervention than others. The nature of the problems a family presents affects workers' decisions regarding appropriate intervention strategies. The character of service provision also varies by geographic region; these differences appear to be related to variations in demographics, community characteristics, and the availability of resources outside Family First programs. Like service characteristics, case outcomes are affected by characteristics of the case and region. Thus, in order to understand the effects of service characteristics on outcomes, we need to control for other variations at the case and regional level. Ordinarily one might develop regression-type models (e.g., logistic regression or hazard models) in which an outcome measure is regressed on a set of service characteristics, case characteristics, and variables representing different sites. However, relationships between independent variables would cause multicollinearity problems. Further, endogenous variables would be included on both sides of the equation. Since service characteristics are endogenous (i.e., caused by other variables within the model), it is likely that some of the variation in outcome measures that should be attributed to the effects of case characteristics or site differences would be attributed instead to the service variables.

Simultaneous equations are a class of techniques designed to handle models that include endogenous variables on both sides of an equation

Table C.1: Variables in the First Stage of the Simultaneous Equations (Unstandardized Regression Coefficients)

	Family First cases in the experiment				All cases in the experiment		
	Duration of Family First service (natural log)	Hours of contact with caseworkers in the first 90 days (natural log)	Hours of contact with parent aides in the first 90 days (natural log)	Number of concrete services	Hours of contact with caseworkers in the first 90 days (natural log)	Hours of contact with parent aides in the first 90 days (natural log)	Number of concrete services
Case characteristics							
Number of prior reports of child maltreatment	—	.039	—	.201	—	—	.180
Prior physical injury	-.076	—	-.402	—	—	-.252	-.355
Chronic neglect	—	—	—	—	—	—	—
Housing problems	—	.126	—	1.158	.644	.481	1.461
Poverty or resource deficit problems	.114	.190	.345	1.327	—	—	.870
Cocaine problems	—	.094	—	.469	—	—	—
Other drug problems	—	—	—	—	.355	—	—
Alcohol problems	—	—	—	—	—	—	.381

	(1)	(2)	(3)	(4)	(5)	(6)	(7)
Parents' chronic mental illness or emotional problems	.124	.134	—	.493	.431	.298	.698
Marital problems, domestic violence, or un-resolved separation or divorce	—	—	—		.364	—	.468
Child care skill deficits	—	—	.355	—	.139	.485	.503
Children's health, development, or learning problems	—	—	.331	.638	.577	.508	1.01
Teenage caregiver	—	—	—	.838	—	—	—
Single-adult household	.023	—	—	.304	.181	.195	.180
Extended-family household	-.062	—	—	—	-.210	—	—
Protective custody within one year prior to referral	—	—	—	—	.297	—	—
Sites							
Chicago East	.285	-.119	.506	-1.618	-.208	.150	-1.256
Chicago South	.392	.164	1.366	-1.456	.102	.738	-.906
Lake Villa/Waukegan	-.082	-.722	.775	-2.005	-.775	.358	-1.586
Peoria	.036	-.211	1.838	-1.451	-.347	1.045	-1.205
Springfield	.022	-1.141	.239	-3.034	-.724	.292	-1.479
Constant	4.417	3.789	1.031	3.799	2.537	.562	2.102
Adjusted R^2	.072	.213	.114	.194	.116	.071	.162

(see Berry 1984; Pindyck and Rubinfeld 1991). In this approach, a system of equations is developed; this system includes one equation for each of the endogenous variables in the model. In our study, simultaneous equations were developed using two-stage least squares (2SLS) estimation. In the first stage, each of the service characteristics in the model was regressed on a set of exogenous variables (the selection of exogenous variables for these equations is discussed below). In order to avoid multicollinearity, each of the first-stage equations contains a unique combination of exogenous variables, with at least one instrument that does not appear in the second-stage equations. In the second stage, predicted values of service characteristics (derived from the first set of equations) are included as independent variables (instruments) in a set of equations designed to predict case outcomes. Exogenous variables are also included in the second-stage equations. Residuals from the first-stage equations are then used to adjust standard errors in the second stage. In this way, service characteristics are purged of their dependence on other variables in the model and we obtain an unbiased estimate of the effects of service characteristics on outcomes, net of the effects of variations in case and site characteristics.

In order to identify exogenous variables for the first-stage equations, ordinary least squares (OLS) regression models were developed for each of the interval-level service characteristics shown in Table C.1. The service variables were regressed on each of the case characteristics shown in that table. Backward elimination was used to identify case characteristics that were significantly related to each of the service characteristics. After plotting the residuals, we found evidence of heteroscedasticity in the OLS models for three of the four service characteristics (duration of services, hours of contact with caseworkers, and hours of contact with parent aides). Since the distributions of these variables were skewed (with long right tails), this problem was greatly reduced by using the natural logs of these variables. Independent variables that remained in the final OLS regression models were included in the first-stage 2SLS equations, along with five dummy variables representing the six sites.

In preparation for the second stage, logistic regression analysis was used to identify exogenous variables that were related to case outcomes. Outcomes were expressed as dichotomous variables indicating whether an event (placement, maltreatment, or case closing) had occurred within one year after random assignment). Again, backward elimination was used to select exogenous variables for the second-stage equations. Variables in the second stage equations are shown in Tables 6.7 through 6.9.

We were interested in the effects of service characteristics on outcomes both within Family First and for all cases in the experiment. Thus, the procedures described above were conducted twice, once with data from the Family First cases in the experiment and again with data from all of the cases in the experiment. We also examined the effects of service characteristics on outcomes before and after site variations were taken into account (in the second-stage models). Thus, four 2SLS models were developed for each of three outcome variables (placement, subsequent maltreatment, and case closing). Results are shown in Tables 6.7 through 6.9.

Appendix D

Variables in the Hazard and Two-Stage Least Squares Analyses

CASE CHARACTERISTICS

A-sequence cases: Only one report of maltreatment was recorded in the DCFS Child Abuse and Neglect Tracking System (CANTS) computer files prior to the referral to Family First (this includes reports made on the same day as the referral). It is assumed that this one report led to the referral to Family First.

Prior physical injury to children: Prior to referral, there were one or more indicated reports of abuse involving death, brain damage, subdural hematoma, internal injuries, wounds, torture, burns or scalding, bone fractures, poison, cuts, bruises, welts, human bites, tying or confinement, sprains, or dislocations.

Chronic neglect: Prior to referral, there were three or more reports, each of which contained one or more allegations of child neglect.

Housing problems: On the 90-day service summary form, the worker identified dangerous housing or homelessness as one of the five most serious problems facing the family in the first 90 days of service, *or* the family had one or more indicated allegations of inadequate shelter in the report of maltreatment that preceded case assignment.

Poverty or resource deficits: On the 90-day service summary form, the worker identified poverty as one of the five most serious problems facing the family in the first 90 days of service, *or* the family had one or more indicated allegations of inadequate clothing or inadequate food in the report of maltreatment that preceded case assignment.

Cocaine problems: On the 90-day service summary form, the worker identified drug abuse problems as one of the five most serious problems facing the family in the first 90 days of service and the worker listed cocaine as one of the drugs involved.

Alcohol problems: On the 90-day service summary form, the worker identified alcohol abuse as one of the five most serious problems facing the family in the first 90 days of service *or* the worker identified drug abuse problems as one of the five most serious problems and listed alcohol as one of the drugs involved.

Other drug problems: On the 90-day service summary form, the worker identified drug abuse as one of the five most serious problems facing the family in the first 90 days of service and the worker indicated that drugs other than cocaine and alcohol were involved.

Parents' chronic mental illness or emotional problems: On the 90-day service summary form, the worker identified chronic mental illness of a parent or emotional problems of parent (e.g., depression, anger) as one of the five most serious problems facing the family in the first 90 days of service.

Marital problems, domestic violence, or unresolved separation or divorce: On the 90-day service summary form, the worker identified one of the following as one of the five most serious problems facing the family in the first 90 days of service: marital or relationship problems, domestic violence, or desertion or unresolved divorce or separation.

Child care skills deficits: On the 90-day service summary form, the worker identified skill deficits in physical care of children or in discipline or emotional care as one of the five most serious problems facing the family in the first 90 days of service.

Children's health, development, or learning problems: On the 90-day service summary form problem, the worker identified one of the following as one of the five most serious problems facing the family in the first 90 days of service: child's acute health problems, child's physical development problems or handicap, or child's retardation or learning deficits.

Teenage caregiver: The worker indicated on the 90-day service summary form that the primary caretaker was 19 years of age or younger.

Single-adult household: According to data provided by the worker on the 90-day service summary form there were no household members age 18 or older other than the primary caregiver. (Primary caregivers were considered adults here, regardless of their age.)

Extended-family household: According to data provided by the worker on the 90-day service summary form, the household included the primary caretaker's parent, sibling, grandparent, grandchild, extended-family member, or an unrelated person.

Protective custody within one year prior to referral: The worker indicated on the 90-day service summary form that a child had been in protective custody within the year prior to referral *or* the DCFS MARS/CYCIS data on children's living arrangements indicated that a placement had occurred within one year prior to referral.

SERVICE CHARACTERISTICS

Duration of services in Family First: Number of days between referral to Family First and termination from the program.

Hours of contact with caseworkers: Hours of in-person contact between caseworkers (or therapists) and family members during the first 90 days of Family First or regular services (as reported on the service summary form).

Hours of contact with parent aides: Hours of in-person contact between parent aides (or homemakers) and family members during the first 90 days of Family First or regular services (as reported on the service summary form).

Number of concrete services: Number of different types of concrete services provided to clients (as reported on the service summary form). Includes services provided directly by Family First or DCFS workers and those that were arranged or obtained for clients through referrals or linkages to other agencies. For a list of the services included see Table 5.3.

Appendix E

Additional Tables

Table E.1: Service Summary Response Rates for Families Referred to Family First Prior to April 1, 1991, by Region

Site	Number of families referred	Families with 90-day service summary forms[a]		Cases requiring extension forms	Families with extension forms[a]		Families with some service summary data (90 day or extension form)	
		N	%		N	%	N	%
Aurora	443	423	95.5	79	75	94.9	424	95.7
Chicago North	411	355	86.4	119	97	81.5	363	88.3
Chicago South	363	332	91.5	151	105	69.5	340	93.7
Chicago East	413	374	90.6	151	115	76.2	378	91.5
Chicago West	410	368	89.8	119	108	90.8	378	92.2
Champaign	357	352	98.6	51	42	82.4	353	98.9
East St. Louis	177	166	93.8	38	32	84.2	169	95.5
Marion	244	238	97.5	80	77	96.3	239	98.0
Peoria	420	414	98.6	58	44	75.9	415	98.8
Rockford	242	230	95.0	92	89	96.7	234	96.7
Springfield	234	215	91.9	96	86	89.6	220	94.0
Total	3,714	3,467	93.4	1,034	870	84.1	3,513	94.6

[a] Excludes cases with substantial amounts of missing data or irreconcilable discrepancies in the data provided.

Table E.2:   Response Rates for One-Time Survey of Workers, by Position and Type of Site

Position	Experimental sites			Nonexperimental sites			Total response rate (%)
	N	Responses	Response rate (%)	N	Responses	Response rate (%)	
Homemaker	70	52	74.3	108	78	72.2	73.0
Caseworker	134	109	81.3	184	147	79.9	80.5
Supervisor	36	31	86.1	76	62	81.6	83.0
Total	240	192	80.0	368	287	78.0	78.8

Table E.3:   Response Rates for Annual Survey of Workers, by Survey Year, Position, and Type of Site

Survey year, position	Experimental sites			Nonexperimental sites			Total response rate (%)
	N	Responses	Response rate (%)	N	Responses	Response rate (%)	
1990							
Homemaker	24	15	62.5	20	17	85.0	72.7
Caseworker	28	22	78.6	46	36	78.3	78.4
Supervisor	7	5	71.4	12	9	75.0	73.7
Total	59	42	71.2	78	62	79.5	75.9
1991							
Homemaker	47	36	76.6	66	48	72.7	74.3
Caseworker	68	42	61.8	111	85	76.6	71.0
Supervisor	11	9	81.8	15	10	66.7	73.1
Total	126	87	69.1	192	143	74.5	72.3
1992							
Homemaker	41	20	48.8				
Caseworker	71	60	84.5				
Supervisor	8	2	25.0				
Total	120	82	68.3				

Table E.4:   Response Rates for Annual Survey of Supervisors, by Survey Year and Type of Site

Survey year	Experimental sites			Nonexperimental sites			Total response rate (%)
	N	Responses	Response rate (%)	N	Responses	Response rate (%)	
1990	20	18	90.0	37	24	64.9	73.7
1991	27	17	63.0	57	39	68.4	66.7
1992	26	13	50.0				

Table E.5: Parent Survey Participants by Wave, Site, and Group

Site	Waves in which respondent participated	Family First cases N	Family First cases %	Regular services cases N	Regular services cases %	Total N	Total %
Chicago East	1991 only	1	1.4	2	2.9	3	2.1
	1992 only	1	1.4	0	0.0	1	0.7
	1993 only	10	14.1	9	13.0	19	13.6
	1991 and 1992 only	4	5.6	3	4.4	7	5.0
	1991 and 1993 only	8	11.3	7	10.1	15	10.7
	1992 and 1993 only	1	1.4	1	1.5	2	1.4
	All three waves	35	49.3	34	49.3	69	49.3
	No interviews	11	15.5	13	18.8	24	17.1
	Subtotal	71	100.0	69	100.0	140	100.0
Lake Villa/ Waukegan	1992 only	5	9.6	5	11.1	10	10.3
	1993 only	7	13.5	11	24.4	18	18.6
	Both waves	34	65.4	18	40.0	52	53.6
	No interviews	6	11.5	11	24.4	17	17.5
	Subtotal	52	100.0	45	100.0	97	100.0
Peoria	1992 only	3	5.5	0	0.0	3	3.3
	1993 only	10	18.2	10	27.0	20	21.7
	Both waves	35	63.6	24	64.9	59	64.1
	No interviews	7	12.7	3	8.1	10	10.9
	Subtotal	55	100.0	37	100.0	92	100.0
Total		178		151		329	

References

Allison, Paul D. (1984). *Event History Analysis: Regression for Longitudinal Data.* Newbury Park, CA: Sage.

American Public Welfare Association, Voluntary Cooperative Information System. (1989–1993). *VCIS Research Notes.* Washington, DC: Author.

Anderson, P. G. (1989). "The Origin, Emergence, and Professional Recognition of Child Protection." *Social Service Review* 63(2):222–44.

Antler, Stephen. (1978). "Child Abuse: An Emerging Social Priority." *Social Work* 23(1):58–61.

Antler, Stephen. (1981). "The Rediscovery of Child Abuse." Pp. 39–54 in *The Social Context of Child Abuse and Neglect,* edited by Leroy Pelton. New York: Human Sciences Press.

Aponte, Harry and Jerome Van Deusen. (1981). "Structural Family Therapy." Pp. 310–60 in *Handbook of Family Therapy,* edited by A. S. Gurman and D. P. Kniskern. New York: Brunner/Mazel.

Arches, J. (1991). "Social Structure, Burnout, and Job Satisfaction." *Social Work* 36:202–6.

B. H. v. Suter. (1993). U.S. District Court for the Northern District of Illinois. Docket 88C559.

Bandura, A. (1982). "Self-Efficacy Mechanism in Human Agency." *American Psychologist* 37:122–47.

Barber, Bernard. (1967). *Drugs and Society.* New York: Russell Sage Foundation.

Barrera, Manuel, Jr. (1981). "Arizona Social Support Interview Schedule." Pp. 69–96 in *Social Networks and Social Support,* edited by Benjamin H. Gottlieb. Beverly Hills, CA: Sage.

Barth, Richard P. (1990). "Theories Guiding Home-Based Intensive Family Preservation Services." Pp. 89–112 in *Reaching High-Risk Families: Intensive Family Preservation in Human Services,* edited by James K. Whittaker, Jill Kinney, Elizabeth M. Tracy, and Charlotte Booth. Hawthorne, NY: Aldine de Gruyter.

Barth, Richard P., Susan Hacking, and Jordana R. Ash. (1988). "Preventing Child Abuse: An Experimental Evaluation of the Child Parent Enrichment Project." *Journal of Primary Prevention* 8(4):201–17.

Barthel, Joan. (1992). *For Children's Sake: The Promise of Family Preservation*. New York: Winchell.

Bartsch, David and George Kawamura. (1993). *Family Preservation Services in Colorado*. Denver: Colorado Division of Mental Health Department of Institutions.

Berger, David. (1979). "Child Abuse Simulating 'Near-Miss' Sudden Infant Death Syndrome." *Journal of Pediatrics* 95(4):554–56.

Bergquist, C., D. Szwejda, and G. Pope. (1993). *Evaluation of Michigan's Families First Program: Summary Report*. Lansing: Michigan Department of Social Services.

Berry, Marianne. (1991). "The Assessment of Imminence of Risk of Placement: Lessons from a Family Preservation Program." *Children and Youth Services Review* 13(4):239–56.

Berry, Marianne. (1992). "An Evaluation of Family Preservation Services: Fitting Agency Services to Family Needs." *Social Work* 37(4):314–21.

Berry, William D. (1984). *Nonrecursive Causal Models*. Newbury Park, CA: Sage.

Binder, A. and G. Geis. (1984). "*Ad Populum* Argumentation in Criminology: Juvenile Diversion as Rhetoric." *Crime and Delinquency* 30:624–47.

Birt, Charles J. (1956). "Family-Centered Project of St. Paul." *Social Work* 1(October 1956):41–47.

Blomberg, T. G. (1977). "Diversion and Accelerated Social Control." *Journal of Criminal Law and Criminology* 68:274–82.

Blomberg, T. G. (1983). "Diversion's Disparate Results and Unresolved Questions: An Integrative Evaluation Perspective." *Journal of Research in Crime and Delinquency* 20:24–38.

Blossfeld, Hans-Peter, Alfred Hamerle, and Karl Ulrich Mayer (1989). *Event History Analysis: Statistical Theory and Application in the Social Sciences*. Hillsdale, NJ: Lawrence Erlbaum Associates.

Blythe, Betty J. (1983). "A Critique of Outcome Evaluation in Child Abuse Treatment." *Child Welfare* 62(4):325–35.

Bowlby, John. (1952). *Maternal Care and Mental Health*. Geneva: World Health Organization.

Bowlby, John. (1969–51973). *Attachment and Loss*. London: Hogarth.

Bowlby, John. (1988). *A Secure Base: Parent-Child Attachment and Healthy Human Development*. New York: Basic Books.

Boyd-Franklin, Nancy. (1989). *Black Families in Therapy: A Multisystems Approach*. New York: Guilford.

Bremner, R. H. (ed.) (1971). *Children and Youth in America: A Documentary History*, vol II. Cambridge, MA: Harvard University Press.

Breunlin, Douglas, Richard Schwartz, and Betty Kune-Karrer. (1992). *Metaframeworks*. San Francisco: Jossey-Bass.

Bribitzer, Marjorie P. and Mary Jeanne Verdieck. (1988). "Home-Based, Family-Centered Intervention: Evaluation of a Foster Care Prevention Program." *Child Welfare* 67(3):255–66.

Bugental, D. B. and W. A. Shennum. (1984). "'Difficult' Children as Elicitors and

Targets of Adult Communication Patterns: An Attributional-Behavioral Transactional Analysis." *Monographs of the Society for Research in Child Development* 49(1, Serial No. 205).

Caffey, J. (1957). "Some Traumatic Lesions in Growing Bones Other Than Fractures and Dislocations: Clinical and Radiological Features." *British Journal of Radiology* 30(353):225–38.

Cherniss, C. (1980). *Staff Burnout: Job Stress in the Human Services*. California: Sage.

Chicago Board of Education v. Terrile. (1977). 47 Ill. App 3d 75.

Christoffel, Katherine Kaufer. (1992). "Child Abuse Fatalities." Pp. 49–59 in *Child Abuse: A Medical Resource*, 2nd ed., edited by S. Ludwig and A. E. Kornberg. New York: Churchill Livingstone.

Cimmarusti, Rocco A. (1989). *A Multi-Systems Approach to Family Preservation: A Curriculum Guide*. Springfield, IL: Child Welfare Training Institute, Department of Children and Family Services.

Cimmarusti, Rocco A. (1992). "Family Preservation Practice Based upon a Multisystems Approach." *Child Welfare* 71(3):241–56.

Cochrane, Raymond and Alex Robertson. (1973). "The Life Events Inventory: A Measure of the Relative Severity of Psycho-Social Stressors." *Journal of Psychosomatic Research* 17:135–39.

Cohen, B. J. (1992). "Quality of Working Life in a Public Child Welfare Agency." *Journal of Health and Human Resources Administration* 15(2):129–52.

Cohen, S. and G. McKay. (1984). "Social Support, Stress, and the Buffering Hypothesis: A Theoretical Analysis." Pp. 253–67 in *Handbook of Psychology and Health*, Vol. 4, edited by A. Baum, S. E. Taylor, and J. E. Singer. Hillsdale, NJ: Lawrence Erlbaum Associates.

Cohn, Anne Harris and Deborah Daro. (1987). "Is Treatment Too Late: What Ten Years of Evaluation Research Tell Us." *Child Abuse and Neglect* 11(3):433–42.

Cook, Thomas D. and Donald T. Campbell. (1979). *Quasi-Experimentation: Design and Analysis Issues for Field Settings*. Chicago: Rand McNally.

Costin, L. B. (1992). "Cruelty to Children: A Dormant Issue and Its Rediscovery, 1920–1960." *Social Service Review* 66(2):177–98.

Cox, D. F. (1972). "Regression Tables and Life Tables." *Journal of the Royal Statistical Society B* 34:187–220.

Crnic, K. A., A. S. Ragozin, M. T. Greenberg, N. M. Robinson, and R. B. Basham. (1983). " Social Interaction and Developmental Competence of Preterm and Full-Term Infants during the First Year of Life." *Child Development* 54:1199–1210.

Crockenberg, S. B. (1981). " Infant Irritability, Mother Responsiveness, and Social Support Influences on Security of Infant-Mother Attachment." *Child Development* 52:857–65.

Cunningham, Maryanne L., Karen S. Homer, Aleksandra S. Bass, and Megan G. Brown. (1993). *Family Preservation in Tennessee: The Home Ties Intervention*. Knoxville: University of Tennessee College of Social Work.

Cutrona, C. E. and B. R. Troutman. (1986). " Social Support, Infant Temperament, and Parenting Self-Efficacy: A Mediational Model of Postpartum Depression." *Child Development* 57:1507–18.

Daro, Deborah. (1988). *Confronting Child Abuse: Research for Effective Program Design.* New York: Free Press.

Daro, Deborah. (1993). "Child Maltreatment Research: Implications for Program Design." Pp. 331–67 in *Child Abuse, Child Development, and Social Policy*, edited by Dante Cicchetti and Sheree L. Toth. Norwood, NJ: Ablex.

Daro, Deborah and Karen McCurdy. (1991). *Current Trends in Child Abuse Reporting and Fatalities: The Results of the 1990 Annual Fifty State Survey.* Chicago: National Center on Child Abuse Prevention Research of the National Committee for Prevention of Child Abuse.

Davis, Inger P. (1988). *Review of Selected Research on Family-Centered, Home-Based Services to Prevent Placement of Abused and Neglected Children.* Unpublished paper. San Diego State University School of Social Work.

Department of Health and Human Services, Office of the Inspector General. (1992a). *State Practices in Using Relatives for Foster Care.* HHS Publication Number OEI-06-90-02391. Washington DC: Author.

Department of Health and Human Services, Office of the Inspector General. (1992b). *Using Relatives for Foster Care.* HHS Publication Number OEI-06-90-02390. Washington DC: Author.

Dix, T. H. and J. E. Grusec. (1985). "Parent Attribution Process in the Socialization of Children." Pp. 201–33 in *Parental Belief Systems*, edited by I. E. Sigel. Hillsdale, NJ: Lawrence Erlbaum Associates.

Donovan, W. L. and L. A. Leavitt. (1992). "Maternal Self-Efficacy and Response to Stress: Laboratory Studies of Coping with a Crying Infant." Pp. 47–68 in *Stress and Coping in Infancy and Childhood*, edited by T. M. Field, P. M. McCabe, and N. Schneiderman. Hillsdale, NJ: Lawrence Erlbaum Associates.

Edna McConnell Clark Foundation. (1985). *Keeping Families Together: the Case for Family Preservation.* New York: Author.

Edna McConnell Clark Foundation. (1990). *Keeping Families Together: Facts on Family Preservation Services.* Information kit. New York: Author.

Encyclopedia Britannica. (1994). "Alcohol and Drug Consumption." *Macropaedia*, Vol. 13, pp. 194–223. Chicago: Author.

Epstein, Laura. (1988). *Helping People: The Task Centered Approach*, 2nd ed. Columbus, OH: Merrill.

Epstein, Laura. (1992). *Brief Treatment and a New Look at the Task Centered Approach.* New York: Macmillan.

Ezell, Mark. (1989). "Juvenile Diversion: The Ongoing Search for Alternatives." Pp. 45–58 in *Justice for Juveniles: Rethinking the Best Interests of the Child*, edited by Ira M. Schwartz. Lexington, MA: Lexington Books.

Fanshel, David and E. B. Shinn. (1978). *Children in Foster Care: A Longitudinal Investigation.* New York: Columbia University Press.

Fein, Edith and Anthony N. Maluccio. (1992). "Permanency Planning: Another Remedy in Jeopardy?" *Social Service Review* 66(3):335–48.

Feldman, Leonard H. (1990). *Evaluating the impact of family preservation services in*

New Jersey. Trenton: New Jersey Division of Youth and Family Services; Bureau of Research, Evaluation, and Quality Assurance.

Feldman, Leonard H. (1991). *Assessing the effectiveness of family preservation services in New Jersey within an ecological context.* Trenton: New Jersey Division of Youth and Family Services, Bureau of Research, Evaluation, and Quality Assurance.

Florida Office of the Inspector General. (1982). *Intensive Crisis Counseling Programs.* Tallahassee, FL: Department of Health and Rehabilitation Services.

Fondacaro, Karen and T. Tighe. (1990). *An Evaluation of Intensive Family-Based Services: Final Report.* Burlington: University of Vermont Department of Psychology.

Frankel, Harvey. (1988). "Family-Centered, Home-Based Services in Child Protection: A Review of the Research." *Social Service Review* 62(1):137–57.

Fraser, Mark W., Peter J. Pecora, and David A. Haapala. (1991). *Families in Crisis: The Impact of Intensive Family Preservation Services.* Hawthorne, NY: Aldine de Gruyter.

Freudenberger, H. (1977). "Burnout: Occupational Hazard of the Child Care Worker." *Child Care Quarterly* 6:90–99.

Gelles, Richard J. (1993). "Family Reunification/Family Preservation: Are Children Really Being Protected?" *Journal of Interpersonal Violence* 8(4):557–62.

Gillespie, D. F. and S. E. Cohen (1984). "Causes of Worker Burnout." *Children and Youth Services Review* 6:115–24.

Giovannoni, Jeanne M. and Rosina M. Beccera. (1979). *Defining Child Abuse.* New York: Free Press.

Glaser, Daniel. (1988). *Evaluation Research and Decision Guidance.* New Brunswick, NJ: Transaction Books.

Goerge, Robert M. (1994). "The Effect of Public Child Welfare Worker Characteristics and Turnover on Discharge from Foster Care." Pp. 205–217 in *Child Welfare Research Annual Review,* edited by Richard P. Barth, Jill Duerr Berrick, and Neil Gilbert. New York: Columbia University Press.

Goerge, Robert M., Allen Harden, and Bong Joo Lee. (1993). *The Physical Movement of Foster Children Placed with Relatives.* Unpublished report. Chicago: Chapin Hall Center for Children at the University of Chicago.

Goerge, Robert M. and Fred H. Wulczyn. (1990). "Placement Duration and Foster Care Reentry in New York and Illinois." Report prepared for the U.S. General Accounting Office. Chicago: Chapin Hall Center for Children (Discussion Paper Series).

Goldstein, J., A. Freud, and A. Solnit. (1973). *Beyond the Best Interests of the Child.* New York: Free Press.

Goldstein, J., A. Freud, and A. Solnit. (1979). *Before the Best Interests of the Child.* New York: Free Press.

Gray, Jane D., C. A. Cutler, J. G. Dean, and C. H. Kempe. (1979). "Prediction and Prevention of Child Abuse and Neglect." *Journal of Social Issues* 35:127–39. [Also appeared in *Child Abuse and Neglect* 1:45–58, 1977.]

Haapala, David A. (1983). "Perceived Helpfulness, Attributed Critical Incident Responsibility, and a Discrimination of Home Based Family Therapy Treatment Outcomes: Homebuilders Model." Federal Way, WA: Behavioral Sciences Institute.

Haapala, David A., Peter J. Pecora, and Mark W. Fraser. (1991). " Implications for Practice, Policy, Research, and the Future." Pp. 289–312 in *Families in Crisis: The Impact of Intensive Family Preservation Services*, edited by Mark W. Fraser, Peter J. Pecora, and David A. Haapala. Hawthorne, NY: Aldine de Gruyter.

Hackman, J. R. and E. E. Lawler III (1971). "Employee Reactions to Job Characteristics." *Journal of Applied Psychology Monograph* 55:259–86.

Hackman, J. R. and R. Oldham. (1976). "Motivation through the Design of Work: Test of a Theory." *Organizational Behavior and Human Performance* 16:250–79.

Hackman, J. R. and R. Oldham. (1980). *Work Redesign*. Reading, MA: Addison-Wesley.

Halper, G. and M. A. Jones. (1981). "Serving Families at Risk of Dissolution: Public Preventive Services in New York City." New York: Human Resources Administration, Special Services for Children.

Harrison, W. D. (1980). "Role Strain and Burnout in Protective Service Workers." *Social Service Review* 54:31–44.

Hartman, Ann. (1993). "Family Preservation under Attack." *Social Work* 38(5):509–12.

Hartman, Ann and Joan Laird. (1983). *Family-Centered Social Work Practice*. New York: Macmillan.

Hennepin County Community Services Department. (1980). "Family Study Project: Demonstration and Research in Intensive Services to Families." Minneapolis: Author.

Hinckley, Edward C. and W. Frank Ellis. (1985). "An Effective Alternative to Residential Placement: Home-Based Services." *Journal of Clinical Child Psychology* 14(3):209–13.

Holmes, T. H. and R. H. Rahe. (1967). " The Social Readjustment Rating Scale." *Journal of Psychosomatic Research* 11:213–18.

Horejsi, Charles R. (1981). "The St. Paul Family-Centered Project Revisited: Exploring an Old Gold Mine." Pp. 12–23 in *Treating Families in the Home: An Alternative to Placement*, edited by Marvin Bryce and June C. Lloyd. Springfield, IL: Thomas.

Howard, Bill. (1992). "The (Over?)Selling of Homebuilders." *Youth Today*, September/October.

Hubbard, Robert L., Mary Ellen Marsden, J. Valley Rachal, Henrick J. Harwood, Elizabeth R. Cavanaugh, and Harold M. Ginzburg. (1989). *Drug Abuse Treatment: A National Study of Effectiveness*. Chapel Hill: University of North Carolina Press.

Hutchinson, Elizabeth D. (1993). "Mandatory Reporting Laws: Child Protective Case Finding Gone Awry?" *Social Work* 38(1):56–63.

Illinois Department of Children and Family Services. (1984–1993). *Child Abuse and Neglect Statistics*. Springfield, IL: Author.

Illinois Department of Children and Family Services. (1991). *Executive Summary, Annual Report*, January 1991.

In the Interest of Ashley K., 212 Ill. App. 3d 849.

In re B.T. (1990). 204 Ill. App. 3d 277.

Institute for Research on Poverty. (1992). "What We Know about the Effects of Foster Care." *Focus* 14(2):22–34.

Jayaratne, S. and W. A. Chess. (1984). "Job Satisfaction, Burnout, and Turnover: A National Study." *Social Work* 29:448–53.

Jayaratne, S., W. A. Chess, and D. Kunkel. (1986). " Burnout: Its Impact on Child Welfare Workers and Their Spouses." *Social Work* 31:53–60.

Jayaratne, S., A. Tripodi, and W. A. Chess. (1983). "Perceptions of Emotional Support, Stress, and Strain by Male and Female Social Workers." *Social Work Research and Abstracts* 19:19–27.

Jones, Marshall B. (1989). "Crisis of the American Orphanage, 1931-1940." *Social Service Review* 63(4):613–29.

Jones, Mary Ann. (1985). *A Second Chance for Families, Five Years Later: Follow-up of a Program to Prevent Foster Care.* New York: Child Welfare League of America.

Jones, Mary Ann. (1991). "Measuring Outcomes." Pp. 159–86 in *Family Preservation Services: Research and Evaluation,* edited by Kathleen Wells and David E. Beigel. Newbury Park, CA: Sage.

Jones, Mary Ann, Renee Neuman, and Ann W. Shyne. (1976). *A Second Chance for Families: Evaluation of a Program to Reduce Foster Care.* New York: Child Welfare League of America.

Kadushin, Alfred. (1978). "Children in Foster Families and Institutions." Pp. 90–148 in *Social Service Research: Reviews of Studies,* edited by H. S. Maas. Washington, DC: National Association of Social Workers.

Karger, H. J. (1981). "Burnout as Alienation." *Social Service Review* 55:270–83.

Kaufman, Joan and Edward Zigler. (1992). "The Prevention of Child Maltreatment: Programming, Research and Policy." Pp. 269–95 in *Prevention of Child Maltreatment: Developmental and Ecological Perspectives,* edited by Diane J. Willis, E. Wayne Holden, and Mindy Rosenberg. New York: Wiley.

Kempe, C. H., Frederic N. Silverman, Brandt F. Steele, William Droegemuller, and Henry R. Silver. (1963). "The Battered Child Syndrome." *JAMA* 181(1):17–24.

Kinney, Jill M., David Haapala, and Charlotte Booth. (1991). *Keeping Families Together: The Homebuilders Model.* Hawthorne, NY: Aldine de Gruyter.

Kinney, Jill M., B. Madsen, T. Fleming, and David A. Haapala. (1977). "Homebuilders: Keeping Families Together." *Journal of Consulting and Clinical Psychology* 43(4):667–73.

Kirusek, J. and E. Sherman. (1968). "Goal Attainment Scaling: A General Method for Evaluating Comprehensive Community Mental Health Programs." *Community Mental Health Journal* 4:443–53.

Kronstadt, Diana. (1991). "Complex Developmental Issues of Prenatal Drug Exposure." *Future of Children* 1(1):36–49.

Lake v. Cameron. (1966). 364 F. 2d 657 (D.C. Cir.).

Landsman, Miriam J. (1985). *Evaluation of Fourteen Child Placement Prevention Projects in Wisconsin, 1983–1985.* Iowa City: National Resource Center on Family Based Services.

Larson, Carol S. (1991). "Overview of State Legislative and Judicial Responses." *Future of Children* 1(1):72–84.

Larson, Charles P. (1980). "Efficacy of Prenatal and Postpartum Home Visits on Child Health and Development." *Pediatrics* 66(2):191–97.

Leeds, Stephen J. (1984). *Evaluation of Nebraska's Intensive Services Project*. Iowa City: National Resource Center on Family Based Services.

Link, M. J. (1990). *Kinship Foster Care: The Double Edged Dilemma*. Rochester, NY: Task Force on Permanency Planning for Foster Children, Inc.

Lipscomb v. Simmons. (1992). 962 F.2d 1374 (9th Cir.).

Littell, Julia H. and Jeanne Howard, with Steve Budde, Cindy Chrisman, Brenda Eckhardt, and Diane Pellowe (1990). *The Nature of the Work with Families in Family First*. Chicago: Chapin Hall Center for Children at the University of Chicago.

Littell, Julia H., Jeanne Howard, Tina L. Rzepnicki, Stephen Budde, and Diane Pellowe (1992). *Intervention with Families in the Illinois Family Preservation Program*. Chicago: Chapin Hall Center for Children at the University of Chicago.

Littell, Julia H., John R. Schuerman, Tina L. Rzepnicki, Jeanne Howard, and Stephen Budde. (1993). "Shifting Objectives in Family Preservation Programs." Pp. 99–116 in *Advancing Family Preservation Practice*, edited by E. Susan Morton and R. Kevin Grigsby. Newbury Park, CA: Sage.

Lundstrom, Marjie and Rochelle Sharpe. (1991). "Getting Away with Murder: Three Child Abuse Deaths Are Believed to Go Undetected Every Day— Because No One Bothers to Autopsy." *Public Welfare* (Summer 1991):18–29.

Lutzker, John R. and James M. Rice. (1984). "Project 12-Ways: Measuring Outcome of a Large In-Home Service for Treatment and Prevention of Child Abuse and Neglect." *Child Abuse and Neglect* 8:519–24.

Lyle, Charles G. and John Nelson. (1983). *Home Based vs. Traditional Child Protection Services: A Study of the Home Based Services Demonstration Project in the Ramsey County Community Human Services Department*. Unpublished paper. St. Paul, Minnesota: Ramsey County Community Human Services Department.

Madden, Robert G. (1993). "State Actions to Control Fetal Abuse: Ramifications for Child Welfare Practice." *Child Welfare* 72(2):129–40.

Magura, Stephen. (1981). "Are Services to Prevent Foster Care Effective?" *Children and Youth Services Review* 3(3):193–212.

Magura, Stephen and Beth Silverman Moses (1986). *Outcome Measures for Child Welfare Services: Theory and Applications*. Washington, DC: Child Welfare League of America.

Maluccio, Anthony N., R. Warsh and B. A. Pine. (1993). "Family Reunification: An Overview." Pp. 3–19 in *Together Again: Family Reunification in Foster Care*, edited by B. A. Pine, R. Warsh, and A. N. Maluccio. Washington, DC: Child Welfare League of America.

Manusco, J. C. and K. H. Hardin. (1988). "Reprimanding: Acting on One's Implicit Theory of Behavior Changes." Pp. 143–76 in *Parental Belief Systems*, edited by I. E. Siegel. Hillsdale, NJ: Lawrence Erlbaum Associates.

Maslach, Christine (1978). "The Client Role in Staff Burnout." *Journal of Social Issues* 34:111–25.

Maslach, Christine (1982). *Burnout: The Cost of Caring*. Englewood Cliffs, NJ: Prentice-Hall.

Maslach, Christine and Susan Jackson (1981a). *Human Services Survey*. Palo Alto, CA: Consulting Psychologists Press, Inc.

Maslach, Christine and S. E. Jackson. (1981b). "The Measurement of Experienced Burnout." *Journal of Occupational Behavior* 2:99–113.

Mayer, Morris Fritz, Leon H. Richman, and Edwin A. Balcerzak. (1977). *Group Care of Children: Crossroads and Transitions*. New York: Child Welfare League of America.

McCroskey, Jacqueline and William Meezan. (1993). *Outcomes of Home Based Services: Effects on Family Functioning, Child Behavior and Child Placement*. Unpublished paper. Los Angeles: University of Southern California School of Social Work.

McCullock, A. and L. O'Brien. (1986). " The Organizational Determinants of Worker Burnout." *Children and Youth Services Review* 8:175–90.

McDonald, Walter R. and Associates. (1990). *Evaluation of AB 1562 In-Home Care Demonstration Projects: Final Report*. Sacramento, CA: Author.

McDonald, Walter R. and Associates. (1992). *County Family Preservation Programs Evaluation: Analysis of Similar Family Preservation Program Evaluations*. Paper submitted to the Office of Child Abuse Prevention, California Department of Social Services. Sacramento, CA: Author.

McGowan, Brenda G. (1983). "Historical Evolution of Child Welfare Services." Pp. 45–90 in *Child Welfare: Current Dilemmas, Future Directions*, edited by B. G. McGowan and W. Meezan. Itasca, IL: Peacock.

McGowan, Brenda G. (1990). "Family Based Services and Public Policy: Context and Implications." Pp. 65–87 in *Reaching High-Risk Families: Intensive Family Preservation in Human Services*, edited by James K. Whittaker, Jill Kinney, Elizabeth M. Tracy, and Charlotte Booth. Hawthorne, NY: Aldine de Gruyter.

Meezan, William and Jacquelyn McCroskey. (1993). *Family Centered Home Based Interventions for Abusive and Neglectful Families in Los Angeles*. Unpublished paper. Los Angeles: University of Southern California School of Social Work.

Meriwether, Margaret H. (1986). "Child Abuse Reporting Laws: Time for a Change." *Family Law Quarterly* 20(2):141–171.

Michigan Department of Social Services. (1993). Report to the House Appropriations Subcommittee on Social Services, May 25, 1993.

Miller v. Youakim. (1979). 440 U.S. 125.

Minuchin, S. (1974). *Families and Family Therapy*. Cambridge, MA: Harvard University Press.

Minuchin, S. and C. Fishman. (1981). *Family Therapy Techniques*. Cambridge, MA: Harvard University Press.

Mitchell, Christina, Patricia Tovar, and Jane Knitzer. (1989). *The Bronx Homebuilders Program: An Evaluation of the First 45 Families*. New York: Bank Street College of Education.

Myers, John B. (1986). "Survey of Child Abuse and Neglect Reporting Statutes." *Journal of Family Law* 10(1):1–72.

National Center on Child Abuse and Neglect. (1993). *National Child Abuse and Neglect Data System (NCANDS)*. Working Paper 2, 1991 Summary Data Component. Washington, DC: U.S. Government Printing Office.

Nelson, Barbara J. (1984). *Making an Issue of Child Abuse*. Chicago: University of Chicago Press.

Nelson, Kristine E. (1991). "Populations and Outcomes in Five Family Preservation Programs." Pp. 72–91 in *Family Preservation Services: Research and Evaluation*, edited by Kathleen Wells and David E. Beigel. Newbury Park, CA: Sage.

Nelson, Kristine, Arthur Emlen, Miriam Landsman, and Janet Hutchinson. (1988). *Family-Based Services: Factors Contributing to Success and Failure in Family-Based Child Welfare Services (Final Report)*. Iowa City: University of Iowa, School of Social Work, National Resource Center on Family-Based Services.

Nelson, Kristine E. and Miriam J. Landsman. (1992). *Alternative Models of Family Preservation: Family-based Services in Context*. Springfield, IL: Charles C. Thomas.

Nelson, Kristine E., Miriam J. Landsman, and Wendy Deutelman. (1990). "Three Models of Family Centered Placement Prevention." *Child Welfare* 69(1):3–21.

Nelson, Kristine E., Miriam J. Landsman, and Janet R. Hutchinson (1986). *Family-Based Services Inventory*. Iowa City, IA: National Resource Center on Family Based Services.

Norman vs. Johnson, Consent decree. (1992). U.S. District Court for the Northern District of Illinois, Docket 89 C1624.

Nugent, William R., Drucilla Carpenter, and Joe Parks. (1993). "A Statewide Evaluation of Family Preservation and Reunification Services." *Research on Social Work Practice* 3(1):40–65.

Oates, Kim. (1986). *Child Abuse and Neglect: What Happens Eventually?* New York: Brunner/Mazel.

Olds, David L. and Charles R. Henderson, Jr. (1989). "The Prevention of Maltreatment." Pp. 722–63 in *Child Maltreatment: Theory and Research on the Causes and Consequences of Child Abuse and Neglect*, edited by Dante Cicchetti and Vicki Carlson. Cambridge: Cambridge University Press.

Olds, David L., C. R. Henderson, R. Chamberlin, and R. Tatlebaum. (1986). "Preventing Child Abuse and Neglect: A Randomized Trial of Nurse Home Visitation." *Pediatrics* 78:65–78.

Olds, David L. and Harriet Kitzman. (1990). "Can Home Visitation Improve the Health of Women and Children at Environmental Risk?" *Pediatrics* 86(1):108–16.

Panel on Research on Child Abuse and Neglect. (1993). *Understanding Child Abuse and Neglect: Summary*. Washington, DC: National Academy Press.

Pearson, Carol L. and Philip A. King. (1987). *Intensive Family Services: Evaluation of Foster Care Prevention in Maryland: Final Report*. Baltimore: Maryland Department of Human Resources, Social Service Administration.

Pecora, Peter J. (1991). "Family-Based and Intensive Family Preservation Services: A Select Literature Review." Pp. 17–47 in *Families in Crisis: The Impact of Intensive Family Preservation Services*, edited by Mark W. Fraser, Peter J. Pecora, and David A. Haapala. Hawthorne, NY: Aldine de Gruyter.

Pecora, Peter J., K. H. Briar, and J. L. Zlotnik. (1989). *Addressing the Program and Personnel Crisis in Child Welfare: A Social Work Response*. Silver Spring, MD: National Association of Social Workers.

Pecora, Peter J., Mark Fraser, and David A. Haapala. (1992). "Intensive Home-Based Family Preservation Services: An Update from the FIT Project." *Child Welfare* 71(2):177–88.

Pellowe, Diane (1992). "Clinical Issues in the Termination of Family First Services." Pp. 112–27 in *Evaluation of the Illinois Family First Placement Prevention Programs: Progress Report*, edited by John R. Schuerman, Tina L. Rzepnicki, Julia H. Littell and Associates. Chicago: Chapin Hall Center for Children at the University of Chicago.

Pindyck, Robert S. and Daniel L. Rubinfeld (1991). *Econometric Models and Econometric Forecasts* (3rd ed.). New York: McGraw-Hill.

Polk, K. (1984). "Juvenile Diversion: A Look at the Record." *Crime and Delinquency* 30:648–59.

Proceedings of the Conference on the Care of Dependent Children. (1909). S. Doc. No. 721, 60th Congress, 2d Sess.

Reid, William J. (1978). *The Task Centered System*. New York: Columbia University Press.

Reid, William J. (1992). *Task Strategies: An Empirical Approach to Clinical Social Work*. New York: Columbia University Press.

Reid, William J. and Laura Epstein (1972). *Task Centered Casework*. New York: Columbia University Press.

Reid, William J., Richard M. Kagan, and Shirley B. Schlosberg. (1988). "Prevention of Placement: Critical Factors in Program Success." *Child Welfare* 67(1):25–37.

Rivlin, Alice M. and P. Michael Timpane (eds.). (1975). *Ethical and Legal Issues of Social Experimentation*. Washington, DC: Brookings Institution.

Rossi, Peter H. (1991). *Evaluating Family Preservation Programs: A Report to the Edna McConnell Clark Foundation*. Amherst: University of Massachusetts Social and Demographic Research Institute.

Rossi, Peter H. and Howard E. Freeman. (1993). *Evaluation: A Systematic Approach* (5th ed.). Newbury Park, CA: Sage.

Roueche, Berton. (1960). *The Neutral Spirit: A Portrait of Alcohol*. Boston: Little, Brown.

Rzepnicki, Tina L. (1991). "Enhancing the Durability of Intervention Gains: A Challenge for the 1990s." *Social Service Review* 65(1):92–111.

Rzepnicki, Tina L. and Stephen Budde, with Jeanne Howard and Diane Pellowe (1991). "Case Planning in Family First." pp. 119–35 in *Evaluation of the Illinois Family First Placement Prevention Programs: Progress Report*, edited by John R. Schuerman, Tina L. Rzepnicki, Julia H. Littell, and Associates. Chicago: Chapin Hall Center for Children at the University of Chicago.

Rzepnicki, Tina L., John R. Schuerman, and Julia H. Littell (1991). "Issues in Evaluating Family Preservation Services." Pp. 71–93 in *Intensive Family Preservation Services: An Instructional Sourcebook*, edited by Elizabeth Tracy, Peter Pecora, David Haapala, and Jill Kinney, Cleveland, Ohio: Mandel School of Applied Social Sciences.

Schuerman, John R. (1993). *The Targeting of Social Programs*. Unpublished paper, Chapin Hall Center for Children at the University of Chicago, Chicago.

Schuerman, John R., Tina L. Rzepnicki, Julia H. Littell, and Associates (1990). "Evaluation of the Illinois Family First Placement Prevention Programs: Progress Report." Chicago: Chapin Hall Center for Children at the University of Chicago.

Schuerman, John R., Tina L. Rzepnicki, Julia H. Littell, and Associates (1991). "Evaluation of the Illinois Family First Placement Prevention Programs: Progress Report." Chicago: Chapin Hall Center for Children at the University of Chicago.

Schuerman, John R., Tina L. Rzepnicki, Julia H. Littell, and Stephen Budde. (1992). "Implementation Issues." *Children and Youth Services Review* 14:193–206.

Schuerman, John R., Tina L. Rzepnicki, Julia H. Littell, and Tammy Jones (1989). "Evaluation of the Illinois Family First Placement Prevention Programs: Progress Report." Chicago: Chapin Hall Center for Children at the University of Chicago.

Schwartz, Ira M. and Philip AuClaire. (1989). *Intensive Home-Based Service as an Alternative to Out-of-Home Placement: The Hennepin County Experience*. Unpublished paper, Minneapolis.

Schwartz, Ira M., Philip AuClaire, and Linda J. Harris. (1991). "Family Preservation Services as an Alternative to the Out-of-Home Placement of Adolescents: The Hennepin County Experience." Pp. 33–46 in *Family Preservation Services: Research and Evaluation*, edited by Kathleen Wells and David E. Beigel. Newbury Park, CA: Sage.

Schwartz, Ira M., Robert Ortega, Shenyang Guo, Gideon Fishman, David Crampton, and John Kerbs. (forthcoming). *Raised by the Government: A Critical Examination of the Child Welfare System in the U.S.* Lexington, MA: Lexington Books.

Shelton v. Tucker. (1960). 364 U.S. 479.

Shotton, Alice C. (1989–1990). "Making Reasonable Efforts in Child Abuse and Neglect Cases: Ten Years Later." *California Western Law Review* 26(2):223–56.

Siegel, E., K. E. Bauman, E. S. Schaefer, M. M. Saunders, and D. D. Ingram. (1980). "Hospital and Home Support during Infancy: Impact on Maternal Attachment, Child Abuse and Neglect, and Health Care Utilization." *Pediatrics* 66:183–90.

Smith, Mary. (1991). "Intensive Family Intervention for Behaviorally Disturbed Children Project: Final Report." Austin: Texas Department of Human Services, Protective Services Division and Texas Department of Mental Health and Mental Retardation, Child and Adolescent Services.

Spitz, R. (1945). "Hospitalism: An Inquiry into the Genesis of Psychiatric Conditions in Early Childhood." *Psychoanalytic Study of the Child* 1:53–74.

Stein, Theodore J. (1985). "Projects to Prevent Out-of-Home Placement." *Children and Youth Services Review* 7:109–21.

Suchman, Edward A. (1967). *Evaluative Research.* New York: Russell Sage Foundation.

Suter vs. Artist M. (1992). 112 S.Ct. 1360.

Szykula, Steven A. and Matthew J. Fleischman. (1985). "Reducing Out-of-Home Placements of Abused Children: Two Controlled Field Studies." *Child Abuse and Neglect* 9:277–83.

Tatara, Toshio. (1993). "Characteristics of Children in Substitute and Adoptive Care, Fiscal Year 1989." Washington, DC: American Public Welfare Association.

Taylor, D. Kay and Carole Beauchamp. (1988). "Hospital-Based Primary Prevention Strategy in Child Abuse: A Multi-Level Needs Assessment." *Child Abuse and Neglect* 12(3):343–54.

Testa, Mark F. (1982). "Child Placement and Deinstitutionalization: A Case Study of Social Reform in Illinois." Pp. 825–71 in *Neither Angels nor Thieves: Studies in the Deinstitutionalization of Status Offenders*, edited by Joel Handler and Julie Katz. Washington, DC: National Academy Press.

Testa, Mark F. (1993). "Home of Relative (HMR) Program in Illinois: Interim Report, Revised 1993." Unpublished report, Chicago.

Thieman, A. A., R. Fuqua, and K. Linnan. (1990). "Iowa Family Preservation Three Year Pilot Project: Final Evaluation Report." Ames: Iowa State University.

Tracy, Elizabeth. (1991). "Defining the Target Population for Family Preservation Services." Pp. 138–58 in *Family Preservation Services: Research and Evaluation*, edited by Kathleen Wells and David E. Biegel. Newbury Park, CA: Sage.

Tracy, Elizabeth M. and James K. Whittaker. (1987). "The Evidence Base for Social Support Interventions in Child and Family Practice: Emerging Issues for Research and Practice." *Children and Youth Services Review* 9:249–70.

Turner, A. N. and P. R. Lawrence. (1965). *Industrial Jobs and the Worker.* Boston: Harvard Graduate School of Business Administration.

Van Meter, Mary Jane S. (1986). "An Alternative to Foster Care for Victims of Child Abuse/Neglect: A University-Based Program." *Child Abuse and Neglect* 10:79–84.

Wald, Michael S., J. M. Carlsmith, and P. H. Leiderman. (1985). *Protecting Abused/Neglected Children: A Comparison of Home and Foster Placement.* Stanford, CA: Stanford University, Center for Study of Youth Development.

Wald, Michael S., J. M. Carlsmith, and P. H. Leiderman. (1988). *Protecting Abused and Neglected Children.* Stanford, CA: Stanford University Press.

Weissert, William G. (1991). "A New Policy Agenda for Home Care." *Health Affairs* (Summer):67–77.

Wells, Kathleen and David E. Biegel (eds.). (1991). *Family Preservation Services: Research and Evaluation.* Newbury Park, CA: Sage.

Wells, Kathleen and Dale Whittington. (1993). "Child and Family Functioning after Intensive Family Preservation Services." *Social Service Review* 67(1):55–83.

Wheeler, Charles E., Grietje Reuter, David Struckman-Johnson, and Ying-Ying T. Yuan. (1993). "Evaluation of State of Connecticut Intensive Family Preservation Services: Phase V Annual Report." Sacramento, CA: Walter R. McDonald & Associates.

Whittaker, James K., Jill Kenny, Elizabeth M. Tracy, and Charlotte Booth, (Eds.). (1990). *Reaching High-Risk Families: Intensive Family Preservation in Human Services.* Hawthorne, NY: Aldine de Gruyter.

Willems, D. N. and R. DeRubeis. (1981). "The Effectiveness of Intensive Preventive Services for Families with Abused, Neglected, or Disturbed Children: Hudson County Project Final Report." Trenton: Bureau of Research, New Jersey Division of Youth and Family Services.

Willis, Diane J., E. Wayne Holden, and Mindy Rosenberg (eds.). (1992). *Prevention of Child Maltreatment: Developmental and Ecological Perspectives.* New York: Wiley.

Wood, Katherine M. and Ludwig L. Geismar. (1989). *Families at Risk: Treating the Multiproblem Family.* New York: Human Sciences Press.

Wood, Sally, Keith Barton, and Carroll Schroeder. (1988). "In-Home Treatment of Abusive Families: Cost and Placement at One Year." *Psychotherapy* 25(3):409–14.

Wulczyn, F. and Robert M. Goerge. (1992). "Foster Care in New York and Illinois: The Challenge of Rapid Change." *Social Service Review* 66(2):278–94.

Yamaguchi, Kazuo (1991). *Event History Analysis.* Newbury Park, CA: Sage.

Yamaguchi, Kazuo (1992). Personal communication with Eric Fong, May 1992.

Yuan, Ying-Ying T. and David L. Struckman-Johnson. (1991). "Placement Outcomes for Neglected Children with Prior Placements in Family Preservation Programs." Pp. 92–118 in *Family Preservation Services: Research and Evaluation,* edited by Kathleen Wells and David E. Beigel. Newbury Park, CA: Sage.

Zuckerman, Barry. (1991). "Drug-Exposed Infants: Understanding the Medical Risk." *Future of Children* 1(1):26–35.

Bibliography of Reports on the Evaluation of the Illinois Family First Placement Prevention Program

Publications

Schuerman, John R., Tina Rzepnicki, and Julia H. Littell. (1991). "From Chicago to Little Egypt: Lessons from an Evaluation of a Large Scale Child Welfare Family Preservation Program." Pp. 187–206 in *Family Preservation Services: Research and Evaluation*, edited by David E. Biegel and Kathleen Wells, Newbury Park, CA: Sage.

Rzepnicki, Tina L., John R. Schuerman, and Julia H. Littell (1991). "Issues in Evaluating Family Preservation Services." Pp. 71–93 in *Intensive Family Preservation Services: An Instructional Sourcebook*, edited by Elizabeth Tracy, Peter Pecora, David Haapala, and Jill Kinney, Cleveland, Ohio: Mandel School of Applied Social Sciences.

Schuerman, John R., Tina L. Rzepnicki, Julia H. Littell, and Stephen Budde. (1992). "Implementation Issues." *Children and Youth Services Review* 14:193–206.

Littell, Julia H., John R. Schuerman, Tina L. Rzepnicki, Jeanne Howard, and Stephen Budde. (1993). "Shifting Objectives in Family Preservation Programs." Pp. 99–116 in *Advancing Family Preservation Practice*, edited by E. Susan Morton and R. Kevin Grigsby. Newbury Park, CA: Sage.

Rzepnicki, Tina L., John R. Schuerman, Julia H. Littell, Amy Chak, and Marva Lopez (1994). "An Experimental Study of Family Preservation Services: Early Findings from a Parent Survey." Pp. 60–82 in *Child Welfare Research Review*, edited by R. P. Barth, J. D. Berrick, and N. Gilbert. New York: Columbia University Press.

Evaluation Reports to the Department of Children and Family Services

Schuerman, John R., Tina L. Rzepnicki, Julia H. Littell, and Tammy Jones. (1989). "Evaluation of the Illinois Department of Children and Family Ser-

vices Family First Initiative Report of First Phase Activities, Progress Report." Chicago: Chapin Hall Center for Children, June, 85 pp.

Schuerman, John R., Tina L. Rzepnicki, and Julia H. Littell. (1989). "Preliminary
Analysis of Service Characteristics." Chicago: Chapin Hall Center for Children, November, 89 pp.

Littell, Julia H. (1990). "Substance Abuse among Family First Clients." Chicago:
Chapin Hall Center for Children, April, 10 pp.

Schuerman, John R., Tina L. Rzepnicki, and Julia H. Littell. (1990). "Evaluation
of the Illinois Department of Children and Family Services Family First
Initiative, June Progress Report." Chicago: Chapin Hall Center for Children,
June, 49 pp.

Staff of the Family First Evaluation. (1990). "Evaluation of the Illinois Department of Children and Family Services Family First Initiative, Report of
Second Phase Activities." Chicago: Chapin Hall Center for Children, September.

Schuerman, John R., Tina L. Rzepnicki and Julia H. Littell with Jeanne Howard,
Penny Johnson, and Karen Rolf. (1990). "Evaluation of the Illinois Department of Children and Family Services Family First Initiative, Progress Report." Chicago: Chapin Hall Center for Children, November, 105 pp.

Littell, Julia H., John R. Schuerman, and Tina L. Rzepnicki. (1991). "Preliminary
Results from the Illinois Family First Experiment." Chicago: Chapin Hall
Center for Children, April, 37 pp.

Littell, Julia H., John R. Schuerman, Tina L. Rzepnicki, Jeanne Howard, and
Stephen Budde. (1991). "Family Preservation Programs and the Placement
Prevention Objective." Chicago: Chapin Hall Center for Children, April, 23
pp.

Staff of the Evaluation of Illinois Family First Placement Prevention Programs.
(1991). "Evaluation of the Department of Children and Family Services Family First Initiative, Progress Report." Chicago: Chapin Hall Center for Children, June, 167 pp.

Staff of the Evaluation of Illinois Family First Placement Prevention Programs.
(1991). "Evaluation of the Department of Children and Family Services Family First Initiative, Interim Report." Chicago: Chapin Hall Center for Children, September, 104 pp.

Chak, Amy, John R. Schuerman, Tina L. Rzepnicki, and Julia H. Littell. (1992).
"A Survey of Parents: Preliminary Findings." Chicago: Chapin Hall Center
for Children, January, 17 pp.

Littell, Julia H., Jeanne Howard, Tina L. Rzepnicki, Stephen Budde, and Diane
Pellowe with John R. Schuerman and Penny Johnson. (1992). "Intervention
with Families in the Illinois Family Preservation Program." Chicago: Chapin
Hall Center for Children, January, 62 pp.

Littell, Julia H., Eric Fong, Tammy Jones, and Hye Lan Kim. (1992). "Effects of
the Illinois Family First Program on Selected Outcomes for Various Kinds of
Cases." Chicago: Chapin Hall Center for Children, January, 29 pp.

Staff of the Family First Placement Prevention Evaluation. (1992). "Case Characteristics, Service Characteristics, and Selected Outcomes in the Family First

Placement Prevention Program: A Report for Program Providers." Chicago: Chapin Hall Center for Children, April (64 reports, 14 pages each).

Schuerman, John R., Tina L. Rzepnicki, Julia H. Littell, and the Staff of the Evaluation of the Illinois Family First Placement Prevention Program. (1992). "Evaluation of the Illinois Family First Placement Prevention Program: Progress Report." Chicago: Chapin Hall Center for Children, June, 161 pp.

Schuerman, John R., Tina L. Rzepnicki, Julia H. Littell, and Amy Chak. (1993). "Evaluation of the Illinois Family First Placement Prevention Program: Final Report." Chicago: Chapin Hall Center for Children, June, 218 pp.

Reports to the United States Department of Health and Human Services Office of Human Development Service

Schuerman, John R., Tina L. Rzepnicki, and Julia H. Littell. (1992). "Progress Report on a Study of the Longitudinal Effects of Family Preservation Programs on Child and Family Functioning." Chicago: NORC, January.

Schuerman, John R., Tina L. Rzepnicki, and Julia H. Littell. (1992). "Progress Report on a Study of the Longitudinal Effects of Family Preservation Programs on Child and Family Functioning." Chicago: NORC, April.

Schuerman, John R., Tina L. Rzepnicki, and Julia H. Littell. (1992). "Progress Report on a Study of the Longitudinal Effects of Family Preservation Programs on Child and Family Functioning," Chicago: NORC, June.

Schuerman, John R., Tina L. Rzepnicki, and Julia H. Littell. (1992). "Progress Report on a Study of the Longitudinal Effects of Family Preservation Programs on Child and Family Functioning." Chicago: NORC, October.

Schuerman, John R., Tina L. Rzepnicki, and Julia H. Littell. (1993). "Progress Report on a Study of the Longitudinal Effects of Family Preservation Programs on Child and Family Functioning," Chicago: NORC, January.

Miscellaneous Papers

Schuerman, John R., Tina L. Rzepnicki, Julia H. Littell, Penny Johnson, Steve Budde, and Jeanne Howard. (1992). "Some Observations on Child Welfare Reform in the 90s." Paper submitted to the United States House Ways and Means Committee, and the United States Department of Health and Human Services Administration for Children and Families. Chicago: Chapin Hall Center for Children, January. 10 pp.

Conference Presentations

Rzepnicki, Tina L. and Julia H. Littell. (1989). "Evaluating Family Preservation Services: The Illinois Family First Initiative." Presentation at the Seventh National Conference on Research Demonstration and Evaluation in Public Human Services, Washington, DC, September.

Rzepnicki, Tina L. and Julia H. Littell. (1990). "Evaluating Family Preservation Services: The Illinois Family First Initiative." Presentation at the NASW Illinois Chapter 1990 Symposium, Chicago, IL, April 28.

Littell, Julia H., Barry Colvin, Tina L. Rzepnicki, and John R. Schuerman. (1990). "Evaluation of the Illinois Family First Initiative: A Randomized Study." Paper presented at the Thirtieth Annual Workshop of the National Association for Welfare Research and Statistics, Bellevue, WA, July 9.

Littell, Julia H., John Schuerman and Tina Rzepnicki. (1990). "The Place of Family Preservation Services in the Child Welfare System: Solution or Distraction?" Paper presented at the Twelfth Annual APPAM Research Conference, San Francisco, CA, October.

Schuerman, John R., Tina L. Rzepnicki, Julia H. Littell, and Stephen Budde. (1990). "Some Intruding Realities." Paper presented at the National Association for Family-Based Services Fourth Annual Conference on Empowering Families in Detroit, Michigan, November.

Rzepnicki, Tina L. (1991). "How to Hit a Moving Target: Issues in Evaluating the Family First Program." Paper presented at the Family First Evaluation Workshop, Chicago, IL, January 18.

Schuerman, John R., Tina L. Rzepnicki, Julia H. Littell, and Stephen Budde. (1991). "Some Realities in the Implementation of Family Preservation Services." Paper presented at conference on Child Welfare Reform Experiments sponsored by the American Enterprise Institute in Washington, DC, February.

Schuerman, John R. (1992). "Family Preservation Evaluation in Illinois." Presentation at the U.S. HHS ACF Child Welfare Training, Child Welfare Research and Demonstration, and Adoption Grantees Conference, Washington, DC, March 19.

Rzepnicki, Tina L. (1992). "The DCFS Family First Initiative: Placement Prevention Program and Evaluation Overview." Paper presented at the Ninth International Congress on Child Abuse and Neglect, Chicago, IL, August 31.

Littell, Julia H. (1992). "Preliminary Findings from the Evaluation of the Illinois DCFS Family First Initiative." Paper presented at the Ninth International Congress on Child Abuse and Neglect, Chicago, IL, August 31.

Budde, Stephen. (1992). "Placement and Family Preservation Referral Decisions by Child Protection Investigators: A Qualitative Study." Paper presented at the Ninth International Congress on Child Abuse and Neglect, Chicago, IL, August 31.

Chak, Amy. (1992). "The Use of Social Support by Child Maltreating Families in a Family Preservation Program." Paper presented at the Ninth International Congress on Child Abuse and Neglect, Chicago, IL, August 31.

Kim, Hye Lan. (1992). "The Influence of Caseworkers' Orientations Toward Child Maltreating Families on Casework Activities and Case Outcomes." Paper presented at the Ninth International Congress on Child Abuse and Neglect, Chicago, IL, September 2.

Rzepnicki, Tina L. (1992). "Do Family Preservation Services Work? Findings from a Large-Scale Experimental Study." Paper presented at the National Association for Family-Based Services Sixth Annual Conference on Empowering Families, Seattle, WA, December 10.

Budde, Stephen. (1992). "Placement and Family Preservation Referral Decisions by Child Protection Investigators." Paper presented at the National Association for Family-Based Services Sixth Annual Conference on Empowering Families, Seattle, WA, December 10.

Index

Adoption Assistance and Child Welfare Act of 1980 (PL 96–272), 6
Analysis of variance (ANOVA), 176–179
Assessment (*See* Evaluation of family preservation services; Evaluation of Illinois Family First)

Basic research, 215
B. H. v. Suter, 219, 220, 221
Bias, placement, 234–235
Bronx Homebuilders Program (New York), 38
Burnout, staff, 128–129

California AB 1562 In-home Care Demonstration Projects, 39–40
California Families First (Davis), 37, 111
Case characteristics
  evaluation of Illinois Family First and, 62–64
  outcomes of Illinois Family First and, 158–159, 162–164, 170, 189, 270
  placement and, 41–42
  regular service families and, 158–159, 163–164, 170, 189
  services of Illinois Family First and, 271
  variables in, 277–279
Caseworkers of Illinois Family First
  administrative data and, 78–79
  attitudes of, 64–65
  burnout and, 128–129
  categories of, 124–125
  characteristic of work and, 130
  characteristics of, 64–65, 125

family problems and, views of, 92–93, 96, 104
  job conditions and, 125–126, 127
  job environment and, 127
  job satisfaction and, 128–129
  morale and, 129–130, 139
  relationship with parents and, 120–121, 183, 186
  training for, 108–109
  turnover and, 130
Chicago East site, 67, 69, 74–75, 78, 88, 90, 92, 97, 98, 100, 101, 103, 115–116, 117, 121, 139, 157, 170, 172, 176, 179–180, 181, 182, 183, 186–187, 189, 190, 230–231
Chicago South site, 69, 88, 92, 111, 121, 145, 157
Child, 5–6, 87 (*See also* Functioning of child/family)
Child abuse/neglect (*See also* Subsequent maltreatment)
  concern of, 3
  definition of, enlarged, 17
  detecting, improvements in, 17
  "educational neglect" and, 17
  family preservation services in preventing, 4–5, 45–47, 241–242
  home-visiting program and, 46–47
  outcomes of Illinois Family First and, 146
  parents' knowledge of parenting and, 47
Child Welfare Advisory Committee (CWAC), 53, 54, 221
Child welfare systems (*See also* specific types)
  concern of, 3

Child welfare systems (*cont.*)
  fragmentation of social services and, 242
  government's role in reformed, 244–246
  "housekeeping" issues and, 243–244
  Illinois Family First and, 190
  in-home versus out-of-home placement and, 246, 247
  least restrictive alternative principle and, 7–9, 12
  parent-child bond and, 5–6
  permanency principle and, 7, 8–9, 12
  protection versus treatment and, 241–242
  reasonable efforts principle and, 6–7, 8–9
  reformed, 244–248
  services in reformed, 246–248
  service technology and, limitations of, 243
  social conditions and, 240–241, 249
  time horizons and, 241, 248
  treatment versus prevention and, 242
Clinical trials for service approaches, need for, 214–215
"Cocaine babies," 18
Cost-effectiveness research, 44–45, 214
Courts, 4, 134–135 (*See also* specific cases)
Cox model, 268–269
Creaming, 23, 236
Crisis intervention, 135–136
CWAC (Child Welfare Advisory Committee), 53, 54, 221

Data quality, 211–213
DCFS (Department of Children and Family Services) (*See also* Regular service families)
  case closure in, 147–148
  contract for evaluation of Illinois Family First and, 53–55
  data provided by, in evaluation of Illinois Family First, 62–65, 71
  data quality and, 211–213
  development of Illinois Family First and, 24
  discussions with, in evaluation of Illinois Family First, 55, 58–59, 62
  exception cases and, 70–71
  implementation of Illinois Family First and, 26–28, 132–134
  lawsuits against, 217–218, 219–221, 222
  MacDonald administration and, 217–218
  provider agencies and, 24, 139, 218
  sites used in evaluation of Illinois Family First and, 66–67, 74–78
  Suter administration and, 218–219, 221, 222
  training carried out by, 108–109
  violations of group assignments and, 70–71
Delinquency, 14
Department of Children and Family Services (*See* DCFS)
Drug abuse, 18, 104, 162

East St. Louis site, 69–70, 88, 92, 93, 111, 115, 117, 157, 188
"Educational neglect," 17
Empowerment, 108
Evaluation of family preservation services
  basic research and, 215
  categories of services/cases and, 214
  clinical trials of service approaches and, need for, 214–215
  cost-effectiveness and, 214
  data quality and, 211–213
  demand for, 199
  experimental versus nonexperimental research and, 206–210
  integrity of research and, 210
  longitudinal effects and, 213–214
  objectivity and, 199

outcomes of programs and, 200–205

problems of, 201–202

quantitative versus qualitative research and, 206, 210–211

term *evaluation* and, 200

treatment versus variations in intervention and, 205–206

Evaluation of Illinois Family First

administrative data and, 63

assessing program and, 65–73

case characteristics and, 62–64

caseworker characteristics/attitudes and, 64–65

contract with DCFS and, 53–55

data provided by DCFS and, 62–65, 71

design of, 53–55

discussions with DCFS/private agency staff and, 55, 58–59, 62

exception cases and, 70–71

interviews with parents in program and, 73–76, 78–79

limitations of, 79

regular service families and, 71, 73

service characteristics and, 63–64, 71

sites used in, 67, 69–70, 74–78

understanding program and, 55, 58–59, 62–65

violations of group assignments and, 70–71

Evolution of Illinois Family First

backlash against family preservation services and, 224–225

consent decree and, 221–222

Illinois Family Preservation Act and, 223–224

implications of, 225–226

from July 1990 to June 1991, 217–221

from July 1991 to June 1992, 221–224

from July 1992 to present, 224–227

lawsuits against DCFS and, 217–218, 219–221, 222

MacDonald administration and, 217–218

Medicaid funds and, 223

"moderate intensity reunification" program and, 222–223, 226

reorganization and, 224

Ryder and, 224

Suter administration and, 218–219, 221–222

Wallace case and, 225

Exception cases, 70–71

Experimental research, 206–210 (*See also* specific aspects of Illinois Family First research)

Families in Illinois Family First (*See also* Interviews with Parents in Illinois Family First)

age, 87–88

caseworker-parent relationship and, 120–121, 183, 186

caseworkers' views of family problems and, 92–93, 96, 104

data collection on, 86–87

empowerment of, 108

ethnicity, 87–88

formal social support and, 182–183

functioning of, 170–172, 176–182, 189

household composition, 88–90, 103–104

income, 90

informal social support and, 101–102, 183

involvement of, in services, 117, 120, 139

parents' views of family problems and, 96–103, 104

problems at referral and, 97–98

referrals and, 85–86, 87, 97–98, 103–104

reports of child abuse/neglect and, 90, 92

self-efficacy of parents and, 102–103, 182, 190, 231

stressful events and, 98, 100

Family, 4, 21, 226 (*See also* Families in
    Illinois Family First; Regular ser-
    vice families; Targeting)
Family-Based Intensive Treatment
    (FIT) Study (Utah and Washing-
    ton), 38–39, 111
Family preservation services (*See also*
    Research on family preservation
    services; specific programs)
  backlash against, 224–225
  child abuse/neglect prevention
    and, 4–5, 45–47, 241–242
  context of, 239
  development of, 18–19
  effectiveness of, limitations of,
    238–239
  family systems approach and, 21
  focus on, 3
  foster care versus, 44–45, 248–249
  goals of, 143, 200, 229–230
  hallmarks of, 19, 138
  integrity of family and, 4, 226
  models in, 20–22
  origin of, 19–20
  other social programs and, 201
  outcomes of, 200–205
  overselling, 239–240
  placement prevention and, 33–43,
    143, 229–230
  protection versus treatment and,
    4–5, 241–242
  purpose of, 200
  referrals to, 235–236
  risk in, 23–24
  short-term, 21, 22, 248
  side effects of, 202–203
  social work's effect on, 20
  specific programs for, 247–248
  subsequent maltreatment preven-
    tion and, 43
  summary of controlled studies of,
    251–266
  systems effects and, 203–204
  targeting families and, 22–23, 237
  time horizons and, 21–22
Family Study Project in Hennepin
    County (Minnesota), 36–37, 37–38

Family Support Project in Los Angles
    (California), 40–41
Family systems approach, 21
FIT (Family Based Intensive Treat-
    ment) Study (Utah and
    Washington), 38–39, 111
Foster care
  "bounce" phenomenon and, 7, 13,
    249
  data on, national, 9–10
  detrimental effects of, 5–6
  family preservation services versus,
    44–45, 248–249
  increase of children in, 4, 9–11
  kinship, 11–13
  placement, 9–11, 14
  reducing number of children in,
    238
  reentry, 11, 13–14
  reports of child abuse/neglect and,
    14–15, 17–18
FPS (*See* Family preservation services)
Fragmentation in social services, 242–
    243
Functioning of child/family
  interviews with parents in Illinois
    Family First and, 170–172, 178–
    182
  measuring improvements in, 200–
    210
  outcomes of Illinois Family First
    and, 170–172, 176–182, 189
  research on family preservation
    services and, 43–44

Government's role in reformed child
    welfare systems, 244–246

Hazard models, 148, 150, 267–269,
    277–279
  exponential, 267
  Kaplan-Meier estimate of survivor
    function and, 268
  monotonic, 267
  nonmonotonic, 267
  parametric, 267
  selecting, 268–269

time dependent, 267–268
variables in, 277–279
Home Based Services Demonstration
Project (Minnesota), 36
Homebuilders, 20–21, 33, 38, 111
Homelessness, 93
Home-visiting program, 46–47
"Housekeeping" issues, 243–244
Hudson County Special Service Pro-
ject (New Jersey), 36

Illinois Family First (*See also* specific
aspects of research on)
advocacy groups of, 24
age of child involved in, 87
challenge of, 138
characteristics of programs and,
130
child welfare systems and, 190
criticisms of, 139–140, 232
development of, 53–55
differences between regular service
families and, 148, 150–159, 162–
165, 169–170, 187–191, 230–231
goals of, 26
growth of, 28–29
Illinois Family Preservation Act
and, 24
multisystems approach of, 25
provider groups of, 24, 108, 139
referrals to, 85–86, 87, 97–98, 103–
104
request for proposals and, 25–26,
27
Illinois Family Preservation Act
(1988), 24, 223–224
Imminent risk of placement, 215, 230,
234
Implementation of Illinois Family
First
authority in, 133–134
conflicts in program goals/philoso-
phy and, 132–133
courts and, 134–135
crisis intervention and, 135–136
criticisms of, 232–233
DCFS and, 26–28, 132–134

initial, 26–28
joint case planning and, 134
success of, 233
time horizons and, 136–138
In-home child placement, 246, 247
Integrity of family, 4, 226
Integrity of research, problems with,
210
Intervention, 4–5, 135–136, 205–206
Interviews with parents in Illinois
Family First
caseworker-parent relationships,
120–121, 183, 186
data compilation and, 79
design of, 73–74, 170
differences between respondents
and nonrespondents, 78
evaluation of Illinois Family First
and, 73–76, 78–79
formal social support, 182–183
functioning of child/family, 170–
172, 176–182
informal social support, 183
informing families, 76
locating families, 75–76
regular service families, 170–172,
176–182, 186–187, 230–231
response rates and, 76, 78
satisfaction with services, 186–187
self-efficacy of parents, 182
sites selected for, 74–75
training for, 75
In the Interest of Ashley K., 219, 220–
221

Job conditions, 125–126, 127
Job environment, 127
Job satisfaction, 128

Kinship foster care, 11–13

Lake Villa/Waukegan site, 69, 74, 75,
76, 78, 88, 90, 92, 97, 100, 101,
103, 117, 119, 121, 157–158, 170,
172, 180, 181, 182, 183, 186, 187,
189, 190, 231
Lawsuits against DCFS, 217–218,
219–221, 222

Least-restrictive alternative principle,
     7–9, 12

Maltreatment (*See* Child abuse/
     neglect; Subsequent maltreat-
     ment)
Maryland model, 25
Medicaid, 223
Michigan Families First, 34
Model slippage, 233
"Moderate intensity reunification"
     program, 222–223, 226
Morale, staff, 129–130, 139
Multisystems approach, 25, 108

Nebraska Intensive Services to Fami-
     lies at Risk, 36
Neglect (*See* Child abuse/neglect)
Net-widening, 23, 170, 188
New Jersey Family Preservation Ser-
     vices (FPS), 40, 43–44, 111
New York State Preventive Services
     Demonstration Project, 35
Nonexperimental research, 206–210
Nonintervention, 4
Norman v. Johnson, 219–220

Objectivity in research, 199
OLS (ordinary least squares) models,
     274
Ordinary least squares (OLS) models,
     274
Outcomes of Illinois Family First
     achievement of case objectives and,
         155–156, 188
     case characteristics and, 158–159,
         162–164, 170, 189, 271
     case closure in DCFS and, 147–148
     case opening/closing/reopening
         and, 156–157, 162, 170, 187, 230
     caseworker-parent relationship
         and, 183, 186
     child abuse/neglect and, 146
     context of family preservation ser-
         vices and, 239
     costs of services and, 190–191

differences between Illinois Family
     First and regular service families
     and, 148, 150–159, 162–165, 169–
     170, 187–191, 230–231
findings and, 229–231
formal social support and, 182–183
functioning of child/family and,
     170–172, 176–182, 189
informal social support and, 183,
     231
limitations on effectiveness of fami-
     ly preservation services and,
     238–239
meanings of data and, 231–233
out-of-home placement and, 143–
     145, 170, 187, 246, 247
overselling family preservation ser-
     vices and, 239–240
risk of placement and, 144, 150–
     152, 159, 187, 188–189, 215, 230,
     234
satisfaction with services and, 186,
     190
self-efficacy of parents and, 182,
     190, 231
service characteristics and, 164–
     165, 169, 170, 271
site variations and, 157–158, 170
subsequent maltreatment and, 145–
     146, 152–155, 159, 162–163, 169–
     170, 187–188, 231
targeting families and, 233–238
variations across sites and, 157–158
Out-of-home placement, 143–145,
     170, 187, 246, 247

Parents (*See also* Interviews with par-
     ents in Illinois Family First)
     bond with child and, 5–6
     family functioning and, view of,
         181–182
     knowledge of child rearing and, 47
     relationship with caseworkers of Il-
         linois Family First and, 120–121
     self-efficacy of, 102–103, 182, 190,
         231

Peoria site, 69, 74, 75, 76, 78, 88, 90, 92, 93, 100, 101, 103, 121, 157–158, 170, 172, 180–181, 181–182, 186, 187, 189, 190, 231
Permanency planning, 7
Permanency principle, 7, 8–9, 12
PL 96-272 (Adoption Assistance and Child Welfare Act of 1980), 6
Placement
 bias, 234–235
 case characteristics and, 41–42
 conclusions of studies of, 33, 42–43, 48
 early studies of, 33–37, 47–48
 family preservation services in preventing, 33–43, 143, 229–230
 foster care, 9–11, 14
 imminent risk of, 215, 230, 234
 in-progress studies of, 41
 least restrictive alternative principle and, 7–9, 12
 out-of-home, 143–145, 170, 187, 246, 247
 permanency principle and, 7, 8–9, 12
 reasonable efforts principle and, 6–7, 8–9
 reasons for, 14
 recent studies of, 37–43, 48
 risk of, 144, 150–152, 159, 187, 188–189, 215, 230, 234
 service characteristics and, 42
 short-term, 21, 22, 235, 248
Protection versus treatment, 4–5, 241–242

Qualitative research, 206, 210–211
Quantitative research, 206, 210–211

Reasonable efforts principle, 6–7, 8–9
Referrals
 to family preservation services, 235–236
 to Illinois Family First, 85–86, 87, 97–98, 103–104
Regression-type models, 271

Regular service families
 achievement of case objectives of, 155–156, 188
 amount of DCFS services to, 109, 111
 case characteristics of, 158–159, 162–164, 170, 189
 case opening/closing/reopening and, 156–157, 162–163
 casework-parent relationship and, 120–121
 continuation of DCFS services and, 121, 124
 data collection on DCFS, 71, 73
 differences between Illinois Family First and, 148, 150–159, 162–165, 169–170, 187–191, 230–231
 evaluation of Illinois Family First and, 71, 73
 family involvement in DCFS services and, 117, 120
 household composition of, 88, 90
 interviews with parents and, 170–172, 176–183, 186–187, 230–231
 out-of-home placement and, 187
 planning of DCFS services and, 111–114
 risk of placement and, 150–152, 187, 188–189, 230
 service characteristics and, 164–165, 169, 170
 subsequent maltreatment and, 152–155, 169–170, 187–188
 techniques and strategies of DCFS services and, 116–117
 termination of DCFS services and, 121, 124
 types of DCFS services and, 114–116
 variations across sites and, 157–158
Relatives, child care by, 11–13
Reports of child abuse/neglect
 drug abuse and, 18, 104, 162
 families in Illinois Family First and, 90, 92
 foster care and, 14–15, 17–18

Reports of child abuse/neglect (*cont.*)
  incidence of, 3–4, 14–15
  increase in, 14–15, 17–18
Research on family preservation ser-
    vices (*See also* specific aspects of
    Illinois Family First research)
  basic research and, 215
  categories of services/cases and,
    214
  child abuse/neglect prevention
    and, 45–47
  clinical trials for service approaches
    and, need for, 214–215
  conclusions of, 33, 42–43, 47–48
  cost-effectiveness, 44–45, 214
  data quality and, 211–213
  early, 33–37, 47–48
  experimental versus nonexperi-
    mental, 206–210
  functioning of child/family and,
    43–44
  in-progress, 41
  integrity of, problems in, 210
  longitudinal effects and, 213–214
  other data and, 281–283
  quantitative versus qualitative, 206,
    210–211
  recent, 37–43, 48
  simultaneous equations using two-
    stage least squares and, 271,
    274–278
  subsequent maltreatment and, 43
  summary of controlled, 251–266
  variables in hazard/two-stage least
    squares analyses and, 277–279
Rockford site, 70

St. Paul Family Centered Project, 20
Self-efficacy of parents, 102–103, 182,
    190, 231
Service characteristics
  evaluation of Illinois Family First
    and, 63–64, 71
  fragmentation, 242
  outcomes of Illinois Family First
    and, 164–165, 169, 170, 271

  placement and, 42
  in reformed child welfare systems,
    246–248
  regular service families and, 164–
    165, 169, 170
  variables in, 279
Services of Illinois Family First
  amount of, 109, 111
  case characteristics and, 271
  caseworker-parent relationship
    and, 120–121
  continuation of, 121, 124
  family involvement in, 117, 120,
    139
  model of, 107–109
  multisystems approach and, 108
  planning, 111–114
  satisfaction with, 186–187
  techniques and strategies of, 116–
    117, 138
  termination of, 121, 124
  time horizons and, 138–139
  types of, 114–116
Service technology, limitations of, 243
Simultaneous equations, 271, 274–275
Social conditions, 240–241, 249
Social Learning Treatment Program
    (Oregon), 37
Social support
  formal, 182–183
  informal, 101–102, 183, 231
Social work, 20 (*See also* Caseworkers
    of Illinois Family First)
Special Services for Children (New
    York), 35–36
Springfield site, 69–70, 88, 93, 115
Stressful events in families in Illinois
    Family First, 98, 100
Subsequent maltreatment
  family preservation services in pre-
    venting, 43
  outcomes of Illinois Family First
    and, 145–146, 152–155, 159, 162–
    163, 169–170, 187–188, 231
  regular service families and, 152–
    155, 169–170, 187–188

research on family preservation services and, 43
risk of, 159, 162–163
"Substance-affected infants," 18
Suter v. Artist M., 222

Targeting
bias in placement and, 234–235
creaming and, 23, 236
family preservation services and, 22–23, 237
"imminent risk of placement" and, 234
limitations in effectiveness of, 236–238
net-widening and, 23, 170, 188
outcomes of Illinois Family First and, 233–238
problems of, 22–23, 215, 236–238
referral criteria and, other, 235–236
Time horizons
child welfare systems and, 241, 248

family preservation services and, 21–22
implementation of Illinois Family First and, 136–138
services of Illinois Family First and, 138–139
Treatment versus prevention, 242
Truancy, 17
Turnover, staff, 130
Two-stage least squares analysis
simultaneous equations using, 271, 274–275
variables in, 277–279

Violations in group assignment, 70–71

Wallace case, 225
White House Conference on Children (1909), 19–20
Work environment, 127